Beauty in Disarray

美は乱調にあり

Beauty in Disarray

Harumi Setouchi

Translated by
Sanford Goldstein & Kazuji Ninomiya

Charles E. Tuttle Company
Rutland, Vermont & Tokyo, Japan

"Beauty exists only in disharmony.
Harmony is deceptive."

—SAKAE OSUGI

Published by the Charles E. Tuttle Company, Inc.
of Rutland, Vermont and Tokyo, Japan
with editorial offices at
2-6 Suido 1-chome, Bunkyo-ku, Tokyo 112

© 1993 by Charles E. Tuttle Publishing Co., Inc.

LCC Card No. 92-85110
ISBN 0-8048-1866-5

First edition, 1993

Printed in Japan

Contents

Notes:
Western word order, i.e., given name followed by surname, is
used throughout the book.

Macrons, signifying long vowels in romanized Japanese,
are used with italicized words within the text.

The kanji and kana on the title page are read *Bi wa ranchō
ni ari*, the Japanese title of the book.

Introduction

IT MAY surprise Westerners to realize Japan had its own well-known women's liberation movement in the late nineteenth century, that first feminist movement extending almost to the end of the Taisho era in 1926. Appearing in 1901 was Akiko Yosano's *Tangled Hair* (Tokyo: Charles E. Tuttle, 1987), startling readers with its narcissistic and sexually oriented poems and a heroine trapped by society's usual subjugations and restrictions:

> In my bath—
> Submerged like some graceful lily
> At the bottom of a spring,
> How beautiful
> This body of twenty summers. (poem 16)

> Softly I pushed open
> That door
> We call a mystery,
> These full breasts
> Held in both my hands. (poem 26)

> These scraps of paper
> Scribbled with poems

In which I cursed and raved,
I press down hard
On a black butterfly! (poem 53)

Twenty, jealous,
Wilting this summer
In the village heat,
I listen to my husband
Taunt me with Kyoto pleasures! (poem 121)

To punish
Men for their endless sins,
God gave me
This fair skin,
This long black hair! (poem 152)

On September 22 and 23, 1911, when a Japanese
translation of Ibsen's *A Doll's House* was performed in
Tokyo at the experimental theatre of the Art Association,
Japanese audiences were stunned by the superb performance of Sumako Matsui as she played a Nora who could
walk away from her responsibilities as wife and mother.
Harumi Setouchi, the author of *Beauty in Disarray*, quotes
the critic Seiseien Ihara:

Sumako Matsui played the heroine Nora. At the opening curtain when she cheerfully came on stage humming, she commanded no attention, her appearance not
the least bit like Nora's. But beginning with the moment when she behaved like a spoiled child to her
husband Helmer, confided her secret to the widow Mrs.
Linde (which suggested Nora's great awakening afterwards), asked her husband to get the widow a job,

innocently played hide-and-seek with her children, and finally up to the scene just before the curtain falls when she cries alone on the stage, "It can't be! It's impossible!" and is gradually terror-stricken after she had been told about Krogstad by her husband even while she still thought, "How was it possible for such a thing to happen?" (because she could not believe what Krogstad had told her while he was threatening her), Sumako changed wonderfully and variously, as if the quietness of water had been transformed into the great stirring of multifarious waves. During that interval there was not the slightest slackening in Sumako Matsui's performance, the movement of her facial expressions so intense the audience was completely captivated by the heroine . . . Above all, despite the fact that I am a man, the scene in which Nora leaves home after her great speech thrilled me because of the adroit cleverness of the play itself (pp. 90–91).

In November of that same year the play was performed at the Imperial Theatre.

Setouchi was eminently qualified to write this historical novel on women's liberation in Japan, which had its roots in sexual politics, socialism, and anarchism, movements in decline following the famous massacre after the Great Kanto Earthquake that devastated Tokyo and neighboring prefectures on September 1, 1923. Among those put to death in the frenzied and prejudicial aftermath of the quake was Noe Ito (1895–1923), the heroine of *Beauty in Disarray*.

It was Noe Ito's puerile poem "Eastern Strand" that first attracted Setouchi and led her to do research on Noe and her connection to women's liberation. In 1961 Setouchi finished her book on Toshiko Tamura (1884–1945), whose novel *Resignation* (1911) reflected the consciousness of the "New Woman." It was at that time that Setouchi came across the name of Noe Ito. Actually Setouchi had just begun work on a long novel about another feminist, Kanoko Okamoto (1889–1939), both Kanoko and Toshiko having in their youth worked on the feminist journal *Seito (Bluestocking)*.

The first issue of *Seito* in September 1911 focused on the marital problems and other difficulties of women. Curious about *Seito*, Setouchi once again examined its issues. "As a result of this reexamination," writes narrator-Setouchi in *Beauty in Disarray*, "I was strongly caught up in the blazing enthusiasm and dazzling way of life in which Noe Ito, the youngest member of *Seito*, spent her youth on the magazine, defended it longer than anyone else did, absorbed from it more than anyone else had, despaired over it more deeply than anyone else, and, finally, using *Seito* as a springboard, resolutely sundered herself from her past to fling herself against the bosom of her lover Sakae Osugi— all at the risk of her life and for the purpose of love and revolution" (pp. 20–21). What fascinated Setouchi was neither Noe's literary talent nor growth as a person "but the elaborate drama of the lives she was entangled in, the extraordinary intensity of each of the individuals who appeared upon her stage, and the bewitching power of the dissonant play of complexity and disharmony performed by all those caught up in these complicated relationships" (p. 21).

In addition to the life of Noe Ito, *Beauty in Disarray* has in-depth portraits of Raicho Hiratsuka (1886–1971), Ichiko Kamichika (1888–1981), and Sakae Osugi (1885–1923). Raicho became famous in 1908 as a result of the Baien

Incident, when she supposedly planned a double love-suicide with the novelist Sohei Morita (1881–1949), whose later novel *Baien (Smoke,* 1909) celebrates the affair. In 1911 Raicho and other young unmarried women from the upper classes founded the Seitosha (the Bluestocking Society). *Seito,* the society's journal, was for women only. Its first number contained Raicho's famous manifesto "In the Beginning Woman was the Sun" *(Genshi josei wa taiyō de atta):*

> In the beginning Woman was the Sun. She was a genuine being.
>
> Now Woman is the Moon. She lives through others and glitters through the mastery of others. She has a pallor like that of the ill.
>
> Now we must restore our hidden Sun (p. 85).

Beauty also contains another Raicho proclamation, one that appeared in the 1914 New Year issue of the famous journal *Chuokoron:* "I am a New Woman," chanted Raicho. "At least day by day I am endeavoring to really be a New Woman. It is the sun that is truly and eternally new. I am the sun. At least day by day I wish to be and am endeavoring to be the sun . . ." Continued Raicho: "The New Woman is cursing 'yesterday.' The New Woman can no longer bear to walk silently and submissively along the road of the old-fashioned woman who has been a victim of tyranny" (p. 164).

Another famous personality in the feminist movement was Ichiko Kamichika, who joined the Seitosha in 1912 while a student at Tsuda College. Later when she became a teacher, she was dismissed because of her association with *Seito.* In 1916 she was a major participant in what became known as the "Hikage Teahouse Incident," in which she stabbed her lover, the anarchist Sakae Osugi. Osugi had fallen in love with Noe and was just beginning to live with her. This event is one of the major dramatic episodes in *Beauty in Disarray*.

Osugi was the leading anarchist of the Taisho era. His first involvement in a cause was in 1906 when he lent his support to public forces against an increase in Tokyo trolley fares. As a result of this support, he was arrested and imprisoned. It was due only to Osugi's imprisonment in 1908 for another event that he was not implicated in the High Treason Incident of 1910, in which key leftists were executed for a conspiracy to assassinate Emperor Meiji (1852–1912). Osugi's love affairs with Noe Ito and Ichiko Kamichika resulted in his being stabbed by Ichiko, an event that led to a divorce from his wife Yasuko. Later he married Noe. On September 16, 1923, while Osugi, Noe, and a nephew were returning home, a police captain arrested the trio. The prisoners were later beaten to death by the captain and his cohorts.

Noe had two children by her first husband Jun Tsuji (1884–1944), the Japanese dadaist, and five children by Osugi. It was Jun Tsuji who had purchased a copy of *Seito* and given it to Noe the following day. As Noe read *Seito*, she was inspired by Raicho's emotional manifesto, including the following: "I want, together with all women, to convince myself of the genius that is lying in women. I put my faith only in that one possibility, and I want the heartfelt joy of the happiness which comes from being born into this world as women" (pp. 85–86).

In November 1914 Raicho felt compelled to give up *Seito*, for family and financial difficulties had caused too much of a strain. Noe, however, decided to take charge of the journal. She was editor from January 1915 until she had to discontinue publication in February 1916.

Beauty in Disarray takes as one of its major subjects the development and growth of *Seito*. Furthermore, at the very core of the feminist struggle during the Meiji and Taisho eras is the drama of several complicated love triangles, in addition to the anarchist and socialist movements of the time.

The life of Harumi Setouchi has also had its dramatic complications. Born May 15, 1922, she was the second daughter of a craftsman of Shinto and Buddhist altar articles. She entered Tokyo Women's Christian College in 1940, married in 1943, and proceeded to China with her husband. When the war ended in 1945, she returned to Japan, separated from her husband in 1948, and divorced him in Kyoto in 1950. Her return to Tokyo in 1951 found her joining the Bungakusha literary group, its leader Fumio Niwa, the famous writer of *fūzoku shōsetsu*, novels dealing with modern urban life. Setouchi's biography of pioneer feminist Toshiko Tamura brought her fame as the recipient of the First Toshiko Tamura Prize in 1960. She continued to write biographies of contemporary political and literary feminists as well as biographical novels, the major one being *Beauty in Disarray*. Japan's literary world was stunned on November 14, 1973, when Setouchi became a Buddhist nun. During a ceremony at the Chusonji temple in Iwate prefecture, she was shorn of her beautiful locks and given the Buddhist name Jakucho. In 1974 she moved from Tokyo to Sagano in Kyoto to live in the Jyakuan hermitage. In 1989 she published a volume of essays entitled *The Glory of Women Who Gained Independence (Jiritsu shita onna no eikō)*. Her energy and public presence remain undiminished. In 1989 she became president of Tsuruga Women's College in Fukui prefecture.

Setouchi remains unique in Japanese literature for her depiction of the struggle of women in love, women in politics, and especially the strong ties women have to the men they love. During the last three decades she has raised the biographical novel to a dynamic art form.

Sanford Goldstein
West Lafayette, Indiana

Kazuji Ninomiya
Niigata, Japan

Beauty in Disarray

Chapter 1

WHEN I THOUGHT of going to Hakata, it was merely out of a desire to stand upon the seashore at Imajuku, noted for its beautiful pine grove at Iki-no-Matsubara. If you look at a map, you will find that the town of Imajuku, which sits upon Hakata Bay on the western outskirts of Fukuoka, is about seven miles from the center of the city. Inside Hakata Bay is a smaller inlet bay called Imazu, and Imajuku is exactly in the middle of that inlet's coastline.

Four or five years ago, on a trip down this coastal highway from Hakata to Karatsu, I must have driven past Imajuku, but I don't have the slightest recollection of having done so. Only after the memory of Noe Ito began to occupy my mind did I become conscious of the name of the small coastal village of Imajuku in the Itoshima district of Fukuoka prefecture.

The name Noe Ito alone will probably not mean anything to those born in the Showa era (1926–89); and even to those born in the Taisho era (1912–26), her name will be practically unknown. But for those who have even the slightest interest in or knowledge about the Taisho era, it is inconceivable that they could not know of the two greatest events at the beginning and end of that era: the trial of Shusui Kotoku for high treason and the Sakae

Osugi murder case. Even among the various massacres that took place in the confusion following the Great Kanto Earthquake of September 1, 1923, no event caused more indignation and consternation among the people in those days than the murder of Sakae Osugi, his wife Noe Ito, and his six-year-old nephew Soichi Tachibana. They had been strangled and beaten to death by military-police captain Masahiko Amakasu and five of his men and then dumped into an abandoned well. Sakae Osugi's too great fame as an advocate of the anarchist and socialist movements in Japan, and the brutality of accompanying his death with the murders of his wife, not even in her thirties, and his young nephew, were the main reasons that the case evoked so much public compassion and resentment. I suspect that those who remember Noe Ito as a victim in the Amakasu Incident may go even further back and recall the famous assault-and-battery case of the zany love affair dubbed the "Shady Inn Incident," after the inn of that name in Hayama, in which Osugi was stabbed by his mistress Ichiko Kamichika. The object of the woman's jealousy at that moment was not Osugi's legal wife Yasuko Hori, but his new flame Noe Ito.

The mere fact that a woman named Noe Ito turned up in these two bloody affairs, both of which created sensations in society within a few short years, is sufficient to make us aware that she committed herself to a dramatic destiny. Furthermore, you will be all the more impressed with the dramatic elements in her life when you realize that the same Noe Ito was one of those sensational "New Women" in the coterie of the Bluestocking Society and much talked about in the magazine *Seito (Bluestocking)*, edited by Raicho Hiratsuka; that Noe Ito shared her fate to the end with *Seito* after proudly taking it over from Raicho;

and that she was also entrusted with the historical role of bringing down the curtain on this magazine. Moreover, before Noe ran off with the anarchist Sakae Osugi, she was the ardently loved wife of Jun Tsuji, the man who had established dadaism in Japan, though according to one family census, she had been married once before. In a period of ten years she gave birth to seven children. The life she lived so fully and colorfully during the brief span of twenty-eight years was so remarkable and brilliant that it contained the measure of the lives of several ordinary women.

It was during the time that I was writing about the author Toshiko Tamura, one of the leading female figures from the last years of the Meiji era (1868–1912) to the beginning of the Taisho era, that I became acquainted with Noe Ito's name. Though I had noticed it listed among the names of the *Seito* staff, to which Toshiko herself was connected, I was not the least bit charmed by Noe Ito's overly subjective impressions, which were composed in a stiff style; by her so-called "short stories," which were cast in a rather immature form; or by her puerile poems published in the magazine, the following one typical:

Eastern Strand

Solitary rock along the eastern strand,
On its brown back
You grebes that have also come to perch today—
Why in that lonely way
Do you cry out?
. . .

See here, grebes! How I wish
You'd die! On that rock—

If you die, I'll die too.
If we must die after all, oh grebes,
Why not hurl ourselves into the maelstrom!

I burst into laughter after reading this poem. I was amazed that even though the magazine had come into being in the last year of Meiji, the staff had been so poorly endowed with talent that they had been forced into publishing such a juvenile attempt at literature.

When I compared this poem with the first article of the Bluestocking Society bylaws, formulated when the group was organized, I was all the more surprised by their naiveté and could not help but smile sardonically:

We will strive for the development of female writers, allow each to exhibit the special gift of her inborn talent, and at some future date aim to produce female geniuses.

By chance I once more came across the name of Noe Ito, which I had hardly given the slightest notice to the first time. This is how it came about. Shortly after I had finished writing about Toshiko Tamura, I began a tenaciously long novel based on the life of Kanoko Okamoto. Kanoko had joined the *Seito* staff a little later than Toshiko and slightly earlier than Noe. Since not only one but two excellent female writers who had attracted my interest had, during a period in their youth, secured positions on the staff of *Seito*, I took another look at the magazine itself.

As a result of this examination, I was strongly caught up in the blazing enthusiasm and dazzling way of life in which Noe Ito, the youngest member of *Seito*, spent her youth on the magazine, defended it longer than anyone else did, absorbed from it more than anyone else had, despaired over it more deeply than anyone else, and, finally, using *Seito* as a springboard, resolutely sundered herself from her past to fling herself against the bosom of her lover Sakae Osugi—all at the risk of her life and for the purpose of love and revolution.

Even when considered in the most favorable light, the literary talent of Noe, who wrote poetry like "Eastern Strand" at the age of seventeen, could hardly be called full of promise. Though she later earned her living quite well from her pen by managing to produce stories and reviews and even translations, she left behind works too poor for later generations to dub her a writer of the first rank.

What attracted me to Noe was neither her literary talent nor her remarkable growth as a human being, but the elaborate drama of the lives she was entangled in, the extraordinary intensity of each of the individuals who appeared upon her stage, and the bewitching power of the dissonant play of complexity and disharmony performed by all those caught up in these complicated relationships. My feelings intensified as I read about Noe in Fumiko Ide's herculean labor *Seito*, and Kureo Iwazaki's elaborately detailed biography of Noe Ito entitled *Woman of Flame*.

By standing on the beach at Imajuku, where Noe Ito was born; by listening to the cries of the grebes, which she had written about in her poem; and by watching the blue waters of Hakata Bay, in which she had swum, I thought I would attempt to get closer to the image of Noe that had so completely captivated me.

When the jet I was on landed at Itazuke Airport, I was greeted by a reporter from the *Nishi Nippon* newspaper office. As soon as I got into his car, the young man, whom I was meeting for the first time, said, "I've been in touch with Mako. I expect she'll see us at the office." At that moment I didn't understand what he meant. Two or three days before my departure for Hakata, I had casually mentioned to Shizuo Kito, an old newspaper journalist who happened to drop by to see me, my reasons for going to Hakata, and he was prompt enough that very same day to arrange for me to contact the *Nishi Nippon*.

Kito, who had been living a long while in northern Kyushu, had told me right off, "Quite a few of Noe's relatives are still living in Hakata. In any event, go meet them. I'm positive the daughters of Osugi and Noe are also living there." Before I left, he even telephoned with journalistic promptness and solicitude to tell me he had already arranged my visit. Nevertheless, I was certainly not mentally prepared to meet Noe's relatives this soon.

Only after we had been driving toward Hakata for five or six minutes, leaving houses with thatched roofs and blossoming cherry trees far behind, did I finally realize that the name I had just heard, Mako, was that of Osugi and Noe's eldest daughter. With Jun Tsuji, Noe had two boys; with Sakae Osugi, four girls and a boy. A glance at the following diagram will indicate the relationships:

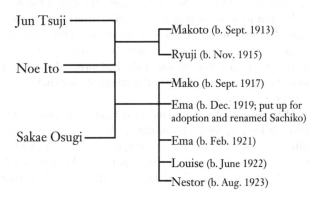

Jun Tsuji ——
Noe Ito ══
Sakae Osugi ——

—Makoto (b. Sept. 1913)
—Ryuji (b. Nov. 1915)
—Mako (b. Sept. 1917)
—Ema (b. Dec. 1919; put up for adoption and renamed Sachiko)
—Ema (b. Feb. 1921)
—Louise (b. June 1922)
—Nestor (b. Aug. 1923)

As you look at this arrangement, noting the ordinary names of Noe's children by Jun Tsuji and the extraordinary names of her offspring by Sakae Osugi, you will be startled by the amazing life force with which she continued to conceive almost without rest.

Osugi had the greatest affection for his eldest daughter Mako, to whom he gave the strangest name of all his children—Mako meaning "Demon Child"—and he often mentioned her in his works. Even when Noe took her other children back to her hometown to give birth to another infant, Mako was the only one Osugi did not allow to go. And on those trips related to his work, he did not think it an inconvenience to take her along.

Late in 1922 Osugi had himself smuggled out of the country, and disguised as a Chinese, he tried to participate secretly in the International Anarchist Conference in Berlin. Because he delivered a speech in Paris on May Day before proceeding to Berlin, his identity became known and he was arrested. He was sentenced to a three-week confinement in Paris's La Santé prison. In his record of that time, "My Escape from Japan," in which he described the whole episode, Osugi commented:

No doubt by now they know about my arrest, thanks to the telegram sent by that newspaper. Adults will merely think I have finally done what I have been intending all along, but even though I have not spoken of my plan to any of my children, they must be worried about me, especially my eldest daughter Mako, for she would instinctively know my condition, despite the fact that she was not told. In my wife's letter the other day, she noted that when Muraki (Genjiro), who has been living in our home, was wrapping books to send to some prisoners, Mako said to him in a low voice, "Don't you have anything to send to Papa?" Since I disappeared after forcing her to spend a few days away from home in order to deceive her, Mako took it for granted that I was again in prison. And even when someone asked her, "Where is your papa?" she either remained silent, not answering at all, or smoothed everything over by talking about something else, but especially at night she speaks casually with her mother about the rumors concerning her father. I thought of sending her a telegram. I actually sat down at my table to try to jot down some simple sentences. But I could not come up with any wording cheap enough. The following strange items came from what I had tried to compose in various ways:

Mako! Mako!
Now Papa's
At La Santé, Paris,
A world-famous prison.

But don't worry, Mako,
For I'm eating delicious European food,
Licking chocolate,
Puffing cigars on a sofa.

And so
Thanks to this prison,
Be joyful, Mako!
Papa will soon return.

So many souvenirs, too heavy in my bag,
And cakes and kisses for my baby!

Dance and wait!
Wait, Mako! Mako!

I spent the entire day loudly reciting these poemlike lines while walking around my cell. Strangely enough, even though I did not feel the least bit sad, large tears emerged from my eyes as I was reciting. My voice trembled, and the tears flowed incessantly.

The passage suggests the figure of a devoted parent writing openly about the daughter he loves.

The collection of Sakae Osugi's complete works, published two years after his and Noe's deaths, contains more photographs of Mako than anyone else. Since almost all the pictures serving as the frontispiece for the volume were snapshots of the day of Osugi's return from Paris on July 12, 1923, only two short months before his final days, Osugi is shown with Noe and Mako, who both came all the way to Kobe to welcome him. He appears totally worn from his travels, despite the bright look on his face, and Noe reveals a lifeless expression, her stomach swollen in just about her ninth month with Nestor, her third child in three years. Only the six-year-old Mako makes the big round eyes she inherited from her father glitter, and no matter which photograph she is in, she looks happy and intelligent.

Mako's fashion was far too chic for those days. Her clothing was European, her hat stylish, and her hair cut in a pageboy bob. Photographs of her give the lively impression of a child in an intellectual urban family that delights in modernity. I realized that very cute little Mako was now almost fifty years old.

It was just about noon when we arrived at the newspaper office. The building, which had escaped damage in the war, had excessively high ceilings, wide stairway landings, and sturdy wooden handrails painted to look like mahogany, all of which made me feel I was in an old-fashioned European manor house. The scene was much too perfect for meeting Mako, the illegitimate child of parents headed for one of the most dramatic fates of the Taisho era, the building itself having remained as it had been at that time. As I was exchanging greetings in the reception room with a few of the men on the newspaper staff, I sensed that someone was at the door, and I looked back just as a woman came quietly into the room.

The face of the small middle-aged woman was fearlessly staring directly at me. Her long thick eyebrows and the remarkably large pupils in her eyes—with their double eyelids glittering as if burning near those eyebrows—pressed down on me with an intensity that suggested those eyes and brows were all the face contained. Her cheeks were hollow, and because all the lines were gathered into her short narrow chin, her face looked for a moment neat and heart-shaped. But I could easily overlay upon that face, so small it could be enclosed completely in both of her palms, the image of the cute little round-faced Mako, whose large button eyes and long eyelashes I remembered from the photographs.

Her age was most apparent around her mouth, her teeth somewhat visible as a result, but the youthfulness that made it impossible for me to imagine that she was nearly fifty was not due to her small size only. Though her features at a glance had in them a trace of sadness, a sudden sign of gentleness, which forced the tight lines of her mouth to immediately soften, flickered in her eyes with a strong light that did not flinch as we exchanged looks, a friendliness and innocent shyness overflowing in ageless freshness in her eyes. Her rich black hair, her dark-blue woolen kimono closed tightly at her slender throat, and her long gray fur overcoat to protect her hands and legs from the cold finally came into view. An intense atmosphere radiated from the unshrinking glitter in her eyes, and the vitality of her small body had a freshness only an intellectual can possess.

The moment before she arrived, I overheard one of the newspaper staff say, "Actually, Mako is notorious for hating to be interviewed. She's a plague to newspaper reporters. She doesn't want to talk about her parents at all, and she even turns away from NHK's microphones, telling them that she had no real connection with her parents. So to get anything out of her . . ." From the very start of my trip, I had no real intention of pumping Mako for various details, so I was moved merely to see before my eyes this fifty-year-old child of a pitiful fate. Mako was the same age as my elder sister, and Louise had been born the same year as me. This amounted to saying that these sisters and I were women who had tasted both the sweet and the bitter of life during the very same generation. When I thought about this fact, I felt in Mako a common, practical housewife of the world seen along any street, the practical wife of a practical man of the world, and I suddenly sensed some intimate attachment to her.

When she became aware of my purpose in coming, she merely nodded and said, "I don't remember anything. But my mother's aunt is still alive, and she may have something to tell you." Mako herself guided me to the place in the city where Kichi Dai lived.

Sitting beside me, Mako came up only to the shoulders

of my five-foot-two-inch frame. The diminutive Mako told me quite frankly, "My daughter living in Tokyo has presented me with a grandchild. She's the daughter I left with my former husband, but nowadays she and I keep in touch with one another. Yes, the husband I divorced has already died. Well, I've had nothing but trouble from my parents." Saying this, Mako humorously made the pupils of her eyes spin around.

From the time she entered school to the time she started working and then got married, Mako had been raised in an age when everything was tinged with militarism, so she had been subjected to unjust pressures and an unjust fate merely because she was Sakae Osugi's daughter. This I could fully imagine from having been brought up during the same period myself.

"Like the time I entered a girls' high school. I had been staying with my grandfather here until I finished elementary school, but I went to high school from the house of an uncle on my father's side who lived in Yokohama. At that time I expected, quite naturally, to take the prefectural high school entrance examination, but my teachers wouldn't let me. Even though I might have passed with good marks, my teachers, needless to say, knew I couldn't get in because I was Osugi's child. That's why I entered the private Koran Girls' High School. So this event, you see, serves as a model for everything else in my life."

Her talking so indifferently of her own affairs, as if she were speaking about someone else, struck home all the more forcefully to me.

"Apparently I was doted on by my father, but I have no memory of that at all. Even those incidents I think I have remembered are from books I read afterwards or are 'images' I got from listening to others, so I feel as if my memories have been made out of them. According to what was written in a book of my father's, a man tailing him by keeping close watch from in front of our house would wonder if my father had given him the slip or not, and he would ask me about him while I was playing outside. When he asked me, 'Is your papa in?' I would say yes, and even when he asked, 'Is your papa out?' I would say yes. And then when he asked me if my father was at home or not, it seems I gave him two yes answers. I was told that the person shadowing my father complained to my parents that he was no match for little Mako. When I was told about such events, I somehow came to believe that I really had those experiences. When I saw my father's books describing those occasions he had taken me to an inn along the coast where he often went to do his work, a kind of vague memory loomed that I had walked along the same seashore with him. All my memories are of this sort. Since my sisters were much younger than I, they can't have had any memories, can they? But, you know, strangely enough, there's only one scene I remember clearly. It was when my father wasn't at home for some reason or other, and we were living in a two-story house. Every time we heard a crowd of people at our front door, my mother's face took on an unusually frightened look, and she forced me up to the second floor, saying, 'Don't come down, no matter what!' I heard Kenji Kondo continually shouting something at the entrance of our house. Mere child that I was, I became frightened, and stretching only my neck out from the upstairs landing, I secretly glanced below. I found my mother sitting resolutely in the very center of the lowest step on the staircase with a bucketful of ashes held tight across her lap.

"That strange posture of my mother sitting smack down

there and that bucketful of ashes have remained remarkably vivid before my eyes. I suppose my feeling of fear and
my mother's somehow reliable figure and that bucket of
ashes were strange even to a child. I guess she intended to
defend us with those ashes if anyone broke into our house.

"Oddly enough, my father left me at home the very day
he was murdered. Perhaps he had a premonition after all,
because wherever he went, he always wanted to take me
with him. But on just that day, he left me behind with our
neighbor, Mr. Roan Uchida.

"My father was very kind to his relatives, so he was
worried about his younger brother's family at Tsurumi,
and he was anxious to visit them as soon as possible. He had
gone out with my mother, intending to bring my uncle's
family back to our house because they had suffered a great
deal during the Great Kanto Earthquake. My uncle,
though, was ill in bed, so for the time being they brought
back only my little cousin Soichi. That was when the
trouble occurred. If on that day my father had taken me
along as usual, I would have been killed with all of them.

"Thinking about the event afterwards, Mr. Uchida told
me that in spite of the fact that I always left with my father
when he went away, it was strange that I hadn't even run
after him on that day. I was playing over at Mr. Uchida's
every day, and I was really there more than I was in my own
house."

I couldn't bring myself to ask Mako, who was speaking
to me in such a free manner, if she remembered anything
further about the day her parents died.

Roan Uchida, in his book *The Last Days of Osugi*, has left
us some notes on Mako's condition during the days before
and after her parents' murder.

On the day they died, Osugi and Noe had departed from their house in clothing so European in style that Uchida mistook them for a European couple working at the Seisho Gakuin Mission School. But even then Mako, who was playing at Uchida's, said, "Oh, Papa and Mama!" and she jumped up and ran out, only to turn back immediately.

"Papa and Mama are going to my uncle's in Tsurumi, and they may be staying there tonight," Mako said, and all through the afternoon she played on at Uchida's. But her parents never returned.

Though practically everyone at home was almost convinced that Osugi and Noe had been assassinated, Mako was still playing cheerfully. Even in the morning, when the coldblooded murders of Osugi and his wife and nephew were finally announced, Mako came over to Uchida's house. He describes it thus:

The members of my family, who already knew about the deaths of Mr. and Mrs. Osugi, finished their breakfast in silence. Since I felt Mako would probably come over to play today too, I warned my children, "Don't say anything about Mako's papa!" Even though they were too young to understand, they nodded wordlessly with an expression on their faces that something terrible had happened.

After a while, just as we expected, Mako came in through the back door as usual. When she saw us, she said immediately, "My papa and mama are both dead. My uncle and grandfather went to get them, so they'll bring them back by car today." The person she mentioned as her grandfather was Noe's uncle, who had rushed up to Tokyo after hearing in his distant hometown in Kyushu about the Osugi tragedy, news of which had spread faster in the districts than it had in the capital.

Coming into the parlor and seeing my wife there, Mako once again said, "Mrs. Uchida, my papa and mama were murdered. It's probably in today's paper."

I had strictly bidden my children, "Don't say anything about Mako's papa!" thinking I didn't want to bruise her poor young heart even a trifle, but clever little Mako already knew everything. Yet she was only an unthinking child of six. Even though she knew about the miserable fate of her father and mother, she was playing innocently as usual. Sensing that Mako was miserable, my child who was the same age gave her all her treasured dolls and stacks of colored paper decorated with lively designs.

Laughing, I asked Mako if she disliked her strange name, as I noticed that although she had retained the name she had changed the way of writing it from "Demon Child" to "True Child." In similar fashion, Ema had become Emiko ("Laughing Child"), and Louise, Ruiko ("Mindful Child").

"Well, my parents' old friends in Tokyo still call me Mako when they see me. It's not a bad name," she said, a bright smile on her face.

While we were carrying on this kind of conversation inside the automobile, we found ourselves at Tsunehiko Dai's house in Chiyomachi. Kichi Dai, the younger sister of Noe's father Yokichi, had married Tsunehiko's son Junsuke. She had taken charge of Noe in her primary school days, and even in those Tokyo days when Noe went to a girls' high school, Kichi Dai had let Noe commute from the Dai house. During her maturing period Noe had been more intimately connected to Kichi than even to her own parents. Now Kichi's home was managed by her grandchild.

We found no one else at home that day due to her great-grandchild's having gone to take a school entrance examination. Kichi was resting quietly in bed in her room at the back of the house. Neat and pretty, her skin white, the elderly Kichi informed us that she was in bed because of a slight cold. Usually so strong that she was seldom laid up, Kichi had, even on her sickbed, fixed her white hair, which was still thick enough to run a comb through, into a prim little bun.

She had classic features. Even at her age her nose was shapely, and she had a lively expression in her eyes, which slanted down slightly. Her wrinkles and freckles were hardly noticeable on her white parchment-like cheeks, and it startled me to find traces of youth and charm on her slender delicate hands, which rested on her chest.

Smiling by my side as I continued to be impressed by the freshness of this elderly woman, Mako said, in a tone she thought Kichi could not hear, "She's quite a foppish old lady. They say she still rubs the slightest bit of leftover warmed saké or egg white into her face and hands. Her grandson's wife laughs at being no match for her youthfulness. Even her hair has to be done each day or she isn't satisfied."

While smiling and looking up at us as we were talking, Kichi occasionally nodded her head in agreement over some point. Nevertheless, she could catch our words if we raised our voices a little, all her responses clear even when she slipped on some expression, her powers of recall amazing, her mind as sharp as ever.

"Oh, I see . . . Yes, is that so? . . . Did you say you came all the way from Tokyo? . . . I see. Oh yes, certainly I have become senile, as you see, and nowadays I am completely useless. I wonder why I am living like this at all . . . What? . . . My age? Well, let me see. I don't know how old I am. Anyway, I've been living a long time already, and I've become useless, and now I'm wondering what I should do. Still, death hasn't come to get me yet. I was born in 1876, so I guess that I'm about ninety. Well, I may even be almost a hundred. I have not counted for a long while . . .

"Are you asking me about Noe? I've already forgotten everything about her. Forgotten everything so that it is all vague and hazy. What I am now remembering in this sort of drowsy way are mostly those memories of Noe in her childhood, and in addition to those memories, though I don't know why, it looks as if I cannot forget those things that touched me to the quick, whether they were happy memories or sad ones . . .

"Are you asking me about Noe? The reason she was living with us in Nagasaki was that her family was poor and they had many children. She was a strong-willed unyielding girl, but she was also a crybaby. My husband Junsuke sold lumber to the Mitsubishi shipyard in Nagasaki. Later he went up to Tokyo, but I've completely forgotten what he did for a living during those Tokyo days. Yes, I guess he was treated kindly by Mitsuru Toyama, and maybe he did some work for a group with a name something like Gen'yosha, some right-wing nationalist society. Yes, that's right. I was his second wife, so his daughter Chiyoko was not my own child. Noe was my relative, so it was quite natural for her not to feel reserved with me, wasn't it? . . .

"Are you asking me about Noe's mother? She was called O-ume, and she was a very wise person. She was perfect from whatever angle and gentle, and no matter from whose point of view, a wonderful person. Our family at Imajuku was called Yorozuya and came of fairly old stock. They say that our family had a prosperous shipping agency in the old days. We made a fine living when I was a little girl. I guess it was about the time Noe was born that our fortune started to decline. Her father Yokichi cared only for music and dancing, so his family was about to go bankrupt. Oh yes, Noe's father was also quite the dandy. Generally, all the Yorozuyas were well known for their faces, and everyone talked about the 'Yorozuya eyebrows' and the 'Yorozuya eyes.' I wasn't the least bit like the Yorozuyas, but all my brothers and sisters were good-looking and popular. And even Mako, when she was brought back to us from Tokyo, when she went to have some fun around Imazu, the Imazu villagers could guess at a glance, 'Ah, she's a granddaughter of the Yorozuya at Imajuku.' I dare say she was really born with Yorozuya eyes and eyebrows . . .

"Are you asking me about Noe's looks? Yes, yes, certainly she was pretty. She was a girl with nice clear-cut features. She liked to read books, and apparently she was not fond of the things that girls usually do, like cleaning and sewing. Still, I told her what a woman's duties were, and I forced her to take turns with Chiyoko in doing the cleaning . . .

"Are you asking me if Noe could swim? Oh yes, if you were raised by the seashore, you'd be able to swim as well as a water sprite. She was good at the crawl . . . When I was a child, I would also slip away from school and swim all day. Then I would lie in the sun on some piece of lumber and dry my wet hair, and when it was half dry, I would put my hair up as if I were quite innocent, thinking I would never be suspected . . . Oh no, I never wore any swimming suit.

Everyone swam stark-naked. Noe loved diving, but Chiyoko was more like what you'd call an athlete today and swam as far as Nokonoshima. It doesn't seem as if the way we spent our days as children and the way Noe did were very different.

"Since we didn't have any really interesting things to do, several times a year when plays came to Shusenji village, she would go to see them, since those plays offered the greatest enjoyment she'd be able to have. She'd go to the Festival of the Dead dancing in a red cotton apron, with cutouts of colored paper proudly sewn on it . . . Well, Noe's love of learning was probably inherited because my mother Sato was so good at reading and writing that she taught the neighborhood children. What's more, my mother had a real taste for songs accompanied by the samisen, and the fondness in Noe's father's blood for dancing and singing was probably inherited from my mother. At village plays and other kinds of entertainment, the first person lively enough to go up on the stage and play the samisen or dance was Noe's father.

"When we moved from Nagasaki to Tokyo, we sent Noe back to Imajuku for a while, and from there she went to an elementary school in Shusenji. When she graduated from that school and got a job at the post office, Noe sent letters to our home in Tokyo day after day, letters so thick that they fell with a heavy thud. Those letters begged us to grant her wish to come up to Tokyo and attend a girls' high school like Chiyoko was doing. Living right next door to us at the time was the novelist Namiroku Murakami. When my husband showed him Noe's letters, the handwriting and the contents were so good that he advised us she showed some promise and that we ought to let her come up to Tokyo, so my husband felt inclined to do so and we decided to take charge of her again. But when she finally did come, Mr. Murakami was quite surprised to see that Noe was a girl. He was convinced on reading those letters that the writer had to be a young man. My husband was really a person who preferred bringing up someone to saving money, and he took a liking to people of character, be they friend or foe. Later on, even though he belonged to the right-wing Gen'yosha group, he felt inclined to take care of Osugi, more, I believe, from my husband's fondness for human beings than from any sympathy with Osugi's doctrines and principles . . .

"Are you asking me about Osugi? Yes, I knew both Osugi and Jun Tsuji real well. I found that while Tsuji was a gentle hesitating person, Osugi was a really fine man. His gentleness, especially toward women and children, was exquisite. Sometimes I wondered why the world feared such a gentle person. Certainly Tsuji was also gentle. All of Noe's men were devoted to her . . .

"Oh yes, are you asking me about Noe's first husband? He was a son of the Suematsu family in Shusenji, and since both fathers were friends, it was natural for the subject of marriage to come up. I've heard that the young man's entire family had settled in America and opened up a shoe store. Noe hesitated in giving her answer, but since she'd be able to go to America, she agreed. But when she found out that she couldn't go to America, she said marrying was out of the question and she began to balk. Nevertheless, during the summer vacation when she was in the fifth grade at the girls' high school, the marriage took place. Somehow, though, I've forgotten all the details concerning the marriage at the time . . .

"I'm good for nothing, since I'm apt to forget everything. I don't even know how I manage to go on living. You took the trouble to come all this way, and I want to give you some memento of Noe, but I've nothing to offer. Well, at any rate, during my life my husband took me to many places I wanted to go to. Yes, he took me just about everywhere. I've probably been to all the famous hot-spring resorts in our country. He even took me climbing with him to the top of Mount Fuji . . .

"Yes? Are you asking me about the time Noe was murdered? I certainly do remember that real well. Before the special edition came out, a newsman let us know about the murder, so my husband and Noe's father rushed up to Tokyo. The members of her family weren't that surprised. I guess they expected it. Noe had the habit of saying that she and her husband would never die peacefully in their beds like ordinary people.

"Oh yes, now I remember. When my husband went up to Tokyo to get Noe and Osugi's ashes, Mr. Toyama was kind enough to lend them his car for as long as they needed it. They told me that several men, Mr. Toyama's followers, protected them as guards. They said there was fear of an attack by some of those right-wingers.

"Yes, that's the way my husband was, and I guess Mr. Toyama was also the kind that took a liking to men of character, even if their principles were different and even if they were his opponents. He treated Noe with affection, and it seems that he gave her pocket money sometimes. Once, thanks to Mr. Toyama's help, Noe went to Shimpei Goto's house to get some money. I remember hearing that Mr. Goto, laughing, told Mr. Toyama everything with the remark 'She's an interesting girl.' It seems that Noe grabbed the money, which had been placed on a table, and as if it were natural to not even bow in thanks, had quietly left. There must have been many times when my husband took the trouble to help Osugi meet Mr. Toyama and Mr. Goto. At first, when Noe ran off to live with Osugi, my husband was very angry with him, but discovering at last that Osugi was a great man, my husband took charge of Osugi's body when he died. You see, a big gravestone, unusual since it didn't have any names on it, was set up in Imajuku for the three victims. What had been put up was merely an unworked stone, but the grave site was big enough to serve as a play area for children, and it became an attraction. Even that grave my husband built. Later the stone was removed due to some city-planning ordinance, but I don't know what became of it, though I heard that someone thought it interesting and in the middle of the night secretly carted it off and put it in his own garden. But not long afterwards, I heard that he fell into his garden pond and drowned. These are the only things I remember . . . Well, I'm really sorry, seeing you have come all this way . . ."

In the Dai home there were two large thick calico-covered albums that Junsuke Dai had assembled. The pictures of Osugi and Mako were carefully laid out, and I also found a photograph of that gravestone for the three victims, a stone that no longer existed but had looked like some queer abstract work of art. From just one of those albums I could surmise the history of the opulent, showy life of the Dai family, and I could imagine the life and character of Junsuke Dai, something of a big shot with his mind bent on business and a fondness for politics.

Mako searched one of the albums for a large photograph of a high school graduation and showed it to me. It was Noe's graduation picture from Ueno Girls' High School. Attired in a long-sleeved kimono and wearing a ceremonial skirt and a formal black jacket decorated with her family crest, Noe, her hair in the long chignon style of graduation ceremonies at girls' high schools of the time, was in the middle of the top row. While all the other students directly faced the camera, Noe was standing with her body sideways, her profile taken as her eyes stared at the sky. The moment the visiting photographer, completely hidden behind the black, red-lined cloth of his old-fashioned camera, had shouted out, "All right, I'm ready to shoot!" and released the shutter by pressing the round rubber ball with a theatrical gesture of his hand, Noe had struck this pose, her manner of looking up at the empty sky either affected or sulky. At eighteen years of age according to the Japanese method of counting, Noe had put on weight, her face, shoulders, and breasts visibly plump.

When Noe went up to Tokyo, she often continued studying through the night for her entrance examinations, all of a sudden deciding to take them to enroll in the fourth-year class at Ueno Girls' High School, where her cousin Chiyoko, two years older than Noe, was in attendance. Noe succeeded. As a result, she finished high school in only two years. This was the fruit of Noe's effort to reduce as much as possible the burden of her uncle Junsuke Dai's school expenses, but it also revealed she was endowed with real talent. In a corner of this graduation picture was a round photograph of Jun Tsuji.

It was in the spring when Noe was in the fifth-year class that Jun Tsuji assumed his post as an English teacher at the school. Pictured as a handsome man with delicate features on a slender face, Jun Tsuji is wearing glasses whose thin frames seem to be made of silver, his kimono neckband joined so tightly at the neck and showing his dark under-garment that instead of looking like an English teacher at a girls' high school, he appears more like a Japanese dancing instructor or a young actor impersonating a female. His features alone give the impression of a nervous person.

We left the Dai home, and while we were on our way to Imajuku, Mako had the driver stop in front of a large house that manufactured Hakata dolls sold wholesale. The lower floor was a kind of storeroom, the clerks visibly quite busy packing these Hakata dolls for shipping.

When we went upstairs directly from the entranceway, we found the second story formed the business office. While we were looking at several Hakata dolls in glass cases lining the walls, someone called out behind and Mako introduced me to a young woman in Western dress.

"This is Louise."

Ruiko, who had changed her name from Louise, sat smiling on a sofa. She seemed quite young, perhaps in her twenties or early thirties at most, but if I remember correctly, she had been born in 1922. When her parents were killed, she must have been a year and three months old.

As I had expected, her pretty oval-shaped face, though longer than Mako's, had the Yorozuya eyebrows and Yorozuya eyes, but her large eyes and round line of chin immediately reminded me of the Osugi I had seen in the photographs. It was either the slender legs under her skirt or the attractiveness of her hairdo bound into a chignon after being combed up at the nape that made me feel she was a strange woman whose youth, like that of a small girl, still remained in her entire body. No sign of age was visible on her smooth wide forehead.

The former owner of the doll factory had been an anarchist living in Fukuoka, and it was this association that had helped Louise acquire a side job painting these dolls. She told me she had just brought in her finished dolls and was going to take back some unglazed ones. I could see the extent of Mako's kindness in silently providing me with every convenience. And Louise also talked in an utterly unaffected way, her face all smiles.

"Well, with parents like ours, we've never benefited at all, have we? Even when I married, my husband's family was dead set against it, telling him to put an end to marrying an Osugi girl, that even a geisha or whatever would be better. The result was he left his family and cut off all connections to them so that now he lives only with me."

Her manner of speaking was also as indifferent as if she were talking about the concerns of someone else. Even this woman, who was much less bound to her parents than Mako had been, had carried on her back from the time she was aware of what was going on around her the burden of the names of her unusual parents.

"At any rate, the times we were raised in were hard times, weren't they?"

When she stood up, I realized Louise was also small. I imagined that both women resembled their mother in build. Was it right to assume that Mako, who had been told that when she was young looked more like her father than her sisters or brother had, had come to take on her mother's features as she grew older? As I gazed into the youthful and beautiful eyes of these sisters who were long past forty and nearing their fifties, I could well imagine their beauty during the heyday of their youth. What with Louise talking about her marriage and Mako's having

referred previously to her second marriage, I guessed that
the unusual passion in the blood of Osugi and Noe had
been inherited by their daughters.

It took less than thirty minutes to get to Imajuku from
there. The car ran along a straight road leading to Karatsu
and before we realized it, we found the sea glittering to the
right of our car window.

The blue of Hakata Bay is whiter and nearer the blue of
sky than the waters of the Seto Inland Sea. Inside the bay
the usually raging waves from the Sea of Genkai had
calmly and quietly settled, and we could see the shadows of
boats gently floating on the clear waters of the sea. The
beach along the coast is narrow, and I was reminded of the
seacoast of Shonan with its smooth flat feeling without
rocks or stones.

No one was on the beach. Our driver told us it was just
at this hour that the area was the quietest and offered the
best view. In summertime this coast is as thick with crowds
as the coast of Shonan, so there is no room to take even a
step.

Around the area where Iki-no-Matsubara appeared,
painted barracks, apparently the remains of a summer
resort, caught our eye. The pine trees grew in such clusters
in so narrow a place that rather than call them beautiful, I
received a somewhat eerie impression from them.

I had expected that the house Noe was born in would be
on the outskirts of the pine grove, but I now found it was
more to the west. The town of Imajuku extended along the
bus route like a sash. Another stretch of narrow road
continued nearer the seacoast than the wide paved road we
were on, and the row of low-built houses on both sides of
that narrow road probably formed the old village of
Imajuku.

When at Mako's direction we turned toward the sea down that narrow road where a police box was located, our car immediately came out on the beach as if we were about to plunge into Hakata Bay. Just beneath the stone wall of a high breakwater, the sea came to a sudden halt. The sandy beach was so covered with fragments of rough stone I felt as pained as if I had been walking over it in my bare feet.

The smooth coastline of the bay revealed a clear gentle curve as if it had been drawn with a compass, Imazu Bay widely nestled in it. Myoken Cape stretched to the east, and jutting out at the end of a headland to the west was the handful of homes of the town of Imazu, one behind the other. The horizon of the spacious Sea of Genkai outside the bay extended beyond as if fusing into sky. As I stood on the shore of this coastline so deficient in variety and so smooth it seemed almost too prosaic, what glittered to overflowing in my visual field was the blue expanse of water and sky, and I felt a yearning as if my heart had been naturally lured beyond that sea spreading out like a fan unfolding. I could only nod my head in agreement as I felt that if anyone stood on this beach every morning and evening, stared at this sleepy tranquil line of coast, and gazed at the approach and return of the tracks of those waves of the sea, that person's heart, be it Noe's or not, would be filled with longing to set out on a journey to some distant world beyond. The wind from the sea was also gentle, but if I gave my mind to it, the sound of waves was continually reverberating into the wind as they quietly beat against the shore.

"This is our old family house."

Mako pointed to a dwelling behind her with its wide wooden wall at the corner of a narrow road. The one-story structure, so low it lay concealed behind this wooden barrier, had probably been built that way to provide protection from the sea wind. It was an unpretentious house in the style of a fisherman's dwelling often seen along the coast.

"Fortunately my aunt has just come from Shimonoseki where she lives, so please meet her. It's too bad you can't talk to my uncle because he's been sick in bed since the end of last year."

I almost gasped at this unexpected good luck. Though there were five children including Noe in her family, only one of the others was a girl, Tsuta by name, two years Noe's junior. And Mako had just said this very Tsuta from Shimonoseki was inside the house. The sick uncle referred to was Noe's second elder brother Yoshibei, her eldest brother Yoshijiro having died young shortly after going to Manchuria. Apparently even Yoshibei was a kind of character, what with his having left home early, living in Saga, devoting himself to inventing and designing, and holding many patents. Late in life he had returned home, had inherited his parents' house, and had led a quiet existence, but Mako said that only last year he had collapsed from a brain hemorrhage.

When I was shown through the house, I found Yoshibei lying in bed in an eight-mat room at the back of the dwelling. The invalid, whose features were conspicuously white, had been born in the twenty-fifth year of Meiji, so I guessed him to be seventy-three. This person too looked far younger than his years, and for an old man he had a soft, genial expression on a face devoid of the unusual blemishes of the aged. Even in bed his figure looked great and imposing. I recalled that the bed on which Kichi Dai had been lying was also rather long and bulky for an elderly person ninety years old.

Tsuta, who had come to inquire after Yoshibei's health and to attend to his needs, had the surname Takabe. She was five years Yoshibei's junior, but with her erect frame and her height noticeably tall for a woman, she seemed much younger. She had a dark complexion, and her upper and lower teeth were missing, but her coloring was healthy. In the beauty and brightness of her large eyes with their long dark lashes and their gently arching length of brow, the charm of her early years could still be seen, unmistakable traces in her of the Yorozuya-type attractiveness. Her dark hair with its sprinkling of gray was artlessly done up in foreign style, and she had on a Japanese cooking apron over her black kimono, indications of her indifference to personal appearance. Once she began, she did not mince words as she spoke openly and frankly, and no matter what I asked, she came through with a response. While she talked, an indescribable light spread over her beautiful eyes, and I felt an easy familiarity growing between us. This generous freedom of behavior and refreshing lack of caution with strangers were common characteristics of all members of the Ito family.

It seemed to me that even Yoshibei, who hardly seemed able to talk, was attending to our conversation, and with an expression that indicated he did not dislike listening, he occasionally smiled as if faintly recalling something.

Beyond was a veranda, a garden which had been tended with great care, and the blue expanse of sea above the wooden wall at the back of the garden. As I was sitting in this room, I could hear the ceaseless sound of waves. The sound I heard was much stronger than when I had stood on the beach, and I felt as if the dull thud of wave after wave was reverberating through my entire body.

"Since my elder sister was only two years older than me,

the two of us, the only sister each of us had, confided everything to one another from the time we were children, and certainly we kept no secrets. Yes, yes, throughout my life I've been put to trouble by Noe. Because from the time she was a child she didn't care about others. Well, she did like studying, and she did quite well at school. From the time she was little, she hated to play with children her age, and she was always doing something by herself. Often at supper time we couldn't find her even after we lit the lamps, so all of us at home were quite worried, but on those occasions when I opened one of the closets, I would almost always find her there. Having brought in a candle, she'd be absorbed in reading every single line in the old newspapers pasted on the walls inside the closet and behind its sliding partition. You see, our family was already poor in those days, so there were no books or magazines in the house, and for that reason I guess she even did things like that. At any rate, reading was what she liked to do more than anything else. Even at that time she was a child who wouldn't do a single thing she disliked, and she thought only of herself. Just studying by herself made her indifferent to everything else, even if it caused our mother trouble or forced the rest of us to cry. Thanks to her, I always had to take the losing part. When we were old enough to know what was happening around us, we realized our father stayed away from home. Yes, certainly from the time our father was young, he had been fond of music, singing, and dancing, and because he was by nature a clever man, he was generally good at fishing, flower arranging, tea ceremony, and cooking. His strong point was in singing to the accompaniment of the samisen, and he was so good on the samisen and at singing ballads he could put even a professional to shame. He was even skillful at dancing. I guess he deserved to be called a profligate because of these things. There were times when he stayed away from home for quite a few years, and my mother had to work hard to provide for her children. My elder sister was our father's favorite child, and she was trained early to play the samisen and to dance. Whenever a troupe of players or anything of the sort came to town, my father dropped whatever he was doing to go, taking my elder sister with him, and he often made her appear on the stage. I couldn't look on with indifference as I saw my mother working alone in the fields around our neighborhood or doing piecework in order to raise her children, so from the time I was little I tried to help her, but my elder sister was totally indifferent as to whether our mother or I was troubled. On top of that, even after Noe became an adult, she continued to mercilessly inconvenience our mother, and she never did any of the duties a child is supposed to do for a parent. Certainly my elder sister was blessed with a lucky and easygoing temperament. The only reason she went to my aunt's home in Nagasaki was to study, and that was because my aunt's place offered a more convenient environment for study than our house did. Noe's writing us that my uncle and aunt treated her harshly was complete nonsense. Even at my aunt's home she was allowed to do as she wished, just as much as Chiyoko was.

"Because my aunt's family went up to Tokyo, Noe came back home and graduated from Shusenji Higher Elementary School about two and a half miles away. She was immediately employed at the local post office for a while, but she was quite disgusted at living in a town of this kind and thought only of going up to Tokyo.

"From the very start she had no interest in working at a post office in a country town, and she took an examination to enter the Kumamoto Communications Bureau. Though she came out first on the written test, her fingers were clumsy, not skillful enough in striking those telegraph keys, and she failed. Well, apparently she was a person unskilled in the use of her fingers. At least she could sew a kimono. When she was a young girl, she didn't take the slightest interest in love or anything like that. She never had the least bit to do with any of the young men around here. Of course, she was bright at school and pretty and attractive, and there were some men who liked her in a friendly way. Generally speaking, though, she studied hard when she was young and had no interest at all in young men.

"She was strong-willed, and though I'm rather talkative now, I was quite reserved in my younger days, since my sister would speak rapidly about whatever she felt like saying to anybody. When she grew up, though, it was just the opposite and she became quiet.

"You want to know about her first marriage? Well, she wrote that our parents and her uncle Dai and his wife had mercilessly decided everything according to what they wished and that she was the victim, but it wasn't that way at all.

"Of course, I'm not denying the marriage was arranged by our parents when my elder sister was at that girls' high school, but marriages of girls in those days were arranged in this way all over Japan, weren't they? The other party was well acquainted with all the members of our family, and even I had often gone to his home on festival days and other occasions. She wrote she had never seen the fellow's face or even known his name, but that wasn't the way it was. Not only that, for although she said she had no intention whatever of marrying him and that our parents heartlessly and forcibly made her, she did once definitely consent. Yes, of course, she never took a fancy to him even once from the very first, but she was fascinated by the prospect of going to America, and she told me that if she did get there, she'd definitely run away from him. So when they celebrated the wedding during the summer vacation when she was in the fifth grade in her high school, she certainly had consented. Even now I remember her hair in the *shimada* style with the bridal hood over it and her short-sleeved crested coat of gauze crepe, and I can remember she was talked about as one of the prettiest brides ever seen in our vicinity. It may sound strange for me to say this, but when she was very young, she didn't spruce up at all and didn't care in the least about her hair and clothing, but she was really pretty then.

"But when she was getting ready for the wedding ceremony, she flared up in anger, saying she didn't like him after all and, as if she were a man, deliberately walked along recklessly kicking up the skirt of her bridal outfit. She so worked off her bad temper on everyone around her she made all of us quite uneasy.

"The day after she married, she came running back home and promptly hurried off to her school in Tokyo. It seems she hadn't allowed the groom to make the slightest move toward her.

"'I wouldn't let even one of his fingers touch me!' she boasted, but we talked it over among ourselves and decided that we had never heard of the existence of such a submissive husband. Well, actually, he was a most unattractive man. All he had to him was that submissiveness, and even I found him distasteful. But as soon as my sister came home, she said quite calmly to me, 'Tsuta, it's better if you marry him instead.' That was her way of talking. And she really thought so. But even I found this kind of man disgusting.

"Though I sarcastically and severely asked how on earth a person like her could live, thinking only of herself and never paying any attention to her family or parents, she arrogantly declared our parents were poor out of their own choice and so it wasn't our responsibility. Nevertheless, with total indifference she continued to inconvenience others. Oh yes, as for me, she gave me lots of trouble until she died, and I never received a single world of thanks from her.

"Later on I settled down in Shimonoseki, and when she was on her way back home from Tokyo, she'd stop off at my place. She always bought her ticket only as far as Shimonoseki. And when she was returning to Tokyo from Imajuku, without fail her ticket was bought only to Shimonoseki. She had decided the remaining portion of her ticket would be handed to her by me, and as for some extra spending money, she had decided that I, of course, would hand that out too.

"Each time she came home, my mother had to work like a horse. Yes, whenever my sister gave birth to a child, whether by Tsuji or Osugi, she came back to Imajuku. You're asking why? Of course, it was because she had made up her mind that the cheapest way of having a baby and getting a rest before and after the birth was at home. My mother, who was already old, often complained about being forced to wash diapers even while having to watch Noe's other small children. Though I told my mother it would be all right to abandon a daughter who had never once since childhood helped her, the fact was my mother was a gentle person, and saying, 'Still, she is my daughter,' continued to look after my sister's needs. Even during the time of a birth, Noe would be reading her books whenever she had a moment to spare, and during that period when she came home, she never washed any diapers or anything else.

"Everyone in our neighborhood whispered about how such a good mother had ever given birth to such a daughter. To make matters worse, there were many times when she came either with Tsuji or Osugi as her husband. When she turned up with Osugi, our father was angry and for a long time broke off with them with the remark that he couldn't show his face to the world, but finally he gave in, and she again began bringing Osugi with her.

"Yes, well, she was lucky with men, wasn't she? Both Tsuji and Osugi were quite kind, and they thought highly of her, referring to whatever related to her by saying 'my dear Noe-san' this or 'my dear Noe-san' that. Both of them were good men, but I guess Osugi was much the better after all. He was more of a man, kinder, more dignified.

"In a way, Tsuji was somewhat feeble and gave one the impression of shilly-shallying. My sister finally complained he was a nincompoop, a good-for-nothing.

"Even now I can remember Osugi with his big body bent down by the side of our well as he washed their babies' diapers. Whenever he came, he worked hard doing this kind of thing, even washing Noe's undergarments for her.

"As for Tsuji, of course, she loved him very much at the beginning. He was quite an expert on the shakuhachi bamboo flute, and I remember how they often played together, my sister accompanying him on the samisen.

"She played it quite well, and she was also good at singing, since she'd been trained in both by our father. After she married Tsuji, she was taught how to sing and play the long epic songs of Japan, thanks to Tsuji's mother, who was quite accomplished in the arts, especially in these epic songs, because she was the daughter of wealthy rice distributor at Kuramae in Asakusa. You see, what my sister learned at home were short ballads and love songs, things like that. You can probably imagine how my mother felt, constantly having to take care of either Tsuji's children or Osugi's. My father and mother were rural people, and no matter which man came they said he was, after all, their daughter's husband, so it seemed they worked as hard as possible.

"After Noe lived with Osugi, our small quiet village came to be thrown into a turmoil. Up until then the police officials stationed in our village had nothing to do after they came to live here, and they were quite happy to come and just go fishing, but the moment my sister began living with Osugi, the officials were put to much trouble. Each time they went to our house, they complained it was just their bad luck to have been ordered to be stationed in such a town. Well, every three days without fail they had to appear at our house to ask us what letters had arrived from Tokyo or if any strange things had occurred. And if at that moment while they were questioning us, my sister and her husband happened to turn up, the police were quite alarmed. For a whole day they would have to loiter around our house as they stood watch outside. And besides that, since my sister and Osugi openly accompanied each other on quiet walks, the police were ready to drop with fatigue from following them. In the long run, my sister won these constables over, and she sent them off on errands and made them watch her children. She always had them carry her luggage from the station.

"As usual, she didn't care about her appearance in the least, and when she came back home, she'd be wearing her shabbiest kimono, intending to have it mended by our mother, and so Noe wore it nonchalantly, the cotton bulging out of the kimono seams. The strings for tying her *haori* half-coat were always twisted pieces of paper. When our mother, unable to look on with indifference, said, 'At least why not set your hair when you come back to the village, since every soul is looking at you!' Noe would declare arrogantly, 'Before long, women will be wearing their hair like mine! Just wait and see.' When I think back to that now, my elder sister's prophecy has actually come true, hasn't it?

"Yes, about the time she was killed, she was often wearing foreign-style clothing. Her hair was bobbed, and she even wore a hat. Osugi was a born dandy, and it being his way to be finicky about clothes, he was extravagant in appearance. I guess my elder sister was influenced by him. Osugi was quite particular about their children's clothing, and Mako-san was made to wear the kind of stylish outfit Osugi liked. So even when we looked after the children here, he made them wear only European dress and brought them wearing the latest fashions. In those days no children in the rural districts wore European clothes, and girls with a Dutch bob were even rarer. Certainly it was quite unusual for a woman to wear European dresses in 1923, even in Tokyo, don't you think? But there was something becoming about my sister in her European attire. She was exceedingly confident that whatever she wore or whatever she did was suitable, so it seems everything and anything became her.

"Oh yes, I just remembered something very interesting about Tsuji. When I returned home after escaping from the family I had married into, my first marriage having failed, it was just then that Tsuji first came to our house and

I happened to meet him. At that time he said he would take me up to Tokyo to make me an actress in the Imperial Theatre, and he kept insisting he could definitely turn me into a success. Even Noe was in earnest about it and encouraged me. It sounds strange to remember that now, but when this was told to me, I somehow felt it wouldn't be a bad thing to appear on the stage, having always liked singing and dancing, and I came to want to go. But for some reason or other my father was against it and wouldn't let me. In those days Sumako Matsui, who acted the parts of Nora and Katucha, had created a sensation all over the country, not to mention the actresses at the Imperial Theatre, so I couldn't deny I had a longing to become an actress. Though my father was fond of singing and dancing and even forced his daughter to dance on the stage as one of his favorite diversions, he nevertheless felt that being a professional actress was worse than being a geisha, obsessed as he was with the old-fashioned idea that no woman should degrade herself by becoming an actress, the word for actress, *kawarakojiki*, equivalent to beggar.

"Oh, is it my marriage you're asking about? The first was when I was seventeen and married a very wealthy man from a neighboring prefecture after he took a fancy to my looks. But since he was a person who had never had to worry about money, he was deceived by a swindler just after our marriage and went prospecting for gold with him after he had told my husband they could find a gold mine in Kagoshima.

"The moment they arrived there, they indulged in all luxuries regardless of expense. They continued their foolish diversions by being spectators at the theatre from morning till night after reserving box seats for a full month and by having geisha parties at teahouses, even asking me to join them, and then when they finally went into the mountains, there was nothing to take out because it was all nonsense from the first, so little by little my husband got in financially beyond his depth and in less than six months found himself quite penniless. The swindler made off with all my husband's money, and I was turned into a prisoner by being forced to stay by myself at the mine while my husband went down the mountain to raise some cash. The money he sent me was seized on the way by his associates, and all of them absconded. The time kept passing and I still couldn't come down from that mine. All the villagers around me kept watching me because everyone connected with my husband had bought everything on credit and had avoided paying their bills at the inns and eating houses and grocery stores. Finally even I ran out of food, and all my clothes were taken away one by one so that I was left only in my kimono undergarment and the long cloth around my loins. For three days, from morning to night, I spent my time in bed. The children who occasionally came to peek in at me soon found me in bed whenever they came and once, thinking I was dead, raised a great outcry.

"Someone advised me there was no other course than to run away at night, so I escaped by the skin of my teeth, but when looking like a beggar I finally found my way to my husband's house, I was told it was no longer ours. My husband had received such a severe shock he had become deranged and entered a mental hospital. While I was nursing my husband, who immediately after enjoying the very heights of luxury had been thrust into the very depths of poverty and who had gone berserk without understanding what was what, my aunt Dai, who had married me off to him, came to see me and suddenly made me go back with her. I was still young and unable to make heads or tails of

what it was all about, but in only one year I had been raised
to the summit of life and flung to its very abyss, and that
was how it ended for us. It was then that I met Tsuji. If my
disposition had been like my elder sister's, I probably
would have ventured up to Tokyo regardless of my father's
opposition and would have let Tsuji make me into an
actress. There's no knowing about one's destiny. I had
learned a costly lesson by my marriage, and I felt no man
deserved to be called such unless he could overcome
adversity when put to the test. My next marriage was to a
person twenty-seven years older than me. My sister said at
that time as if treating me with contempt, 'Why on earth
marry a man whose age is so different from yours! Will it
satisfy you?' And since I couldn't forget her words, I also
said to her when she married Osugi, 'Why on earth do you
want to marry a man who has so many women around him?
Will it satisfy you?'

"She said quite calmly, 'As for those women, I don't care
how many there are. Because I'll be the one to monopolize
him before long!' Well, it absolutely turned out the way
she said. That was really strange. And even about her death
she told me, 'After all, we won't die normally on straw
mats. In all probability we'll be murdered when we least
expect it. So if that time should come, never be confused or
grieve over me. Even if we should be killed, we ourselves
will be happy because we have always done what we felt was
worth doing.' Even those words turned out to be true. Yes,
at that time we were informed by the Dentsu news agency
even before the special edition of the newspapers came out.
Perhaps because we had often been told of such a possibility by my sister, we merely thought, 'Well, at last it's so,'
and we were neither too surprised nor too suddenly
saddened. Even our parents told me they felt the same way.

"My second husband ran a house in a red-light district in Osaka and later in Shimonoseki. Although my sister had principles, she never criticized our business. Nor did Osugi. Instead, though, their taking money from us seemed like the most natural thing in the world. They often came to our house in Shimonoseki. At first my husband, his age being what it was, couldn't understand them in the least and didn't like to associate with them, and so after receiving my sister's letter, I always went to the station to meet them and handed them some money there, and that was how I met them to talk over many things. But gradually my husband was able to understand them, and my sister and Osugi came to see us at home. Yet what troubles we had after they arrived! Without fail, we would be summoned by the police and even asked what time they woke up and when they ate. The questioning took all day, and it disgusted us! During their stay with us, two or three detectives would be standing around our house watching. It was an absolute torment! So finally when my sister reached the station, she herself telephoned the police and told them they had just arrived. In the end there was the spectacle of the police carrying her luggage and riding the children on their backs and sending all of them up to our house.

"Speaking about misery and happiness, I have never been as miserable as the time my sister and her husband were killed and my father and uncle Dai came back from Tokyo with the children. Because my sister was killed twenty days after the birth of her last child Nestor, this last baby couldn't even hold its head properly. The older children were two-year-old Louise, three-year-old Ema, and Mako, who was seven. Yes, I'm counting their ages in the Japanese way so they were even younger. My father was carrying the baby in one arm while holding Louise's hand with the other, and my uncle was leading Ema and Mako with both his hands.

"Each time they arrived at one of the stations between Tokyo and Shimonoseki, many newspaper reporters suddenly crowded onto the train, taking pictures and interviewing them, so it must have been unbearable. When I went to Shimonoseki Station to meet them, it was so jammed I couldn't even get near. It wasn't only the reporters, for the place was crawling with busybodies trying to catch a glimpse of the children, and the entire station was in great confusion. When I finally reached them after pushing my way through the crowds, I found my father totally exhausted and the baby, who hadn't received enough milk, almost senseless.

"Mako was stomping her feet on the ground screaming, 'I hate having my picture taken!' Attracted by her cries, Ema and Louise started bawling frantically. We couldn't do anything to make them stop. There wasn't even any water to mix the condensed milk with. But just then across from us a woman also with a baby held out her thermos of hot water. I too began crying, thinking we had really found a friend just when we needed one. After finally dissolving the condensed milk in hot water and giving it to the baby and pacifying the other children, we once more boarded the train and at long last started off. I cannot forget the misery I felt at that time. For the first time I was really enraged by the cruelty of my sister's death, forcing her to leave behind such lovely children.

"Already in those days my husband was in complete sympathy with my sister and her husband, so all the articles in the newspapers and magazines that came out at the time on Osugi and her he clipped out, no matter what was covered, and he put them neatly away. He never wanted the children to see them as long as they were alive. But saying these articles might be of some use, he kept diligently cutting them out and accumulating them. Yes, the pile of clippings was handed over to Ema after she grew up—she had been raised in our home. The child who looked most like my sister is Ema, who now lives in Shimonoseki. Clearly she most resembles Noe in her younger years.

"In those days we were troubled by the fact that many people wanted to do something for these children. We were surprised that even in that era so many people still wanted to raise the children of Osugi and Noe. All of them were decent, the offers coming only from rich men and scholars and other respectable persons. There were ever so many proposals to which they appended explanatory notes and inventories, like lists of their property and rough sketches of their homes. But confronted by these wild schemes, my father firmly held out against letting even one of the children go anywhere, and he was determined to raise them himself. Even though my elder sister had put my father through terrible troubles while she was alive, she was his favorite daughter, and in the long run he had unconsciously been influenced by her, so I believe he couldn't bring himself to hand her children over to others.

"Though I was Noe's only sister, the life I lived was quite different from hers. After I married a second time, I was never in need of money, and because of our difference in age my husband overlooked everything I did and let me do as I wished with all the luxuries he gave me. Nevertheless, my way of thinking was different because of our difference in age, so without really being able to understand him, I was not that satisfied somehow.

"I tried to compensate for the loneliness and emptiness

I felt by making use of luxury and diversion, so matters became worse. The only thing I didn't do was take a lover, but as for other possibilities, I drained the cup of pleasure with everything and anything that men do. Every day I went to the theatre and I went to teahouses with my friends and I even called in geisha. I gambled. I drank saké. And besides all that, I decked myself from the top of my head to the tips of my toes in the most extravagant luxuries. I put on so many diamonds and draped myself in furs to my heart's content. When our house burned in the war, we became quite penniless, but due to the fact that I had been content at least once in my life, I no longer have any interest in anything or in desiring anything.

"Oddly enough, my husband, who had been thoroughly put out by my conduct, finally became partial to my sister and once after returning from a visit to her place in Tokyo kept saying, 'Everyone keeps mentioning that Noe's a woman who's more dreadful than a man, but when I went to Osugi's, I found, on the contrary, there's no woman equal to her in femininity. In her gestures and in her consideration for others, she's really womanly. I really understand now why all the men are crazy about her. When I compare you with her, even though you look like the embodiment of all that is womanly, you are truly a masculine woman!' That was what he was complaining about. Everyone in our family line lived long, many to be eighty or ninety. If my sister had not died in this way, she too would have lived on and on in good health.

"Though I couldn't give birth to even one child, my sister had seven children in ten years and died, according to the modern way of counting, when she was only twenty-eight. That alone shows how much vitality she had. Only twenty days after the delivery of her child, she went to

Yokohama with Osugi during one of those dangerous times after the earthquake. Sometimes, even now, though it's my own idea, I feel Noe and her husband wouldn't have been killed if the Great Earthquake had occurred half a year later. To tell the truth, they were preparing to abandon some of their ideas, thinking about their children's future and saying they would put an end to their dangerous affairs. They really did tell us that . . . Good heavens! It's gotten dark outside. Dear me! I forgot myself in talking so carelessly about the things I did, and I've made you listen to my own absurd and trivial matters. Please forgive me!"

When we returned to Hakata, the lights downtown were already glittering. Mako had the driver turn down a dark street near Hakata Station and said to me, "Please come in and meet my child."

When we entered the old two-story house with its earthen floor, the dwelling apparently in the style of a residence in a shopping district, several men and women sitting in a wooden area near the entrance were painting Hakata dolls. I realized Mako's business was now the making of these dolls. Having caught the sound of our voices, a young girl with a big round face grinned as she came down from upstairs and standing by her mother's side greeted me.

Far taller than her mother and still growing was Mako's youngest child, who was in the sixth grade and who had once said to her parent, "My granddaddy was a great man, wasn't he? That's what my teacher told me." Above her smooth cocoa-brown cheeks were the unmistakably inherited Yorozuya eyebrows and eyes. Was it my own sentimentality that made me feel the child's face looked less like her sensitive mother's than it did the photograph of Noe as a wild young girl?

Chapter 2

IT WAS APRIL in the spring of 1911 that Jun Tsuji met
Noe Ito for the first time. The execution of Shusui Kotoku
and others for high treason had been carried out on
January 25, and only two months later the spring was so
ominously cold that even in the color of the cherry
blossoms just after they had bloomed and even in the
spring breeze one sensed the image of blood, the smell of
decay.

On that spring day the entrance ceremony at Ueno
Girls' High School was held. The *oshima* kimono Tsuji
wore, bequeathed him by his father, had been hemmed up
by his mother before Tsuji had set out. Because the
kimono had been inherited from his father, its folds were
considerably worn, but the *hakama* skirt, originally of
superior Sendaihira silk, was neatly bound low around
Tsuji's waist, and he had on a *haori* of black *habutae* silk,
though the color of its crest was somewhat dulled. In that
outfit Jun Tsuji's shoulders looked narrow and drooping,
the skin of his oval face pale. The thin silver frames of the
glasses he wore made his delicate face with its classical
features seem nervous, but his eyes and their corners
sloping downward gave an impression of mildness.

Behind Jun Tsuji, being led by the assistant principal

into the auditorium where the pupils were already standing in rows, the murmurs of the girl students broke out, those murmurs spreading to every corner of the hall with a commotion and speed like rippling waves. When the assistant principal, who was walking in front of Tsuji, seemed to deliberately clear his throat, the noise instantly subsided, along with those voices saying "Sh! Sh!"

"He really looks terribly old."

"No. He's still young."

"He's like an artiste!"

When he caught these whispers out of the clamor that had suddenly died down, Tsuji suppressed a sardonic smile. His unusually keen sense of hearing had been inherited from his mother.

Almost all the chairs were occupied by other teachers sitting in rows near the windows at the side of the platform. Lined up in front were seats for the headmaster and his assistant and for the new appointee too. As if everyone had been waiting impatiently for these three persons to sit, the ceremony began.

Tsuji was no longer that young to feel nervous in being exposed to the glances of several hundred girl students. Born in 1884, he was twenty-eight according to the Japanese way of counting, but since he had dropped out during his second year of middle school, he had come through some unusual difficulties, studying English by himself while frequently changing jobs. What with being forced to endure a hard life from the age of twelve or thirteen, he had never known what it was to be young. Marked somewhere on his face was a dark shade of pessimism, and he was apt to be thought older than he actually was.

The strange odor which had pierced his nostrils the

moment he had entered the hall had increased in intensity so that he felt more and more nauseous, every pore on his skin seemingly impregnated. He thought the smell a mixture of the body odor of the girls crowded into the auditorium and the aroma from their hair oil.

"Well, it's inevitable you'll feel nauseated by that female smell for a week. So do your utmost to prepare for it."

As Nakano, his friend who had helped get him into the school, had said, Tsuji was experiencing that "female smell." While Tsuji wondered during the formalities of the ceremony how long he would continue as a teacher in the midst of this female odor, he experienced a sensation like the sudden nausea one feels before taking up chopsticks in front of a plate piled high with food.

It was to support his mother, brother, and sister rather than for the sake of earning a living that he had sought a job as a teacher at a private school when he was nineteen by the Japanese way of counting, and at twenty he had become an elementary school instructor with a special license to teach one course, several years having followed in an instant. His beginning monthly salary of nine yen had been no more than a trifle, even though an additional salary for long service had been attached. This girls' high school was privately run, and it would probably be a somewhat leisurely place, his monthly stipend almost forty yen. Attracted only for these reasons and not for any real love of devoting his life to teaching, he had transferred to this school. If possible, he wanted to confine himself all day in his study, to bury himself among his favorite books of all times and places, to immerse himself in them from morning till night.

Ever since he could remember, he had loved books. His mother Mitsu, born at Kuramae in Asakusa as the daughter of a distributor of rice to retainers of the daimyo class, had been raised with extraordinary care and training, at the time of her marriage bringing among her possessions from her parents' home many kinds of *ezōshi*, illustrated storybooks flavored with Edo culture. The moment Tsuji began to understand what was going on around him, he was drawn into the world of these strange fascinating stories of the *ezōshi*, and from the age of seven or eight, when he was able to read, he was infatuated with the extraordinary adventures in *Saiyuki*, a long novel set in Ming dynasty China. Both the *ezōshi* and *Saiyuki* expanded the boy's dreams infinitely. At the end of a period of random omnivorous reading, the romantic lad of twelve or thirteen was a precocious peevish type whose favorite book was *Tsurezuregusa*, a collection of short sketches, anecdotes, and essays.

His father Rokujiro, once a vassal of the shogunate, had been an apprenticed law student and had become a minor government official. He had served in the legal division of the Tokyo municipal government and, when Tsuji was seven or eight, was working in the Mie prefectural office. In Tsuji's tenth year his father's duties were again shifted to Tokyo, the family living on Sakumacho in Kanda, and there the father suddenly died. Left behind in addition to Tsuji were a younger sister and brother. The mother, raised in luxury since her birth, was weak at managing the family budget after her marriage, and with the death of her husband no funds remained in reserve.

Having withdrawn in his second year from Kaisei Middle School, Tsuji found himself the sole support of his family, maintaining his mother, brother, and sister when he was fourteen or fifteen. Even while he had to work, he attended Athenée Français and the People's English Acad-

emy; furthermore, he commuted to lectures at the Liberty
English Academy at Hitotsubashi in Kanda. By listening
there to the lectures of Yubi Aoyagi and Inazo Nitobe,
Tsuji became acquainted with the names of Carlyle and
Goethe, and his eyes opened to translated works of literature. His random reading was shifted from Japanese and
Chinese literature to European works. *Saiyuki* was transformed into Baudelaire, extended to Hoffmann, and drawn
on to Poe. *Tsurezuregusa* became Lao-tze and Chuang-tsu,
shifted to the Bible, turned into Stirner and Sterne, and
from Senancour extended to the heights of Leopardi.
Besides reading, Tsuji tried his hand at short stories and
made some secret attempts at translating. At the same
time, it was inevitable that he would be concerned with the
current trend toward socialism, which in those days was
advancing like surging waves. He read whatever he could
lay his hands on, from anarchistic to Marxist literature, and
he was a devoted reader of the *Heimin Shinbun*, edited by
Shusui Kotoku. As a new appointee at Ueno Girls' High
School, Jun Tsuji was already a young literary enthusiast
with an erudition born from this kind of spiritual background and with many complicated folds of a nihilistic
mentality.

After the tedious greetings and admonitory comments
of the headmaster and guests, a girl stood up in the front
row diagonally across from Tsuji. The assistant principal's
voice was heard, indicating the congratulatory address was
to be given by the student-body representative.

The girl, short and plump, her cocoa-brown cheeks
flushed and shining against her downy hair, was staring
straight ahead with pitch-black pupils one would instinctively wish to peer into, both ends of her full lips raised as
she walked with long strides toward the freshmen students.

Almost all the pupils, ribbons in their low pompadours, were dressed in maroon *hakama* skirts with crested black cotton *haori*, the uniform for ceremonial days.

She was the only girl who wore her hair in foreign style, gathering it together simply at the nape, the ribbonless hair strikingly black and abundant. Something slovenly and unrefined was evident in the way she had joined the neckband of her kimono and had put on her *hakama*.

She turned stiff as she delivered her short commonplace message of congratulations, and concluding by saying she was Noe Ito, representing all the students, she swept back to her seat. Apparently relieved at having finished her task, Noe was even more flushed, the pupils of her eyes moist and glittering.

Tsuji had paid no attention to the contents of Noe's prosaic remarks, but he had quite agreeably attuned himself to the beauty of her tense penetrating voice.

As she sat down, their eyes happened to meet. Noe made her dark eyes widen and, as if astonished, looked Tsuji straight in the face. Her eyes frankly communicated the drift of a mind full of curiosity, Tsuji parrying that lively movement with the vitality of one observing a fresh piece of fruit. The eyes of the girl, which were so voluptuous they reflected the pure childish curiosity and excitable sensitive agitation he had lost long ago, were softly tantalizing Tsuji's breast with a velvet-like touch. After the formal reply by the representative of the new students, which was twice as long as Noe's address, the principal introduced Jun Tsuji as the new teacher of English.

As he stood and walked toward the stage, he had a strange and vivid sensation of being stared at from behind by Noe's dark passionate eyes.

In no time at all Tsuji became an object of student

adoration. Even those students who at the start had spoken ill of him as wavering and feminine suddenly and easily changed into devotees once they attended the new teacher's classes. Tsuji's English pronunciation was completely different from that of the old principal, who had been instructing them until then. When the young Tsuji read from the very same English textbook, he conveyed to them for the first time exotic and musical sounds. He wrote on the blackboard some of Poe's poetry which was not in their book and had them copy it. Noe and her fifth-year classmates, in ecstasy over "Annabel Lee" and "The Raven," learned the poems by heart.

At first Tsuji was surprised that the Noe he saw from his position as teacher was so poor in English. He expected she would be quite capable in all subjects since she had read the congratulatory address as the student-body representative, but her command of English was below the class average. Noe, small in stature, sat in the front row near the teacher's platform, and observing him as if her jet-black pupils were aflame, she stared at her teacher's face without even blinking. No matter which classroom he entered, the eyes of one or two students from among the many tens stared straight at him on the platform, but not one of those glances could obliterate the flamelike intensity burning in Noe's eyes. It was not long before Tsuji was told by Nakano, who was in charge of Noe's class, that the girl had suddenly been allowed to enter as a fourth-year student the previous year by a special selection committee, that she was poorest in English because she had until then been living in some out-of-the-way place in Kyushu, but that she was an extraordinary student with something of a natural gift for literature. Tsuji easily surmised Nakano cherished some great expectation from this flicker of talent in Noe. When Nakano showed him the school newspaper edited by her, Tsuji for the first time came to have a better opinion of the girl. That mimeographed newspaper which was brought out almost solely by Noe herself was, while immature, bolstered by a youthful single-minded passion overflowing with the vigor of purity. Already her essays and descriptive impressions, even while their touch was stiff and puerile, were products of an eye that could see with originality.

"It's decent enough, isn't it?" said Tsuji to his colleague, and for a while he still found himself following Noe's firm masculine prose on the mimeographed sheet.

From the time Tsuji began teaching her, Noe's progress in English was extraordinary. Putting aside the study of her other subjects, she immersed herself only in English. Her classmates, much quicker than their teacher Tsuji, stared in wonder at the way Noe's English improved so remarkably. There were occasions during his classes when even Tsuji, elaborating some grammatical point or offering an explanation of a particular translation, noticed Noe's enthusiasm and progress as he directed his glance at her flamelike eyes. The persons most involved were quite at ease, the last to notice they were already deliberately being whispered about by some of the more perceptive girls sensitive to the delicate pattern of feelings between Noe and Tsuji.

In those days Tsuji felt no attraction to Noe as a woman other than finding her "an interesting student." Eyebrows and eyes pressed closed to each other on her dark face, her eyes aflame and her thick lips voluptuous, Noe was emitting from every part of her body an odor and feeling like that of a wild beast warming itself in the sun. To Tsuji's eyes, with their taste for Edo culture, especially for the elegance of the downtown quarters, Noe's untidy negligence of dress was a reflection of her rustic and even dirty background. However, as her teacher he could not be indifferent to her avaricious pursuit of knowledge and the delicate susceptibility with which, like litmus paper moistened with water, she revealed a vivid reaction with precision and speed to everything he taught her. He found it interesting that without exception all the women teachers disliked her, saying she was quite assertive and conceited about everything she did and there was nothing pleasant about her. Tsuji rather felt Noe's stubbornness and serious rebellion wild and lovely.

Gradually he found himself stimulating Noe's talents outside the classroom and enjoying his endeavors at helping the hidden sprouts within her expand.

He would leave his own manuscripts with Noe, who late after classes were over was mimeographing in a corner of the teachers' room. "I've finished this. If you can use it, go ahead." Hardly daring to breathe, Noe read his translations of Gourmont, Shestov, and Wilde, and while reading his reviews of the recent works of Jun'ichiro Tanizaki and Kafu Nagai, she was unaware she was being taught how to appreciate literature. She became all the more engrossed in the school paper just to be able to receive Tsuji's manuscripts. Finally the rumors of her classmates reached her, but these made Noe with her unyielding spirit all the more rebellious, all the more daringly attracted to Tsuji.

She had come to feel she was not in school at all if on even a single day she did not see his face. She began to regard things the same way he did and to regard them with his sensibilities. Having from childhood adhered to her own strong ideas, Noe was at this late date quite indifferent to the opinions of others. After school she mimeographed the school paper out of the sheer desire to have Tsuji look at it, and once she finished her work, she went to the music room to search for him. She knew that usually every day until evening he played the piano there. Though he was a teacher of English, he revealed an extraordinary passion for music, and without fail he would turn up at all the student concerts, his own performance on the piano and organ as skillful as that of the music teacher. Noe had already heard from Tsuji himself that his playing of the many-holed shakuhachi bamboo flute, in which he had even more ability than he had on the piano, would have put a professional to shame. Sometimes Tsuji would capriciously turn back to Noe, sitting behind him as he was playing the piano, her chin cupped in her two hands, her body never stirring, and he would make her sing. Though she was at first somewhat shy, she would soon begin a Schubert nursery song she had learned at school, or the chic lyric of a love song she had been taught by her father, or some provincial sad lullaby. Her clear voice was lovely and maidenly and more than made up for the trace of wildness in her features.

Tsuji was quick to accompany her on any of these songs, and thinking to startle her he taught her some English hymns. Eventually the students came to catch sight of the figures of Tsuji and Noe keeping each other company on the way to and from school. By the time Tsuji accidentally realized it, he always found Noe walking beside him. Whether by investigation or other means, Noe had some great animal instinct for Tsuji's activities. But at those times the conversation of the two strollers was somewhat stiff and formal, quite far removed from any whispers of love. Usually it was talk of the kind in which Noe would give her impressions of the book she was reading at the moment and Tsuji would offer a proper response. Her facial expression, which had somehow looked gloomy and introverted, became brighter, her behavior much more lively and buoyant.

In those days Tsuji was secretly enjoying a slight infatuation with a girl quite unlike Noe. Okin-chan, the daughter of a saké-dealer in Yoshiwara, was a genuine Tokyoite. Her graceful figure was perfectly suited to her kimono of yellow silk with its black neckband, her *shimada* coiffure with its cloth chignon band of dappled scarlet typical of a woman of the downtown quarter. A beautiful girl who looked as if she had stepped out of one of Kyoka's novels, she also resembled a girl in love with literature, a devotee of a Kyoka story. Though she had left Ueno Girls' High School in midcourse, she was two or three years older than Noe.

Up to that time Tsuji had been attracted to several women, for example, the girl he had been friends with since childhood, her father a man who put on magic lantern shows; the daughter of an elderly minister of a church he had in his boyhood temporarily visited as if he were in a daze; and the wife of a diplomatic official living in Mukojima, whom Tsuji had taught English conversation a few times a week as a side job before he was employed at the girls' high school. With each of these women he had felt some mutual attraction bordering on love, but every instance had ended merely as passing infatuation. What had made him more timid toward women than one might have thought was the fact that he had not lived comfortably enough to wholly abandon himself to love, and there remained a lack of balance between his knowledge, more mature than might have been expected from someone his age, and his own inexperience in the real world. Even while he kept sending long love letters every day to the saké-dealer's daughter, whom he had met by chance, the fact remained he could not even bring himself to hold her hand.

Though Okin was not intellectual, she was literary enough to forward a thick reply to his letters of affection, so their relationship had lasted a comparatively long time, and they were sufficiently content to believe themselves in love. Occasionally Okin came to Tsuji's office because the school was her alma mater, and she even spent time talking with her old classmates. Noe, with a sensitivity common to those in love, was quick to suspect the relationship between the two, but her only displeasure was in wondering why Tsuji could like such a dull downtown type whose single qualification was a beauty similar to that of a toy doll. Noe was totally unaware that the jealousy of a girl in love had instinctively made her dislike this beautiful girl. Nor was Noe yet conscious that her affection for Tsuji was love.

From the time her parents had abruptly brought up the subject of marriage while she was at home during her summer vacation when she was a fifth-year student, Noe became all the more rapidly intimate with Tsuji. Against her will she had gone through the marriage ceremony in her hometown, and returning to Tokyo by herself after cutting short her summer vacation much earlier than expected, she went on foot directly to Tsuji's house and cast before him the disaster that had befallen her. The commonplace features of the man called Fukutaro, who had just returned from America, and his dullness in which nothing intellectual could be sensed summoned forth in her as she sat before Tsuji a hatred several times the disgust she had felt at home.

"My uncle's to blame! He was blinded by the condition that the other party would pay for my schooling, so my uncle arranged everything in his own way. And now that things have gone this far, my uncle blames me, saying if I refuse, my parents and our family name will be put in a very bad light."

Tsuji had the impression that in less than a month Noe, who was appealing to him with tears of mortification, had suddenly matured to take on something of the savor of a woman. The problem of her marrying, even while she was averse to it, and her anguish had unconsciously stimulated the body and soul of the woman in her and had probably roused into wakefulness this feminine vitality that had lain dormant within her. Tsuji sensed a kind of charm, absent until then, in the somewhat tight thin line along her cheeks and around her shoulders, and he observed the face of the crying and agitated woman, an ugly face yet one increasing in loveliness. She had hesitated to mention it but finally confessed she had already gone through the ceremony.

"I was so terrified I wouldn't let him take a step near me, and I just ran away."

Quite overwhelmed, Tsuji kept staring at her. Was it really possible for a woman to keep her husband at bay even after marrying him? Could a man exist today who remained silent while his wife dragged him down with such an insult?

Clearly feeling Noe was asking for help, Tsuji found the only thing he could do was listen silently to her resentment and her whimpering grievance. Should he thoughtlessly offer his hand, it was quite evident to him that Noe, who had already reached the point of ignition, would transfer the blazing fire of her passion to him, and in no time at all they would together go down to ruin in flames.

In any event, Noe, who had gone through the wedding ceremony, was already a married woman. And probably her name had been placed in the family register by the man who had said he would pay for her schooling. Though Tsuji felt pity for her, to get involved would prove troublesome. The worldly wisdom he had gained through long years of economic distress whispered to him to back away from her. At the same time, however, Noe's misfortune and anguish in being sacrificed to a kind of marriage of convenience and her inability to study freely as she wished due to her family's poverty, which was like his own, aroused in Tsuji a sympathy and compassion he would not have felt about another person's affair.

Noe became so emotionally stirred by the mere fact of Tsuji's mother serving her tea and cake that she began shedding even larger tears.

Inside this house with rooms of only six, four-and-a-half, and three mats, Noe's words, which continued their emotional complaint, could be heard perfectly by Tsuji's mother and sister. After Tsuji had seen Noe off and come back, he found his mother Mitsu sitting on the very cushion Noe had used only a moment ago in his three-mat study.

"Poor thing, isn't she? And still a child."

"Yes, but it can't be helped."

"That child, she likes you, doesn't she?"

"Well, I don't know."

"She's quite unsophisticated, but she's a little charmer."

"You think so? She has the blood of the old Kumaso clan in her. If you touch her carelessly, you may get burned."

"You ought to be settling down."

No longer willing to pursue the subject, Tsuji reached over for his favorite bamboo flute and turned his back to his mother. Before he put his lips to the mouth of the instrument, he waited impatiently while she cleared away the tea things and went out of the room. The piece he played was the famous "Bell of Emptiness," one of the three great traditional melodies for the shakuhachi.

His fascination with the sound of the flute had started from his seventh or eighth year. Next door to their house, which belonged to the Mie prefectural government his father was working for, there lived at that time a junior official who was quite good on the shakuhachi. His Kyoto wife could play ballads on the samisen, and Tsuji's mother Mitsu, who had rigorously acquired during her childhood the knack of playing *nagauta*, the long epic songs, frequently visited her neighbor to perform together. On those occasions Tsuji went with her and listened in rapt attention to the neighbor's flute. During Tsuji's middle school days when he was back in Tokyo, he found a cheap shakuhachi at a secondhand shop in Shitaya, and by following the neighbor's example he somehow came to be able to produce a few notes. It took him a month to make some flutelike sounds and about half a year to accomplish something like the passage of a song the way he thought it ought to go. Neglecting his studies, he lost himself in playing the flute from morning till night. His mother, who from the first loved songs accompanied by the samisen, suggested, "If you like the bamboo flute so much, why not take lessons regularly from a teacher?" The person Mitsu chose for her son was Chikuo Araki, the famous shakuhachi master of the Kinko School. In a tight-sleeved kimono patterned in white and blue splashes, Tsuji called on him one day to boldly ask for permission. Chikuo, who was already past seventy, allowed this unusual boy to become his disciple.

All of Chikuo's students ranked above the middle class, some of them even belonging to the peerage. In no time at all Chikuo clearly perceived that this poverty-stricken newcomer, his youngest disciple, whom he had allowed on a whim to enter his school, had unexpected genius. Immediately Tsuji became the disciple Chikuo loved beyond all others. But when this young prodigy expressed the desire to establish himself as a shakuhachi performer, the master flatly opposed him. "After all, shakuhachi is a dying art. Someone as young as you are shouldn't spend his entire life on that kind of thing. Do it as a hobby."

Tsuji eagerly went to Chikuo's home for his lessons on each day of the month with a three or an eight in it. Those lessons continued without interruption until Chikuo moved to Imado and it became too difficult for Tsuji to make the trip.

With his father's death it was impossible to play the shakuhachi at leisure, as Tsuji was continually driven to earn a living, but he again went back to the flute when he was twenty-one. At that time he was so highly praised as a performer that he was invited to give concerts at various places far and near.

His favorite instrument for the present was one made by Chikuo's most distinguished disciple, Kado, Tsuji's second master.

While Tsuji listened to the tones he produced on the shakuhachi, the agitation from Noe's visit that had so disturbed his peace of mind gradually subsided.

The night wind passing over the wooded area and meadow sparsely dotted with human habitations swept into this quiet home on a hill at Somei. The heat of the afternoon was at last gone, and before Tsuji realized it, the cries of insects were coiled round the sounds of his flute.

Tsuji had set himself free on the wind of night, his mind lucid as water. The serenity of tranquillity—which could not be violated by anyone at this very moment—was a handful of happiness, which he had at last acquired at twenty-eight years of age. Though this was a rented house with only three rooms in which three persons lived, his mother and her children, Tsuji was satisfied with it. Probably because the owner was a gardener, he had been careful, even though the house was small, to select timber of the finest quality when he built it, Tsuji's three-mat study at the back of the house having been made into a detached room in tea-ceremony style surrounded on all sides by a veranda.

Hanging in the alcove was an India ink drawing of the Goddess of Mercy Kannon by Chikuden, and adorning the opposite wall a portrait of Spinoza framed in lignitic Japanese cedar, and below the picture a desk. On it were only a few books, some European works, and some Japanese and Chinese classics. Tsuji's personal needs and meals were sufficiently looked after by his mother and sister. Though his remuneration from the high school was by no means large, his income was the highest in his life until then and the most reliable. If he desired a woman, he could easily buy an ignorant yet gentle prostitute with the money from his side jobs.

He had long lost any interest in making his life successful. Nor was he concerned any more about social reform. A mere glance at the ominous silence and icy indifference of the social reformers since the trials for high treason had made it quite evident to him that the realization of their ideals was even more remote. His three-mat study and bamboo shakuhachi which would not inconvenience anyone were satisfying enough, a handful of happiness for the young nihilist. He had been blessed. To become entangled in the destiny of a girl from the country whose soiled neckband smelled would have been unbearable. He was by nature, he thought, a wanton, like water. Water conforms to the shape of its container and without a moment's delay swerves into the slightest opening. Was not the strategy of water that of escape? To escape made one the victor.

While playing with perfect clarity a classical melody, Jun Tsuji found sufficient justification in his heart to leave Noe to her unhappy fate.

That summer day in 1911 in which Noe for the first time in her life was immensely troubled as she stood at a crucial turning point in her destiny was a memorable day worthy of special mention in the history of women in Japan. While Noe was suffering from the oppression of her family and their lack of understanding, some people in an obscure corner of Tokyo were steadily beginning preparations by which they would ignite the signal fires for the liberation of women, allowing them to extricate themselves from long-established customs and live freely as human beings. With Raicho Hiratsuka as chief editor several young women were bustling about in a terrible sweat under a scorching August sun for the publication of the women's literary magazine *Seito*.

It was several days after Noe had visited Jun Tsuji, the third day of the new month of September. Having spread out the morning papers on his bed as usual, Jun Tsuji raised his head with a cry. In the advertisement section on the front page of the *Asahi*, his eyes had come across a notice for a strange magazine jammed in between announcements of such famous journals as *Chuokoron*, *Taiyo*, and *Nihon Oyobi Nihonjin*.

Seito immediately reminded Tsuji of the word blue-stocking, which had its origin in the salon of Lady Montagu in the fashionable world of eighteeth-century London. Someone had once translated the word bluestocking as *aotabi*, or Japanese-style blue stocking. The advertisement had declared it the only female literary magazine in Japan. Tsuji felt something fresh and intellectual in the spirit of the women editors who, anticipating the sneers and taunts of the world, had called themselves "bluestockings."

Tsuji promptly purchased a copy of *Seito*, which appeared in the bookstores several days later. It was unmistakably a magazine for women's liberation though literature so fresh and bold it was much more than he had anticipated or hoped for. He immediately surmised that its editor Raicho Hiratsuka was Haruko Hiratsuka, who three years earlier in a suicide attempt with Shohei Morita had created quite a stir in the incident labeled "Wandering in the Snow at Shiobara." Tsuji, who was by nature a feminist, believed himself interested in and warmly sympathetic to Haruko Hiratsuka's speech and behavior since that incident three years ago. He also remembered the moment on the last day of August three years ago when he had opened his *Asahi* and had read on the society page an article under a large headline extending over several columns:

CULMINATION OF NATURALISM
GENTLEMAN AND LADY
SUICIDE ATTEMPT
LOVER A BACHELOR OF ARTS
AND NOVELIST
MISTRESS A GRADUATE OF A
WOMEN'S COLLEGE
[omission]

CAUSE OF THEIR DARING ATTEMPT

Bachelor of Arts Morita had graduated two years earlier, gained distinction as a talented student, and become well known after publishing a few novels. Though he had a young wife and child at home, he happened to be a colleague of Haruko (written with a different Chinese character) at a certain high school for girls, and so they had become ill-fated lovers, and due to their having the same literary tastes, they had reached a point of inseparable intimacy with one another. On the other hand, it was impossible to live together openly since he had a wife and child, and with real bitterness against their ties in this floating world, they resolved to commit their double suicide. First, Bachelor of Arts Morita, after eliminating his major difficulty by leaving his wife and child in her hometown, departed from Tokyo with Haruko in search of a place where the two could die, but luckily or not, they were unable to find one and were finally apprehended by the police. Though there have been many love-suicides from ancient times, it is actually unprecedented for a man and woman who had received an education at the highest academic institutions to imitate the foolishness of common people. It must be said that it is a news event that represents the ultimate in naturalism and gratification of the passions. And yet was it not madness that when the two lovers were seized by the police at the summit of Obana Pass, the man declared, "My conduct demonstrates the sacredness of love. I have done nothing wrong in the sight of God and man."

Such was the tone of the article, all newspapers imitating it and violently censuring the "folly" of the two lovers. Yet the chance encounter of these two people was different from the newspaper's account, for they had become acquainted at the Women's Literary Circle sponsored by Choko Ikuta, with Sohei the lecturer and Haruko a member of the audience. Though a talented student of Soseki, Sohei Morita was almost consigned to social oblivion because of this affair, yet it was due to Soseki's kindness that from January the following year *Smoke*, a confessional I-novel dealing with this event, was published serially in the *Asahi*. In Sohei's novel, in which he tried to show the truth of the affair so erroneously conveyed by this article and others, the relationship of the two persons remained to the very last platonic. As heroine, Haruko is portrayed as a completely different type from women seen up to that time, a woman aroused by the demands of a modern ego, her excessive self-consciousness of speech and behavior often strange, eccentric. Her abrupt and unexpected conduct in everything took on a fresh charm and made the hero look upon Haruko as an enigmatic, sphinxlike woman.

In the novel the hero finds himself dragged along by a woman who will never say she loves him, and finally, even while realizing the woman will never love him, he attempts a double suicide with her on a snow-filled mountain. The woman is so overly self-conscious that even before this confrontation with death, she writes a suicide note: "I have carried out the plan of my life. I perish through my own will. No one can interfere with me."

Smoke resurrected Sohei as a literary figure, but readers found the affair even more incomprehensible, and Soseki himself, all things considered, treated it contemptuously as no more than an idle love story. Haruko Hiratsuka wrote a severe rebuttal of *Smoke*, but it was almost totally ignored.

It was through this event that Jun Tsuji recognized in the unknown Haruko Hiratsuka the possibility of a new woman awakened to an ego that had not been seen in any of her sex up to that time, Tsuji cherishing his interest in and sympathy for Haruko, whom he had never met.

It required little intelligence to know that an unmarried woman so scandalously written up in the newspaper and so thoroughly struck down by the world was already no better than someone put to death by society. Now, however, three years later, that woman, the common butt of a public scandal, had proudly lifted her head to bring forth a splendid magazine. With the unexpected feeling of wanting to applaud her, Tsuji found himself turning over *Seito*'s pages.

In the table of contents lined up with the name of the well-known writer Akiko Yosano were the names of Shige Mori, wife of Ogai, and Haruko Kunikida, wife of Doppo, and also cited was Toshiko Tamura, who had just made a brilliant debut in January that year by having her work named the best novel in a contest sponsored by the Osaka *Mainichi* newspaper. Also listed were such unknowns as Ikuko Araki and Kazue Mozume. From Tsuji's point of view all the compositions were immature, all in forms impossible to classify as literary. Nevertheless, he felt in them a tense and passionate sincerity that forcefully moved him:

Rambling Thoughts

The day has come when these mountains move.
Though I say so, no one believes me.
For only a short while have mountains been dozing.

In days of old
Mountains moved, burning in flame.
Still, this you need not believe.
All women who have been dozing are now awakened
and moving.

I wish I might write solely in first person singular
I am a woman
I wish I might write solely in first person singular
I I

As might be expected, this opening selection of Akiko Yosano's poem sang out forcefully and unreservedly about the aspirations and dreams of the magazine.

Though Raicho Hiratsuka's inaugural message, which chanted aloud in soprano-like tones, revealed various logical contradictions in its long passages, it had sufficient charm to arouse in its readers a powerful response:

In the beginning Woman was the Sun. She was a genuine being.
Now woman is the Moon. She lives through others and glitters through the mastery of others. She has a pallor like that of the ill.
Now we must restore our hidden Sun.

The following day Tsuji gave Noe his copy of *Seito*. The moment she glanced at Raicho's words, she was passionately impressed:

I want, together with all women, to convince myself of the genius that is lying in women. I put my faith only in that one possibility, and I want the heartfelt joy of the happiness which comes from being born into this world as women.

We are no longer waiting for heaven's revelations. Through our own endeavors we will lay bare our natural inner secrets and make these our own spiritual revelations . . .

On that day we will possess the entire world, everything in it.

On that day we will be Rulers alone throughout heaven and earth, and on our own feet we will become genuine persons who will be self-existent and independent at the very core of Nature without the necessity of self-examination. And we shall know how pleasant and how abundantly satisfying it is to be in splendid solitude and loneliness.

No longer will Woman be the Moon. On that day she will be, after all, the Sun of her beginnings, a genuine human being.

We will erect a huge circular Palace of Gold radiating high on the Crystal Mountain to the east of the Land of the Rising Sun.

Women! Never forget that when you draw your portraits, always select a vaulted ceiling of gold!

Even though I perish midway on our quest, even though I sink to the bottom of the sea like a shipwrecked sailor, I will raise both my benumbed hands and with my last breath cry out, "Women! Advance! Advance!"

As Noe read aloud these words of Raicho as well as Akiko's poem, her jet-black eyes were overflowing with large tears. At this very moment when women were awakening as women, when they were extricating themselves from worn-out customs established long ago, hoisting their own flag and walking bravely by standing on their own feet, she alone was caught up in ancient conventions, bound by the chains of her old household and fettered to a loveless marriage.

Noe felt that the yearning for women's awakening and liberation pervading the pages of *Seito* would arouse the sympathy of each and every woman in Japan. A vision came to her of all women linking arms and encircling the earth like a garland, and she became so mortified and ashamed in seeing only herself left alone outside that line of women her body trembled.

Tsuji was moved more than he expected by Noe's sensitive response to *Seito*. Though he wanted to avert the danger of lending a helping hand to the grievances which came from her circumstances, he felt it his duty as her teacher to ease the pains he was witnessing and to lend some assistance to the proper craving of a soul longing for maturity. On their way to school and back or in the deserted music room after classes were dismissed, Tsuji, with *Seito* as his text, explained to Noe the history of the awakening of women in Japan.

In 1899, when the Girls' High School Decree was promulgated, there had been only about twenty such schools, but that year the number increased sharply to 250. As for colleges, Umeko Tsuda established Women's English College and Yayoi Yoshioka, Tokyo Women's Medical College, both in 1900. The following year Japan Women's College was created by Jinzo Naruse, and the Fine Arts Academy for Women by Tamako Yokoi. Still, even though ways of learning were opened to women in the Meiji era, no more than a handful of the privileged elite had been able to partake of these benefits. Just to receive an education at a girls' high school, how many miracles and how much exertion was needed for girls like Noe, raised in rural areas and in poor families!

On the other hand, before and after the Russo-Japanese War, publishing began to be established as an enterprise, and magazines solely for women were put out in rapid succession. Among them were *World of Learning for Women, New Learning for Women, Women's Circle, Women's World, Paragon of Womanhood, Women's Literary World, Mauve, Women's Companion, Women's Review, Women of the World, World of Women,* and *Women's Pictorial.* Yet these magazines were classified first into young women's literary magazines whose quality was low and content tinged with romanticism, and then into those of a practical order to teach housewives home economics. Although these magazines were not viewed as a strong active force in stimulating the advancement and awakening of women, at this time the trend in the European publishing world was to introduce ideas on the emancipation of women.

"Miss Ito, have you read Hideko Kageyama's *Half of My Life?*"

"No, not yet."

"You'd better read it. Viewed from the history of the awakening of women, Hideko Kageyama is the heroic woman who lit the signal fires for the first time in our country. She's from Okayama, and she was active in the movement for democratic rights."

"Is she living now?"

"Certainly she is. She's fallen in love and been married many times and has given birth to ever so many sons. She even fell in love with a man much younger than she was, Sanshiro Ishikawa, who was her husband's houseboy, student disciple, and comrade in the socialist movement."

Tsuji continued talking while enjoying Noe's reaction, her thick-fleshed nostrils distended, a habit she had when she became excited, an urgent expression on her face as she listened without blinking her eyes.

"Hideko Kageyama spoke up vehemently, especially for women, but there were no women of talent to follow her, so the position of women didn't improve. Finally, ten years after her book, the idea of women's liberation in foreign countries was introduced by men in the socialist movement. In 1904 Toshihiko Sakai and Shusui Kotoku translated Bebel's *Women Under Socialism,* and I think it was in the following year that Koken Yamaguchi published Bebel's *Evolution of the Relationships Between Men and Women.* Sakai translated Carpenter's *Love's Coming of Age* as well as Engels's *The Origin of the Family, Private Property, and the State.* The recent novels of Naoe Kinoshita, *Confessions of a Husband* and *A Pillar of Fire,* are easy to understand, and they're worth reading as books dealing with the woman question as a social problem."

"I read a novel by Mr. Kinoshita. In it the hero Shunzo Shirai is wonderful."

Her eyes glowing, Noe had finally interrupted Tsuji. As she was listening to him, she realized the extent of her ignorance and even felt desperate about it. At the girls' high school which she had so yearned for and struggled so hard to enter, what could she possibly learn? She did not know anything. And when she realized she did not, she came to feel hopelessly confused in her helpless desire to know more and more.

"I want to read all those books. Would I be able to understand them?"

"For the most part, yes. I'll lend them to you since I have them."

While talking to her in this way, Tsuji was thinking that the reason he felt himself attracted to this girl who gave off a wild scent like that of an animal warming itself in the sun was probably due to the fact that he was responding to the flamelike desire yearning for expansion inside her, that he was merely trying to fully "educate" her and cultivate the talent she was endowed with, and that he was desiring somehow to touch the heated blood of the Kumaso clan running through her.

In the second semester Noe, like someone who had become desperate, abandoned her studies at school to immerse herself in the books on women's liberation she had borrowed from Tsuji. At the same time, she forced herself to drink whiskey, which she could hardly down, and cutting classes, she wandered along the streets. No matter what she did, these were nothing more than fruitless attempts at rebellion, for actually she was living on the money she received monthly from the family in Kyushu into which she had married.

In the year 1911 we were suddenly exposed to the "New Drama." On both September 22 and 23, when *Seito* appeared, the experimental theatre of the Art Association completed its new building on Dr. Shoyo Tsubouchi's grounds at Yochomachi, and the opening performance was held. Staged for the first time in our country was Ibsen's *A Doll's House*, translated by Hogetsu Shimamura, the unknown actress Sumako Matsui as Nora gaining an unprecedented favorable reception:

Sumako Matsui played the heroine Nora. At the opening curtain when she cheerfully came on stage humming, she commanded no attention, her appearance not the least bit like Nora's. But beginning with the moment when she behaved like a spoiled child to her husband Helmer, confided her secret to the widow Mrs. Linde (which suggested Nora's great awakening afterwards), asked her husband to get the widow a job, innocently played hide-and-seek with her children, and finally up to the scene just before the curtain falls when she cries alone on the stage, "It can't be! It's impossible!" and is gradually terror-stricken after she had been told about Krogstad by her husband even while she still thought, "How was it possible for such a thing to happen?" (because she could not believe what Krogstad had told her while he was threatening her), Sumako changed wonderfully and variously, as if the quietness of water had been transformed into the great stirring of multifarious waves. During that interval there was not the slightest slackening in Sumako Matsui's performance, the movement of her facial expressions so intense the audience was completely captivated by the heroine . . . Above all, despite the fact that I am a man, the scene in which Nora leaves home after her great speech thrilled me because of the adroit cleverness of the play itself.

Tremendous rave reviews for Sumako as Nora, including the above by Seiseien Ihara, followed one after another without letup, and in November the same year, the play was again staged at the Imperial Theatre. Sumako's Nora was refined further than it had been in September, resulting in an unprecedented triumph.

Seito, which had inserted in its inaugural issue an article on *Hedda Gabler*, could not be expected to let this drama on the awakening of women go unnoticed, and for its January number the following year it brought out a special edition on *A Doll's House*.

Noe's uncle had moved to Osaka during that time, so Noe and her cousin Chiyoko were placed under the care of the assistant principal at his home and had no freedom to see the play. Through rumor and *Seito*, however, Noe knew about Sumako Matsui, who played Nora, and she could not help but feel excited. Tsuji also explained from a literary and social standpoint what Ibsen's Nora had accomplished for women's liberation in foreign countries, and he answered Noe's questions about "Noraism," as it came to be called.

As she read *A Doll's House* and came to know about the heroine, Noe could not fail to be all the more angry over the helplessness of her own situation. Though the circumstances were different, she could not discard as another person's affair the determination of Nora, who was abandoning her home, her husband, and even her children, and who as the curtain fell was about to live her own life. Noe was unable to keep herself from comparing these events to her own condition, in which she was firmly bound hand and foot by her family and convention, and like a doll had been forced to marry.

Like Nora, Noe wanted to live freely by herself, someday shaking off both her family and her relatives. While increasingly hardening her secret resolve to rebel, she was yearning for her graduation day, which was drawing nearer moment by moment.

A new year dawned, Noe eighteen and Tsuji twenty-nine by the Japanese way of counting.

The very day Noe graduated she would have to return to her hometown and enter the family she had married into, and that day was steadily approaching. She had made up her mind that if only she graduated, she would not return to her hometown under any circumstances. She had not yet formulated any plan beyond graduation. To live with a husband she did not love in the family she had married into was loathsome to her, and she would not, even if it meant dying. She had once thought of sailing to America with her husband and running away from him there, but in all likelihood Fukutaro's journey had been called off. No longer did any attraction remain to induce her to stay with him.

Still, March came quicker than she thought, and graduation day on the twenty-sixth was approaching. When she desperately finished her graduation examinations, she absorbed herself in thinking only of how she might manage to slip away from Chiyoko and remain in Tokyo. The most reasonable plan she thought of was to start for home with Chiyoko, give her cousin the slip on the way, and hide somewhere for several months until the storm subsided. Where could she hide? At that moment Tsuji's small house at Somei flashed into her mind. She felt Tsuji's mother, who was apparently kind and gentle, and his younger sister, who seemed strong-willed yet open-hearted, had been favorably disposed toward her. Would they not, if she asked, harbor her as a kind of maid, after she revealed her situation to them? However, when she speculated on how Tsuji, the most important person to her, would feel about it, Noe lacked confidence and hesitated. Though he was exceedingly gentle and friendly, he had not taken one step beyond the strict line of their being a teacher and student. No matter how flattered she felt about their relationship, she could not believe his feelings toward her were more serious. And she realized she also had to consider his connection to the beautiful girl at Asakusa. Noe was not aware of the fact that at the bottom of her heart, where she guarded her desire to receive refuge in Tsuji's house, another feeling beyond that of wishing for a nest in which to hide was also at work. Still, her pride stubbornly prevented her from asking Tsuji about sheltering her because she knew she had not gained his love, other than his affection for her as a student.

Before she had formulated a practical plan, her situation took an unexpected turn. Due to the fact that Chiyoko's grandfather had died suddenly, an order came from her uncle for the two girls to promptly return home on the twenty-seventh, immediately after the ceremony on the twenty-sixth. Noe wept throughout the night, unable to catch even a wink of sleep before the graduation.

Tsuji was not seen at the event, and even when the commemorative photograph was taken, he did not turn up.

Since Noe was quite nervous about Tsuji's absence, she could not remain calm during the ceremony. She slipped away while the thank-you party for the teachers, the leave-taking, and the various other activities were following one another, and in the unusually beautiful attire of a crested coat and ribbon in her low pompadour, she visited Tsuji at his home in Somei.

He came outside, saying he had a slight cold and fever.

"My bed isn't even taken up yet. How about going for a walk?"

"Is that all right for your health?"

"Yes. I'm fine now. I was just thinking of going out."

He quickly left the house ahead of Noe. This area with its few houses was surrounded by hills and groves, the trees and grass tinged faintly with the green sprouts of early spring.

As they stood in a grove at the top of an incline,

Asukayama Hill at Oji was blurred in the distance. At the bottom of the slope, opposite a ravine, was a temple whose bell Tsuji had always said was better in tone than that of any other temple. He continued walking after pausing to wait for Noe, who was apt to lag behind. Occasionally she stumbled and fell.

"What's the matter with you?"

His hands supported her. Her entire body momentarily gave way, a shudder running through it. Flustered, he released his hold. Noe's face was crimson, her eyes dazzling.

"Last night I didn't sleep at all, so I feel dizzy."

"That was a dumb thing to do. You shouldn't have done such a stupid thing."

He sat down on the grass in the grove. With his hand he beat down some of the dry grass near him and put down his handkerchief, which had hung at his waist, for her to sit on.

"Let's sit here. That way we won't be so tired."

In her ceremonial skirt Noe obediently sat on the handkerchief. Extending from the bottom of her long skirt were her legs in black stockings, her brand-new lace boots glittering.

"You have really small feet."

Tsuji spoke as if he had noticed them for the first time. Although Noe was not tall, one had the feeling she was strongly built, her skin fresh and firm. From the impression she gave to others of being wild and animated, those delicate feet were to Tsuji's eyes strangely appealing and lovely.

"My hands and feet are really tiny. Look!"

She held both hands in front of him. They were small childlike hands which somehow did not seem suitable as the hands of Noe, who wrote out her characters firmly like a man. On the back of her hands and short fingers, the flesh was swollen soft and full, and in one after another of the joints there was a cute dent, as if pressed down by a pencil. For all their shortness the fingers tapered off at their tips to turn into graceful appendages with low knuckles. Even though she had been raised in straitened circumstances, those hands suggested the rich stock of Noe's old family line. They were not the strong hands of laborers who had continued to work over the generations. Without realizing what he was doing, Tsuji took hold of her hands. They were cold and chilly.

"Are you cold?"

"No."

As she was shaking her head, tears again welled up in her eyes. Since she remained with both hands in Tsuji's, she could not wipe her tears away, and with her eyes as they were she kept them wide open and looked up into Tsuji's face, her tears continuing to flow down. That crying face under a strain like that of a child was so innocent Tsuji felt it nonsensical for this girl to be called a married woman. Suddenly he was carried away by the impulse of wanting to embrace her round shoulders and draw her closer to him. He knew that at the present moment she would probably be more comforted by his caress than by any number of soft words. However, when she leaned her head against his shoulder as if she were totally exhausted, he ended by failing to put any power into those arms even though he was supporting her by placing his hands lightly around her shoulders. The heat glowing in her skin was transmitted even through her kimono to his palms.

When she stopped crying after a while, she withdrew her face from him as if she had at last composed herself. Her eyelids were swollen red from crying, her cheeks softened like leather that had become moist, even her movements languid—all these details stimulating him.

The area was completely dark, and both the strong slope of the temple roof in the valley beyond and Asukayama Hill at Oji were enveloped in evening haze and blurred like slides in a magic lantern.

Now Noe had no more words with which to make an appeal to him. She had already repeated the same words any number of times, and she did not know how to make him listen to her. In the long run, the sole comfort Tsuji's silence had offered her was that nothing further could be done.

"Are you all right? Can you go back?" Tsuji asked, standing up just as they were about to part.

"Yes."

"It's bad not to sleep."

"I know."

"There's only tomorrow left now ... Did you hear about the exhibition of the posthumous works of Shigeru Aoki to be held at Takenodai tomorrow? Have you time to see it?"

"I'll go," Noe replied as if clinging to him. Her train was to leave after one in the afternoon. If they went in the morning, there would be enough time.

As expected, due to her two or three sleepless nights, she rested soundly that night. She did not even dream.

The moment Noe awoke the next morning, she dressed hurriedly and ran out of the house without even telling Chiyoko where she was going. She had promised to meet Tsuji at the Sakuragicho streetcar stop in Ueno. When she got off the car, she found he had already arrived.

They walked side by side without either of them speaking. Since it was still early morning, the park was very quiet, not a soul around. As Noe listened to the sounds of their footsteps, she was seized with the feeling she was finally about to leave Tokyo that very day, and she was ready to burst into tears again. For some time Tsuji did not say anything. He went along silently, his oppressive and cold attitude strangely different from his usual manner.

The art museum had just opened, and it was very quiet inside. As she stood before the pictures of this genius who had been born in her hometown and had risen in the world, a painter whose works she had always longed to see, Noe could not look at them with appreciation.

While Tsuji moved slowly along, taking steps as if remembering he had to, Noe moved on hurriedly to the next painting. Even after she finished looking at the pictures, no impression whatsoever remained of them. At any rate, it appeared that the two had been inside at least an hour. Before they realized it, people were crowding into the hall.

When they came outside, Tsuji went on ahead, walking rapidly without a word as if he were still angry. He walked so fast Noe had to follow at a quick pace. The cluster of trees in the large park was so thick they felt they would get lost in this deeply wooded area if they followed the path below. Before they realized it, they found themselves concealed in the midst of the quiet forest where no noise from the street could reach them.

Exhausted, Noe came to a stop and with her hands against the tree beside her tried to catch her breath. Tsuji immediately retraced his steps several paces in front of her. His narrow eyes from behind his glasses were strangely glittering. His usually pale face was paler than usual. Suddenly Noe was being tightly embraced. Her back, pressing against the tree, was in pain. She had no time to cry out because her lips were being shut tight. She was seized by the feeling her entire body was ripping open, flying away with a sound like that of fireworks exploding. It became quite dark in front of her, and the next moment she saw countless numbers of fireworks aflame. The power in the man's arms was great, his lips cold, his tongue hot.

When Tsuji loosened his grip, Noe crouched down powerlessly on the spot, her body hugging the tree. The strength had gone out of her knees, and for a while she could not stand. Countless fireworks still piling atop one another continued to burn in front of her eyes.

The shadows of those flames flickered and squirmed even on Tsuji's face, and she found it difficult to catch sight of his real expression. He did not utter a word. As he looked down at Noe crouching and trembling at his feet like a wet pup, he felt his blood grow cold in an instant. Already deep at the bottom of his heart he was seized with the feeling he had made a mess of everything. In spite of having controlled himself up to that time, just when they were to separate in only two or three hours, he had been negligent and had sloppily cut through the rope of self-control, actions he already regretted. He had finally been tripped up by this little girl's childish enticements. The apprehension of his probably being increasingly burdened with the troublesome and heavy destiny of this kind of girl ran in cold waves down his spine. Having once caught fire, his instincts, nevertheless, betrayed his reason, and he was obsessed by the impulse to at least once ascertain the smell of Noe's flannel-like skin and the heat of the blood that had burned its way up even through her kimono.

"Are you angry?"

How trite and affected! Hurt by his own words, he bent down in front of her and again drew his arms across her round shoulders. Immediately, with the suppleness of a stem no longer able to support its heavy blossoms, Noe collapsed against his bosom, her legs giving way inside her skirt. Unconsciously she had balanced her body so that she could easily be embraced.

By the time the two hurried to Shimbashi Station, the train had already left as scheduled, even the well-wishers gone, and on the platform only Chiyoko, half in tears, was waiting. There was nothing to do but switch to the night train.

In the evening when Noe and her cousin again came to the station, Tsuji was already there. While Chiyoko was talking to several of her friends, Noe suddenly mentioned she had forgotten to buy a model train for her nephew.

"If you hurry out now, you'll have time. You still have forty minutes," said Tsuji, as if tempting her. With the feeling that she wanted to be alone with him if even for a moment, Noe ran from the station. He was silent and did her the favor of following her. As they walked side by side toward the Ginza from the front of the station, they hunted through some stationery shops and toy stores, but no model train could be found. Since her intention from the start had merely been to be alone with Tsuji, she had no reason to make an enthusiastic search.

"It seems we can't locate one."

"We don't have to look any further."

Saying these words as if she were angry, Noe began turning back. At the moment she herself did not really know what she was irritated about. It was impossible to believe she wanted to be embraced by a man in the midst of a crowded thoroughfare on the Ginza. And yet how dull-witted Tsuji was! He should have guessed how she felt. By the time they rushed back to the station as if they were running, the assistant principal and Nakano had turned up. Again Chiyoko was uneasy, thinking that Noe might have once more disappeared. There was no longer any time to exchange words with Tsuji. When the train was ready to depart, the girls dashed out and ran after it, but Tsuji stood behind alone on the platform without making a move.

At Osaka, Noe's aunt Kichi also boarded the train. Her uncle had started for Kyushu earlier. Averting her face from her aunt and Chiyoko, Noe pretended to be looking out the window. All she could think was that second by second she was getting further from Tokyo and Tsuji. As the train increased its distance from Tokyo, she grew miserable, feeling that Tsuji's embrace was no more than the diversion of a momentary impulse. When the train reached Shimonoseki, she made use of the short interval at the station to write Tsuji a postcard in front of the mailbox on the platform.

"I've finally come this far."

When she had written that much, she was seized with emotion, her tears so abundant she could not even see the characters she was jotting down. Now she could not help but realize that no matter how the other party felt, she was in love with Tsuji.

It was a morning less than two weeks since Tsuji had seen Noe off at Shimbashi Station. Still in bed in his study, the newspapers spread out before him, Tsuji heard the voice of a young girl talking to his mother.

"My, how beautiful! The cherry blossoms are completely over in Kyushu."

Noe! Thinking it impossible, Tsuji could not believe his own ears! She could not have turned up at this time. Yet the girl's voice was certainly hers. Going directly into the garden through the wicket gate by the side of the front entrance led to the six-mat room. His friends usually visited him that way through the garden.

The voices of his mother and Noe, who had gone into the garden, reached his pillow all the more clearly.

"Since you've only just arrived after spending the entire night shaken and jostled on the train, you must be thoroughly exhausted."

"Yes . . . but I'm all right. Returning to Tokyo is so wonderful nothing else matters."

Noe's bright carefree voice came to him.

Hurriedly putting his bed in order, Tsuji went out of his study.

"What's wrong?"

Looking up at Tsuji, who had called to her from behind his mother, Noe reddened to the roots of her hair. She was much more conspicuously worn than before she had left Tokyo, her eyes a size larger. As if she had been waiting impatiently for the moment when Tsuji's mother left the room, Noe suddenly lay face down on the mats and began crying.

By the ninth day after returning home, she had already run away. She told Tsuji that she had concealed herself in the boardinghouse of a childhood friend teaching at an elementary school in Fukuoka, that from there she had appealed for help in a letter to Nakano, who had been the teacher in charge of her class, and that he had sent her the traveling expenses.

"Well, have you called at Nakano's home yet?"

"No. After I reached Tokyo, I felt I wanted to come here first."

Again Noe reddened to her ears as she lowered her eyes. When Tsuji guessed it was her self-respect due to her love for him that had made her request the travel money from Nakano and not himself, he found her tender and appealing. At the same time he felt a restless agitation welling up inside him for being unable to undo what he had done to her. If only he had held back his embrace at Ueno that day . . . He thought it both childish and aggravating that Noe's stupidity, which obsessed her with the idea she had been tempted only from the man's side, kept her from realizing he had been aroused by her own unconscious coquetry.

Mitsu had sympathized with Noe's situation earlier than Tsuji, who could not make up his mind about giving the girl shelter. Having been brought up as a native Tokyoite in the downtown section, Mitsu believed harboring a bird in distress that had taken to flight was quite simple, the most natural of all actions.

"Isn't she pathetic? Let's have her stay with us until the matter's settled."

With Mitsu's words Noe came to live at Tsuji's from that day.

Yet Tsuji felt a danger lurking in letting her stay on at their home. Anyone could tell she was in love with him merely by looking at the earnest pupils of her eyes so passionately aflame each time they turned toward him. For Noe's teacher to lapse into a sexual relationship with her, whose name had already been entered into a family register as the wife of Fukutaro Suematsu, would be the ruination of Tsuji's life. Furthermore, he realized there were limits to his self-control in living under one roof with Noe, burning with the passionate blood of a young southern girl who had in her the unrefined purity of the country and who with her entire body was leaning hard against him.

He sounded out his friend Nakano to entrust Noe to the assistant principal with whom she had lodged until her graduation. Nakano, a young enthusiast of literature, moved deeply by the love between his highly gifted student and his close friend, was more excited by the situation than any of the parties concerned. It was the considered opinion of Tsuji and Nakano that the assistant principal, who was second to the latter in admiring Noe and who had first been perceptive enough to recognize Tsuji's talent, would probably help them out.

Already at that time, however, a request to search for Noe had been made to the police by her uncle Junsuke Dai, and both the principal and his assistant were more afraid than anything else that the school would be dragged into the affair. Tsuji's frank discussion with the assistant principal was met by a resistance more severe than he had encountered from anyone else.

"That you, a teacher, should have seduced your own pupil is unpardonable!"

Stormed at from the start, Tsuji was dumbfounded. He realized the headmaster and his assistant and even Nakano had taken it for granted a sexual relationship had already been established between Noe and himself. It was useless to justify his conduct.

He was taken to task as a contemptible man who had seduced Noe, had forced her to leave home through mutual consent, and had tried to make the school bear the responsibility for everything.

Guided by the policy of "safety first," the headmaster said with excessive politeness, "To be perfectly frank, we have been repeatedly told by Mr. Suematsu, Noe's husband, that if you do not return Noe-san, he will appeal to the law. Well, you may love as you like, but if you want to carry out your affair to the bitter end, I beg you to resign from the school."

"I understand. Please allow me to resign no later than today."

After automatically saying these words, Tsuji himself was startled. He cursed himself. And cursed himself again. Once more, in less than a year, he had flung away the comparatively peaceful life he had finally gained. The die was cast. Into what further tight corners would he ultimately be driven by the burning eyes of that young girl?

In spite of the situation Tsuji could not ward off the sudden impudent laugh he was seized with. By turning his back on the headmaster and his assistant, who were nonplused by his burst of laughter, Tsuji eliminated himself forever from Ueno Girls' High School.

It had been a reckless statement. The moment his violent emotions subsided, he became uneasy about his livelihood from the following day. Strangely enough, however, he had neither any lingering attachment to the school nor repentance for leaving it. That he was sacrificing his job for the sake of a young girl he had no reason to feel this attached to might have been called more comic than moving. Tsuji felt himself another person, his own cold eyes deriding himself for his quixotic behavior.

"But even if nothing comes from my affair with Noe, I was already disgusted with being a teacher. Try thinking about that. My clinging to this miserable kind of job for ten years since I was nineteen reveals how superhuman my patience has been. That girl smelling of earth with her soiled kimono neckband is no more than a necessary springboard. Whether or not I had an affair with her, in the long run I would have been driven one morning into the act of thrusting down my letter of resignation.

"Be that as it may, you were too reckless. You ought to have been much more tactful.

"Isn't it good to be reckless? For the most part, I haven't been too reckless up to now. I haven't been too adventurous. I'm almost thirty. And as for these past years, were they spent generally as the heyday of a blooming youth? Everything was done in a calculated way! A senseless, monotonous, commonplace, stingy lifestyle! A stereotyped life in which morning followed night and noon morning! A life in which neither miracles nor adventures occurred! I'm fed up with it already!

"And so you're going to burden yourself with that poor girl for your entire life? That headstrong, selfish, vulgar, jealous, blubbering, slovenly girl with apparently no conception of frugality?

"But isn't that what we call a woman? Not once until now have I freely and openly unfolded my feelings. I have been living timidly on the principle of 'safety first,' cowardly cautioning myself only of the trouble of being injured. The toxin of unfulfilled desire is already pent up in my entire body and is just about ready to explode. You can easily set it on fire. Isn't the wild blood of a Kumaso clan girl more suitable for an arsonist than the white hands of a refined downtown type?

"Is that your justification for your treatment of Okinchan?

"That downtown girl's too delicate. Too pretty. I have no confidence in making her happy. Any man except me would be able to. But as for that Kumaso clan girl . . .

"I see. You don't have to explain further. In short, you're enamored of Noe. If you don't like it put that way, an illusion of the possibilities in that girl has been . . . "

As he tried to set his thoughts in order, Tsuji, without

returning directly home, continued walking alone in the woods of Somei he was so fond of. While he did this for about two hours, he came to feel himself emancipated, as if his body had become lighter and refreshed, as if he had finally been cleansed all over. Somehow or other he would manage. Taking advantage of this opportunity, he would live only as he himself wanted to. For a very long time all his desires had been eaten up by that monster called "a petty life." Even Stirner has said, "No one can dominate or command others. It is good to do only what you yourself can do. You ought to be clearly aware of the sphere of your own abilities and the sphere of another person's abilities."

"Let me live according to Stirner's philosophy! Let me live according to Stirner's philosophy!"

"*Sensei.*"

Called to a stop, Tsuji looked back.

Noe's body in shadow from the trees in the grove, her face dappled by sunlight, she was staring at him with her jet-black eyes as if she had been intent on some thought.

"What's the matter?"

"I was worried because it's so late . . . and I wondered if you might not be here . . ."

Noe had known Tsuji had an interview about her that day with the assistant principal and others.

"Come over here."

Noe stared at Tsuji as if she doubted her ears, her shoulders trembling in alarm, and contrary to his expectation, she moved back a step. Since she had come up to Tokyo, he had not even grasped her hand. The feeling or humiliation that his embrace had been only a game after all had been deeply wounding her the last several days. That was the only way she could interpret his intention of turning her over to the assistant principal at his home.

"What's wrong? Come over here."

Tsuji stepped up to Noe, who stood petrified where she was.

For the first time she offered fierce resistance in his arms. But Tsuji in a composed manner thoroughly overpowered the struggling girl and pressed against her lips, which were like overripe silverberries under a hot sun.

When he finally released his lips from Noe, who was totally exhausted, he said in a low voice, "I've resigned from school."

"What!"

"They said that if I was going to love you, I had better resign."

"*Shensei!*"

Born in Kyushu, Noe pronounced teacher *shensei* instead of *sensei*. She had tried hard not to use this word carelessly but now she was beside herself. And in a more obvious dialect than she had indicated a moment ago, she said, "*Shensei!*" and calling out clung to him of her own free will. With her round hot body pressed against him with all her might, Tsuji toppled over even as he was embracing her. He heard the sound of her wild blood igniting the fuel in the interior of his body which had overflowed to the ignition point, gasping in search of egress.

The love of a girl not yet twenty with a man who was almost thirty united in one flame to set that day off from all others, and that love flared up with terrible force. When Tsuji, who up to that time feared morality and law and the opinions of others, found himself in this situation, it became quite funny to him. With a fresh sense of liberation, as if he had at one powerful stroke cut off by himself the thick rope that had coiled and bound him threefold, he lost himself in happiness for some time.

Having as their guest been given the largest room in the house, one of six mats, Noe came every night to pay a secret visit to Tsuji in his study.

Mitsu immediately discovered their new relationship, but did not show the slightest surprise, thinking it a natural development. Yet she made Noe scrub and wash and sew like her own daughter, though previously she had treated Noe like a visitor. One day she had Noe carry a mirrorstand and washbasin to the veranda, and skillfully shaving the nape of Noe's neck and the downy hair on her face, which no razor had touched since her birth, Mitsu kindly set Noe's overabundant and straight black hair into the stylish *yuiwata* coiffure.

Before they realized it, the six-mat bedroom became unnecessary, Noe jointly sharing Tsuji's three mats. Tsuji found himself addicted to her fresh young body, which was resilient, firm, and tense, and bursting into flamelike heat as he made his way deeper into her. Noe's youth, eighteen years by the Japanese way of counting, did not know what exhaustion was. When her sallow skin adhered to the man's like some thick wet petal of a flower in a strange land, it was not easily stripped off. Its freshness was like a spring deep in a mountain recess, the more drawn from the more abundantly welling, and each time it was scooped up, it overflowed without limit.

With no need to go to school, Tsuji sometimes found himself intoxicated with her until dawn, sometimes the two of them freely and insatiably craving one another as if they were the first human beings secluded behind a curtain of shrubs under sunlight filtering through trees deep inside a midday forest.

In about a month Noe's cheeks became firm, the pupils of her eyes much more dark and moist. For the first time since his birth Tsuji was tasting with the cells of his entire body what it meant for a person to be alive. He also realized in the culmination of carnal pleasure the sweet and dangerous invitation to death. Many times in the midst of a caress, he had been ravishingly carried away by the illusion of wanting to breathe his last after tightening his hands around Noe's smooth neck.

"I'll make Noe live in the full meaning of that word. I'll cultivate her to the limits of woman's possibilities. I'll drag out of her every talent and gift dormant within her. I'll definitely make her into a wonderful woman by pouring into her all my knowledge, even my life."

In the dim light of dawn, while swaying Noe's heated body which had finally lost consciousness after the extremity of his nightlong caress, Tsuji continued whispering to himself, his eyes charged with a strange light, hollow eyes like those of an aging magician.

Chapter 3

IT WAS A hot afternoon in early July in 1912 (the forty-fifth year of Meiji). Piled high on a desk that day in the editorial office of *Seito*, located in a back room of the main building of the old Mannenzan Temple at Horaicho, Komagome, in Hongo, were letters from readers all over the country.

Seito, which had already put out its tenth issue since its beginning number in September the previous year, had found it necessary to begin preparing its first-anniversary edition. The response and success in this practically full year of publication had been totally unexpected by the staff, even by its chief editor Haruko Hiratsuka, whose pen name was Raicho Hiratsuka. The word *Seito* had now spread far and wide over the entire nation, and no newspaper reader could fail to know that the stimulating and fashionable words "New Women" referred to those who wrote for *Seito*.

When Haruko recalled how she had rushed about in a sweat preparing the introductory number in the heat of those hot summer days of the previous year, she felt as if the time were only yesterday. Sifting through the mail, she looked toward Yoshiko Yasumochi, who at a desk opposite her was absorbed in counting on an abacus.

Seito, whose first run of one thousand copies had been brought out fearfully, was by now in excess of two thousand an issue. In charge of finance, Yoshiko Yasumochi had recently cited the figure three thousand, boldly confident they could dare print so many for the anniversary edition. It has been said that even women's magazines with the aim of merely making a profit can easily manage to establish themselves if they print this many copies. The mere fact that *Seito*, begun by a staff of nonprofessional unsophisticated young ladies, was already approaching that number in less than a year was proof of the magazine's achievement.

Sweat was oozing along the forehead of Yoshiko, who was looking down, wisps of hair dampened by her perspiration and stuck fast to her temples giving off the impression of an oppressive warmth. Even though a slight breeze swept into the room from the wide-open veranda windows, the breeze itself was lukewarm and muggy, so it was not the least bit cool. The cries of cicadas in the treetops of the vicinity were annoying and seemed to stir up even more heat.

Haruko remembered that last summer she had done her edition on the cool wide premises of Kazuko Mozume's house at Sendagicho in Hongo. Kazuko Mozume, an influential staff member who had worked with Haruko from the first issue, had already left *Seito*. Tei Kiuchi and Hatsu Nakano were also gone. These last two had resigned out of preoccupation with their own private lives; as for Mozume, the recent atmosphere surrounding *Seito*, which appeared too frequently in the press, became unsuitable to the conservative element in her family.

The leaders who had shared in the hardships since the founding of the magazine had finally been reduced to two,

Haruko and Yoshiko. Looking at the plump shoulders of Yoshiko, who was still moving her fingers along the abacus, Haruko was wondering if she would have ever made the step toward publishing *Seito* had it not been for this woman. When they had finally decided to publish it, Haruko Hiratsuka had not foreseen it would receive so much attention from the public, women throughout the nation enthusiastically welcoming it. When for no reason at all she had gone to visit Choko Ikuta and had entered by way of the garden as usual, Choko had suggested as they talked, "Why not try to bring out a literary magazine only for women?" That had been the real beginning. And while they talked, Choko had gradually become quite excited about the scheme.

"It's possible to have a magazine of about 130 pages, you can print a hundred copies, and the cost will be about a thousand yen. As for expenses, well, you can discuss that with your mother. I guess she can put out that much for you." Even while Haruko was being given such advice, she found herself becoming interested in a magazine of this type.

Although the affair of her double-suicide attempt three years ago with Sohei Morita was finally beginning to be forgotten by the public, the various psychological wounds received from that event had not necessarily healed. If looked at from her own point of view, *Smoke*, which Sohei had published after the incident, had been written only for his convenience, she herself feeling he had not made one deep cut into the truth which only the two of them knew well. All there was to the book was a beautiful compactness. In short, not a single line in it delineated Sohei's expectation and sinister design that if only he could succeed in luring a girl out to some lonely mountain far

from Tokyo, she would easily lean against his bosom. Even
the description of their climbing the mountain in snow,
the grand view from the summit an unearthly moonlit
palace of ice, had not been the least bit depicted by Sohei's
pen, and these omissions had only given Haruko further
dissatisfaction. While Haruko, who had been strong enough
to calmly walk the three- or four-mile road each day to
practice meditation at a Zen temple, had easily climbed the
snowy mountain path as if she were walking on level
ground, Sohei, his motor nerves dull, had slipped with
each step, tumbled into snow up to his waist, and tottered
after her with a miserable awkwardness that was comic and
by no means romantic. But not one line in his novel had
recorded such details. While Haruko was even angrier by
the description of herself as no more than a nymphoma-
niac or a woman suffering from a nervous breakdown, she
was also indignant about the way they had tried to settle
the affair, the way in which Natsume Soseki, his followers,
and Sohei's colleagues spoke about her as they attempted
to ward off the criticism of society by arranging a marriage
between Sohei and herself.

When she thought of their calm attitude brought on by
practical deception, degrading even her attempt to risk her
own life, the scant affection remaining for Sohei had been
completely wiped away. An active vitality, bringing forth
in the nihilistic Haruko "something stirring with life" out
of those days and nights of idleness, began in her after that
long interval. It was Yoshiko Yasumochi, a friend of
Haruko's elder sister at Women's College, who had spurred
even more those feelings in Haruko that had begun to
budge. Yoshiko had no intention of returning to her
hometown in Shikoku after graduating from college, and
she happened to be staying temporarily at the Hiratsuka

home of her classmate while trying to find a job in Tokyo. Told by Haruko of the plan suggested by Choko Ikuta, Yoshiko instantly jumped at the suggestion and became even more eager about it than Haruko herself. When the still hesitant Haruko finally felt inclined to attempt it after being dragged into the scheme by Yoshiko's zeal, Haruko's mother Tsuya offered one hundred yen saying, "This, at any rate, is the money I kept for your marriage expenses." Teijiro Hiratsuka, Haruko's father, was a high-ranking government official who had become director of the Audit Bureau, and not only was he intelligent enough to do a translation of Bluntschli's *Allgemeines Staadstrecht*, but he was such an idealist after his marriage that he permitted his wife to go to such schools as Sakurai Women's Academy and the Kyoritsu Professional School for Women. When Haruko reached the age when she could perceive the situation she was in, she knew she was being raised by her grandmother, after recalling seeing the figure of her mother going off to school. Because Tsuya was this type of mother, she fully understood she ought not to begrudge any constructive assistance toward the publication of *Seito* to help Haruko recover from her affair with Sohei. Urged on by Yoshiko's zeal and practicality, Haruko had gradually been directed toward the publication of *Seito*.

"Oh, at last I've finished. Even though the circulation is increasing rapidly, the rate at which we're collecting our bills is bad, and our mailing expenses are terribly high, so we aren't showing much of a profit."

"You don't have to worry about it."

From an earthen teapot she brought out of a corner of the room, Yoshiko poured some wheat tea into Haruko's cup and her own. Even though two or three other staff members usually appeared at the office and some unknown readers of the magazine dropped in, it was exceptionally quiet that day, probably because the heat made one hesitate to go out.

"Look here! This many threatening letters have again come in."

Placing on her palm some postcards and envelopes she had tied into a bundle, Haruko showed them to Yoshiko. Before they realized it, *Seito*, which had begun with their simple intention of bringing out a literary magazine, had in less than a year been entrusted with a mission as if it existed for the liberation of women. It had so naturally come to take on that character they could not clearly indicate when this had happened. Was it possible to say it was due to the fact that these young women who at least wanted to write "something" and publish it in a magazine were self-awakened persons who had had this "something" within them to publish? In that era when it was considered a woman's virtue to hide behind the male, to submerge herself inside her family, and to never let out one single thing about herself, for a female to write unflinchingly about troubles with parents and husbands and mothers-in-law, or to boldly compose audacious love stories, or to create love poems from a married woman to another man was behavior already outside the frame of common sense and morality. Furthermore, the women connected to *Seito* were said to drink saké and beer at their own gatherings, so the public had been even more astounded. With the vigorous movement of the "New Drama" occurring at almost the same time as the publication of *Seito*, introduced were such heroines as Nora and Magda, whose conduct could not be measured by long-established conventional morality, so heated discussions for and against these characters became confused with the criticism of the

"New Women" of *Seito*, some people coming to view *Seito* members as "destitute females going to extremes," their sex not submissive to men. In addition, various indecent conjectures formed by the curiosity of the vulgar were made of there being only young women in the group, these irresponsible rumors circulating widely.

Even those members who at first had come together quite innocently awoke gradually to the fact that their slightest actions were so immediately seized upon by the spiteful eyes of the public that malicious gossip and scandal were unexpectedly fabricated, and for the first time these women were forced to realize that the position and power of their sex were not the least bit recognized by society. Inevitably the speech and behavior of the staff tended to become aggressive, and out of an instinct for self-preservation they solidified their union by mutual affection and strengthened their will to fight against any and every censure in order to overturn the unfair positions into which women had been placed and to recover their own natural dignity.

At just such a time there followed in succession events that incited the public even more and caused further misunderstanding. These were the "Wine of Five Colors Episode" and the "Incident of the Yoshiwara Visit." Involved in both these occurrences was Kazue Otake, who had been invited to join the staff in the spring and wrote in *Seito* under the name Kokichi. The eldest daughter of Etsudo Otake, a master painter residing in Osaka who had been allowed to display his works at an art exhibition sponsored by the Ministry of Education, she had come to Tokyo to enter the Women's Academy of Fine Arts and happened to be staying at the Kami-Negishi home of her uncle Chikuha Otake, who had also been permitted to enter the same exhibition. She left the academy without graduating and mingled with the young painters and literary men of the Shirakaba School who frequented her uncle's house, and under the liberal supervision of Chikuha, known as a man about town, Kazue was enjoying the maximum freedom allowed girls at that time, her days spent in happy self-indulgence. When she saw the letter of solicitation sent by *Seito* to Chikuha's wife, Kokichi learned of the magazine's existence, and contacting it of her own free will she became a member.

This eighteen-year-old girl, whose body was larger than the average female's but whose mind remained as naive as a child's, dressed in the striking manner of a boy, her stylish kimono and *haori* of dark-blue Satsuma cloth in the same pattern of white splashes, her uncle's mantle thrown over her shoulders. Because she had been raised too indulgently, she was more sensitive to and greedy for affection than other women were. Ill-adapted to her large physique was a delicate and abnormal nervous system that could be extraordinarily and easily damaged. Some vilified her by saying her acting like a spoiled child was disgusting, but Kazue's idiosyncratic personality was highly esteemed by the editors, even her questionable and unbalanced words and actions deeply interesting them and welcomed in a friendly way.

At first sight Kazue was utterly charmed by Haruko's beauty and intelligence. During this period the tendency toward lesbianism among female students had apparently become a kind of fad, and even in Toshiko Tamura's *Resignation*, which in January of that year had won first prize in a newspaper competition for novels, lesbianism had been openly depicted.

Haruko fully responded to Kazue's passionate devotion,

the two of them looking to all the world like a perfect pair of lesbian sweethearts. That love between a man and a woman was strictly forbidden as immoral in the eyes of a severe public and that homosexual love between men or women was not viewed as particularly unusual was probably because homosexuality touched a moral blind spot in those days in which heterosexual love could only be understood as something carnal. Even within the *Seito* group, the lesbian love of Haruko and Kazue was publicly avowed, and that in itself received no censure from any of the members:

"Let me see! Let me see! Oh, I want to!"

My heart trembled. One night while I was totally unaware of what was going on, Kokichi, to preserve her love for only one woman, secretly slit her own soft flesh with my dagger and broke a thin vein. I had to see it at any cost.

The long bandage was unwound, one rotation after another. Pink flesh was barely visible from the transparent rift of skin in a straight line about two inches in length. The blood was no longer flowing. I tried hard to suppress the movement in the deep pit of my stomach. And then while I gazed steadily at the wound, I imagined before my eyes the flame of a candle burning straight as an arrow, the sharp dagger blade which coldly reflected that somber light, and the color of passionate blood.

"Why did you do such a thing?"

"I'll finish binding it again," and she drew back her hand.

"It was you that cursed me. Like that Russian girl," I jested in my uneasiness.

"You say I cursed you? I?"

"What happened to the blood? You sucked it up?"

"I'm keeping it."

The wound was sterilized with carbolic acid. Out of consideration for her, I bandaged her arm as it had been . . . Yes, yes, that was so. Yes. The evening of the eighth day after. I was counting from the thirteenth of May, which ought to be a day of remembrance for the two of us. My heart was again filled with the memory of our meeting that night. How violent my embrace was in which I tried to let Kokichi become the flesh of my world! I don't know. No, I do not know how in an instant the entire body and spirit of Kokichi blazed up to become fire . . .

Haruko was so open about their relationship she had published this kind of passage in an essay, the two women feeling no shame about their homosexuality.

Haruko Hiratsuka had essentially a refined and elegant beauty that reminded one of a noble lady in a dynastic regime. In the exquisite texture of her somewhat dark and delicate face, her radiant and rather large, thick lips prevented her brown eyes from looking too large, cool, and sharp, and also kept the freshness of her well-shaped nose from revealing too cold a look. Her abundant black hair was divided in two, directly in the center of her wide brow, then bound back into three strands below the nape. This Western-style hairdo, which seemed so artless, was best suited to Haruko's quiet, intellectual features. Even though her body was small, it was well proportioned, the line from her abdomen to her waist reminding one of the unexpected dauntlessness of a female panther. There was a delicacy from her shoulders to her breasts, and a slight girlish impression still remained in her that somehow served to maintain an appearance of purity. She had in these refreshing features a quality that attracted both men and women to her at a glance. Due to the fact that in her school days she had secretly devoted herself to Zen meditation and "the real nature of seeing," she always carried herself well, and the beautiful pupils of her eyes without stirring or wavering were concentrated directly on those of the person opposite her.

The young girls who gathered together with Haruko as the central figure were more or less drawn toward her personal charm that came mainly from outward appearance, the feeling of affection they cherished toward her bordering on homosexuality. Like a sunflower in a garden, Haruko, while she was always being looked up to by many of the flowers around her, raised her own head high as she followed the sun, which was her ideal.

While Kokichi, that is to say, Kazue, treasuring an intense and extraordinary attachment to Haruko, frequently came to the *Seito* office, she also took it upon herself to solicit advertisements, and she would sally forth to seek ads at the Maison de Konosu, a cafe on Koamicho in Nihombashi.

The Konosu had become a gathering place for writers and artists of the Pan Society, and Kokichi, often there with those writers whose company she enjoyed, became acquainted with the proprietor. One night just to amuse her, he showed her how to pour into a glass "wines" of five different colors. It was nothing more than a kind of cocktail, and because he poured them in order of their density—liqueur, peppermint, maraschino, vanilla, and cognac—the colors red, blue, white, green, and auburn decorated the glass in five lateral stripes. Kokichi was enchanted by this magical cocktail of such vivid hues, and as if swallowing a rainbow, she washed it down at a gulp.

Kokichi, whose childlike curiosity about everything was strong and who was as impressionable as a youngster, would grab hold of anyone at all and proclaim as with a flourish of trumpets she had downed to the last drop a "wine" of five colors. The event was immediately bandied about, and before anyone realized it, the episode was turned into a sensational headline, "New Women Befuddled with Five-Colored Wine," journalism making much of the story and giving the impression such women were impossible and absurd.

Only a few days later when Haruko and Hatsu Nakano paid a visit to Kokichi at the home of her uncle, the painter Chikuha Otake, he said to them in his excessive mirth while drinking saké with these three young persons as his companions, "You women talk big about liberating the fair sex, but you ought not to speak if you don't know the mode of living of the prostitutes at Yoshiwara. Why not let me take you on a tour of inspection now? Do you have the courage to come?"

What with his suggestion, the women, half out of curiosity and half out of amusement, left for Yoshiwara with this master painter who knew the ways of the world. They went to a house Chikuha often frequented, the Daimonjiro in Yoshiwara, called in the prostitute Eizan, who was Chikuha's favorite, engaged in small talk, and returned after several hours the same night.

This event too, however, thanks to Kokichi's innocent and exaggerated chatter, quickly spread to their male friends. It was unfortunate that the story reached Ken'ichiro Ono, a reporter for the Tokyo *Nichi Nichi* who was living in the same neighborhood. Immediately dramatizing the gossip in a witty way, Ono let the episode appear in a third-rate newspaper. The scandal so raged in which the New Women of *Seito* were engaging in profligacy by gulping down wines of five colors and visiting the red-light district of Yoshiwara that even men were shocked, the criticism focusing on this group of delinquent women destroying laudable customs.

From that moment on, protests and threatening letters against *Seito* and Haruko kept piling up on the editor's desk; at the same time many encouraging letters arrived from admiring female readers who wondered why it was bad for women to do what men had always done, so the turmoil became even greater. At any rate, due to the accidental occurrence of these events one after the other, *Seito*'s name became all the more famous, and the number of sales continued to climb.

Yoshiko Yasumochi, who was so reliable and steady she was nicknamed "Old Auntie," offered the criticism that disrepute of this kind came from the rash actions of only some members of the group, and she severely reprimanded Kokichi as well as Haruko. Because Kokichi happened to be suffering from lung trouble and went to Nankoin Hospital at Chigasaki to recuperate, the former tranquillity of the editorial room was restored.

When this edition was completed, Yoshiko was also to go immediately to Nankoin Hospital. She had been an earlier patient there than Kokichi, even renting a cottage inside the hospital's wooded grounds and doing some work for the hospital during the summer.

While dividing the letters into two bundles and alternately reading from each pile and discarding them, Haruko suddenly raised a startled face and held out the envelope with the letter she had just finished.

"Say, read this. She's got quite a strong personality, hasn't she?"

The letter had been in a bulging envelope with as many as three stamps on it, the masculine handwriting written with a pen. Inscribed on the back of the envelope was "Noe Ito, Imajuku village, Itoshima district, Fukuoka prefecture."

"Is she living in Kyushu?"

"No. Apparently she's in Tokyo now. Her Tokyo address is inside."

Several letters a day came seeking advice from the chief editor, but even Haruko and Yoshiko, accustomed as they were to these communications, were not a little attracted to the letter that day from an unknown girl by the name of Noe Ito. The rebellious spirit and anguish of a girl inevitably forced to marry against her will due to a lack of understanding by her family were spelled out in vivid passages full of passion.

"Even though she seems to be only seventeen or eighteen, it looks like she's got a reasonable head."

"Her sentences are also fairly decent."

"Somehow, I'd really like to cultivate the talent of a reliable girl with brains."

Haruko wrote out a reply on the spot, telling the writer to at least come in for a visit.

The morning Noe Ito received Haruko Hiratsuka's reply written in a skillful hand, she rushed to Jun Tsuji's three-mat room, where he was still reading a book in bed.

"It came! A reply came!"

"I told you it would, didn't I? Read it."

It was Jun Tsuji himself who had made Noe address her letter to Haruko. Tsuji was not particularly surprised, a touch of a smile on his face. *Seito* had been considered no more than a dilettante pursuit of bourgeois daughters, so with the steady publication of the magazine, which, it had been rumored, would fold by its third issue, Jun Tsuji's goodwill had deepened all the more toward this publication which had delighted him from the start, and he was inwardly supporting it. Even though he had, of course, heard the disreputable gossip and criticism of late, Tsuji, who knew the tricks of the sources from which journalism obtained its news, did not for that reason want to misjudge these women. He had felt Noe needed to lift her eyes away from herself to the outside world. She was slowly becoming impatient and even almost hysterical about being unable to come to terms with her parents in her hometown, her condition still that of a runaway, so he had recommended she write to Haruko about whatever she had on her mind.

Tsuji himself had not once gone to the school he had resigned from, his entire day spent reading his favorite books and advancing a little at a time his translation of Lombroso's *The Man of Genius*. Even though the expenses for Noe's food were no more than a trifle, it was clear as day his family budget with no fixed income was on the verge of collapse.

At the present time, the third month since Noe's arrival, he had reached rock bottom in his already meager savings, his books disappearing a few at a time from his shelves. He had to pretend not to see his mother occasionally carrying in secret some cloth-wrapped parcels to a pawnshop. Even though he was not indifferent to the pressing economic collapse of his home, the value and pleasure of his unlimited freedom, in which he was tasting all at once the unfettering of every restriction, did not allow him the latitude to think about other matters.

"What will be will be. Let us continue on to the very end."

At such moments, by linking Stirner's thought with the egoism of enjoying the fulfillment of each minute, Tsuji firmly decided to see for a little while longer with his own eyes the very pit of this poverty.

However, the more Noe weakened under Tsuji's caress, the more attached she felt to him and the more pain she experienced about the unsettled marriage negotiations in her hometown. At the same time she was conscious of a restraint and guilt for the strain on his family finances, which were reaching total depletion before her eyes. Although Tsuji's mother and sister still endeavored to keep up the cool pretense of standing on ceremony toward her without showing their poverty, Noe felt all the more deeply agonized, as if her body had been sharply cut. When she thought that Tsuji's unemployment was directly due to herself, she felt more than a little responsible for the family's destitution. Five or six days later, advised to by Tsuji, Noe visited Haruko at Mannenzan.

On meeting Noe for the first time and finding the small childlike girl looked only about sixteen, Haruko was surprised this charming youngster and the woman who had written the solid letter were one and the same. In an innocent and agreeable manner, earnestly and fearlessly, Noe complained of her sad plight. She even revealed quite candidly the house she was so indebted to and staying at was that of Jun Tsuji, who had been her high school teacher and had lost his job because of her. As might have been expected, however, Noe remained silent about their physical relationship. Even while listening this far, Haruko could not possibly have imagined such a connection between them because of her first impression of Noe's childlike manner and Tsuji's age. On meeting Noe and seeing for herself the girl's intelligence and single-minded aspiration, Haruko felt something of a sense of mission to educate such a person in *Seito* and admirably draw forth all the possibilities of the talent dormant within her. Encouraging Noe and offering her support, Haruko explained the situation Noe was in was not hers alone but the problem of all women in Japan who were still behind the times, the problem of the errors of long-established conventions in social situations and feudalistic morality. Shown the bundle of letters piled on Haruko's desk, letters from readers in every section of the country, their distress the same as Noe's as they sought counsel about their personal affairs, Noe was quite stirred.

"Your fight will never end merely as your own single, solitary battle. We must build a society in which not only you yourself are delivered from the restraints of convention but one in which all women are finally set free from the heavy pressures of mistaken conventions from the past and from the family system."

Deeply moved by Haruko's beauty, intelligent tone, and gentleness, which were more than Noe expected, she returned delighted to Tsuji's home. After reporting in detail about the interview, she whispered to him, her face still excited, the expression in her eyes as if entranced, "What a refined and splendid person she is! I wonder if even someone like me could become like her one of these days."

Haruko's encouragement motivated Noe, and she left again for Imajuku to settle the question of her marriage once and for all.

When she reached home, the negotiations were not disposed of as easily as she had felt they would be. She was told that even the repayment of her educational expenses, which she had already received and used, was impossible for her family. Both her uncle and parents informed her it was out of the question to ask Fukutaro to release her from the marriage after so long a time, and finally they cried out their complaints about her. To make matters worse, Fukutaro had not yet abandoned his marriage to her even though he had been this scorned, and he would have gladly welcomed her back if she returned to him.

"You've done such a shameful thing to us! We've been so humiliated we can't even walk outside to meet the villagers!"

What Noe found most unbearable was her mother's crying. Exhausted by these day-in and day-out disputes with her family, Noe felt as if she were going mad.

Was it better to resign herself and with the feeling that she was already dead remain married? When she had thought this far, her love and attachment to Tsuji fiercely blazed up in her entire body to demolish that ridiculous idea. Having gone and separated from him, she realized all the more keenly the weight of their three months together. She already felt bound to him body and soul. How could she dare to betray Tsuji, who had given her his love at such a terrible sacrifice? Even though she wanted to run away to Tokyo, she did not have a single yen, and she was being carefully watched. Unable to stand the situation any longer, Noe informed Haruko Hiratsuka by letter of all that had passed and appealed to her in desperate tones that if things went on as they were, nothing remained except to die.

Having received Noe's communication, Haruko was even more surprised. When she recalled how unyielding Noe had looked, how overflowing had been her wild,

energetic enthusiasm, Haruko thought Noe might be
seized by a fit of passion to kill herself.

Carried away by her own uneasiness, Haruko resolved
then and there to visit Tsuji. She wanted to inform him of
Noe's present situation, listen to his opinion, and further
discuss the problem with him. When with much difficulty
she actually paid her call, Tsuji was out. Haruko informed
Mitsu of the object of her visit, left her card, and returned.

The following day Haruko received Tsuji. On this first
meeting she felt favorably disposed toward him. Though
on the surface he seemed weak-willed, he looked like a
young man of a highly nervous yet sensitive temperament
who was in some way elegant and quiet and sober in his
tastes. She perceived an extraordinary refinement even in
what he happened to say casually, his speech and manner
conveying something stylish and chic, as if he had been
bred in downtown Tokyo, and Haruko, herself a native
Tokyoite, discovered something instantly suggested to her
in addition to his words. She sensed that Tsuji was enter-
taining toward her a deep understanding and goodwill, and
she felt such affection for him she found it all the more
difficult to realize this was their first encounter. Haruko
thought Noe, who not only had this kind of protector but
lover as well, was fortunate. From her conversation with
him Haruko surmised that Tsuji had been devoted to Noe
and had aspirations for the seeds of a talent still as
unknown as some creatures of the seas or mountains.
Haruko also listened frankly to Tsuji's confession that he
had reached the very bottom financially.

"At any rate, let's summon Noe-san back to Tokyo.
Somehow I can at least manage her travel expenses. I'll also
think about a job for her after she returns." Having said

this with assurance to Tsuji, Haruko also requested his cooperation.

On receiving her travel funds from Haruko at the beginning of August, Noe was finally able to escape from her village. Once more held securely against Tsuji's bosom, Noe said she would never go anywhere else again, her voice broken by sobs.

From Noe's attitude and behavior during her return to her hometown, the people around her, after taking into account the firmness of her resolution, seemed to resign themselves this time and annulled the match with Fukutaro. Noe did not even ask how they had managed to pay back the money she had spent.

Having at last settled in Tsuji's home as his wife, Noe, even in the midst of the uneasiness that day by day they were getting closer to the very pit of distress in their family finances, was intoxicated with the happiness that apparently belongs only to newlyweds, and for the time being nobody in the world attracted her attention except Tsuji.

Haruko Hiratsuka went to Chigasaki partly to pay a sick call on Kokichi and partly to avoid the summer heat in the city, and Yoshiko Yasumochi also moved there, partly to take a side job at Nankoin Hospital, so it appeared the entire editorial staff of *Seito* had transferred to Chigasaki.

That summer in which Noe in a kimono with a dark neckband, her hair bound into the chignon of a married woman, joined her playing of the samisen to Tsuji's bamboo flute and was enraptured body and soul on her honeymoon was also the brilliant and dramatic summer in which Haruko chanced to meet her destined lover Hiroshi Okumura.

Hiroshi Okumura was born in 1891 (the twenty-fourth year of Meiji), the young man then twenty-two years of age by the Japanese count and five years Haruko's junior. Rather than call him young, it would be more suitable to refer to him as a good-looking boy with rosy cheeks. His skin was white, his eyes were gentle, and his face suggested something of femininity or the ladies' man. In contrast to Haruko, who, ever since she had begun to discern the true aspect of things around her, had been brought up accustomed to seeing the brilliant glitter of a chandelier hanging in their drawing room and leather-bound books shining in gold letters in her father's library, Hiroshi had lived quietly with his family, consisting of himself, his retired father so old he might have been taken as the grandfather, and his gentle mother, all inside an excessively large residence with a storehouse at Fujisawa. An only child, Hiroshi had been extraordinarily delicate and sensitive from boyhood on, and because his constitution would not allow him to eat even a slice of meat, he had been a vegetarian from his earliest years. Having often been mistaken for a girl since his hair was cut in a Dutch bob, he had no desire for friends. He seldom tired of looking at the woodcut prints of Hiroshige and Harunobu piled in oblong chests in the storehouse. When he did grow tired of these, he went out secretly for some fun in the red-light district near his home. Such houses as the Yamatoya, the Tsutaya, the Matsuzakaya, and the Miuraya were arranged in rows, and prostitutes smelling of thick white face powder competed in taking the cute Hiroshi in their arms, their cheeks pressed against him. When he was handed from one prostitute to another, the young Hiroshi's hand occasionally happened to touch something overflowing and rich under the exposed upper part of the woman's long undergarment. Having been treated like a little girl because of his looks, he did not think these visits anything to be ashamed of; instead, he was afraid of and disgusted with the mischievous and vulgar rough boys his own age.

From his early years so sensitive was Hiroshi to the beauty of nature and so much mystified and inspired by the blooming of flowers, the trembling of leaves, and the movement of his own fingers that he was easily reduced to tears. He was a child reluctant to kill even a single insect, the mere sight of this action in another making him shout out and burst into tears.

"It might be better for him to become a Buddhist priest," his aged father whispered, observing him. Even though his elderly parent no longer had any regular income, he put it this way: "Although he need not work so hard, I hope he will not lessen the property we already own."

The good looks given Hiroshi from his early years were turned more and more into the prettiness of a young girl, and he had many experiences of being adored by upper-classmen and by young officers who lodged at his house. Among these persons was the governor of a subprefecture who lived nearby and who in conduct disgraceful for one his age lost himself in the beauty of Hiroshi, young enough to be his own son. Assuming the air of a guardian after becoming acquainted with Hiroshi's family, the governor raped the boy in an incident occurring on a festival day. With no knowledge of the real situation, Hiroshi's parents were pleased to think a guardianship from someone as powerful as a subprefectural governor would in the future prove beneficial to Hiroshi, who had few relatives, and in obedience to the governor's request they gave him and his family a part of the large house to live in. Disgusted by the homosexuality of the governor, who stole into his room at night, Hiroshi was unable to bear the situation any longer, and finally, after withdrawing the savings that was in his own name, he came up to Tokyo with nothing but the clothes on his back.

Already in those days he cherished the desire of becoming a painter, but even while attending art school, he enjoyed his self-indulgent adolescent life at a boarding-house. His elderly parents finally learned the real situation after Hiroshi left home, so they and the subprefectural governor did not get along as well as before, the quiet life again returning with only the old people living in the large house.

Brought up too much indulged and cared for, Hiroshi had none of the masculine ambition and fighting spirit needed in the struggle for existence. Filled with a dream-like yearning for art, he was content to paint pictures and, if possible, compose songs and poems, so he became a staff member of Yugure Maeda's magazine *Shiika*. Instead of a scar being left on his heart by the consumption of the girl at Kamakura who was Hiroshi's first love during his middle school days, he thought her an example of a beautiful life colored with idealism.

One morning after the middle of August, Hiroshi, having returned to his father's house to avoid the summer heat, set out for Fujisawa Station to pay a sick call on this girl at Kamakura. His line of vision was suddenly absorbed in watching the hands of a young man in kimono apparently two or three years older than himself standing by a window in the waiting room and smoking. Hiroshi was able to make out the characters *Zamboa* on the cover of the just-published magazine the young man was holding. This poetry magazine edited by Hakushu Kitahara struck Hiroshi's eyes with a freshness no lover of literature like himself could escape noticing. When he realized it was the most recent issue, one which was not yet being sold in the bookstores in his neighborhood, Hiroshi was like some impatient child seized with the desire to read. When the handsome Hiroshi, his hair long and a beret on his head as if he were a literary enthusiast, suddenly addressed the young man, the stranger was not the least bit surprised and said, "Oh, you want this? Please take it. I've finished it," and easily handed Hiroshi the magazine.

As Hiroshi was breathlessly turning the pages, the man asked while suppressing a yawn, "Do you know any place nearby where I can eat breakfast? I'm returning from a night at the Miuraya, and I'm starving."

Out of consideration for having been given the magazine, Hiroshi could not flatly refuse, so he led the man to a small restaurant in front of the station and treated him to a late breakfast. Throwing off all formality, the man said, without even asking Hiroshi his name or revealing his own, "Look. How about going with me to Nankoin Hospital? I'm going to pay a sick call on a woman friend. But there are some unusual women there, and you may find it amusing."

As Hiroshi was tempted by the aura of this carefree man, the romantic image of Nankoin's entirely white-walled building again floated attractively before him, a building he had seen only from afar.

"Should I?"

"Let's go. You're not busy anyway, are you?"

The two young men immediately boarded an electric train for Chigasaki. At this time Hiroshi did not yet know the man was Yokichi Nishimura, owner of the Toundo Publishing Company, which was putting out *Zamboa*. Since Nishimura was to undertake the publication of *Seito* in September, he was combining this visit of inquiry after

Kokichi's health with a discussion of the enterprise with Haruko Hiratsuka, who was going to be in Chigasaki. It was only out of the caprice of the moment that he had invited along this handsome lover of literature who had treated him to breakfast.

A cool sea breeze swept in through the wide-open windows of Nankoin's white-walled drawing room, the lace curtains ballooning out. On a table in the center of the room was a potted dwarf pine about ten inches tall with overspreading branches. Timidly walking behind Yokichi Nishimura but with a smile playing about his white face, Hiroshi Okumura entered the room.

From beyond the vivid green of the pine which suddenly caught Hiroshi's attention, the face of a woman who sprang to her feet greeted his eyes head on. The pupils of her brown eyes, shaped long and large, looked steadily and directly into his own without blinking. He felt as if he had been struck by electricity, and for a moment he could not budge an inch. Although that glance was as short as it takes to wink, it seemed to Hiroshi that he had been pierced by those two fixed eyes for several minutes. He thought it a considerably long time after he entered the room that the woman's face and figure had attracted his glance.

After he was introduced by Nishimura, Hiroshi finally noticed two other women in addition to the one called Haruko Hiratsuka. Both instantly vanished from Hiroshi's mind, the fat woman Yoshiko Yasumochi, her eyes somewhat strange looking, and Kazue Otake, who, though larger than a man but with a dark childish face, behaved like a spoiled brat. For the first time Hiroshi realized the name of the man he had come with was Yokichi Nishimura.

"I haven't even asked yours yet."

With these words by Nishimura, Hiroshi introduced himself for the first time.

"I'm Hiroshi Okumura," he said.

Kazue Otake shouted wildly and burst into laughter, her entire body shaking. Haruko's eyes still fixed on Hiroshi, and her thin lips slightly opened at the edge.

Hiroshi could focus his glance only on Haruko's smile. His heart cried out, "It's exactly like the Mona Lisa's! No, it resembles the fiancée of the Duke of Orange, Princess Marie, in Van Dyck's painting. Ah yes, the face of a Botticelli woman is also her type." A mere glance at the fresh beautiful face of Haruko Hiratsuka had literally charmed him.

Though Haruko was smaller than the two other women, she was much more dignified. She looked neat and trim in a summer kimono of bold coarse cloth with tapering vertical stripes, her light-blue cashmere Japanese skirt bosom high.

Hiroshi left the hospital after their rambling talk that day. Knowing nothing of the real world, he acknowledged himself a young literary enthusiast, but he was not much interested in *Seito* or the New Women that had been creating a sensation in society, and even when he heard the Mona Lisa-like woman he had met that day was Haruko Hiratsuka, he could not connect her to Raicho Hiratsuka, *Seito*'s editor. Of course, he knew nothing about her attempted suicide with Sohei Morita several years earlier. The Haruko he happened to meet that day was no more than a woman with neither background nor title, an ideal woman whose face he had conjured up in dreams as if she had broken loose from a famous painting. He had already lost interest in inquiring after the health of the girl at Kamakura, and he returned home to spend the rest of the day sketching the image of Haruko he still kept in his memory.

This chance encounter, which was so profoundly shocking to Hiroshi, left in Haruko as well an extraordinary agitation she had never experienced before. Throughout her twenty-six years, she had not once had an experience that could actually be called love. As for her affair with Sohei, he alone had taken the active role toward her at a time she was under such conditions that her mind, stretched and strained by the extraordinary vitality of directly seeing into herself in Zen meditation, was apparently spreading a net of curiosity toward all the phenomena of the world.

Ever since she had received Sohei's first love letter, Haruko had been logically constructing in her mind a love affair not the least bit emotionally glowing, and she had pretended she was behaving intensely like a woman in love. In short, her love affair was no more than a childish adventure in which a well-bred, well-protected petite bourgeoise, no matter how boastfully she had talked about love, felt herself drawn toward an illusion of love known by her only as idea, and she was trying to peep into the reality of a love that would never defile her body. After that affair was over, she easily gave her virginity to a young monk she had known at the Zen temple, and in such a way as to have actually seduced him herself. She neither loved the man nor had she been drawn toward his body. The event meant only that she could no longer control a curiosity which made her glance resolutely beyond the door of sex conceived only as an abstraction.

Radiant in beauty and intelligence, Haruko had been accustomed to being greeted by the eyes of ardent admirers no matter where she went. In general, almost all the people who saw her, be they men or women, were enchanted by her quiet intellectual beauty. Used to the eyes of these admirers, she could see with the clarity of day, even before her own feelings were stirred, the movement of their hearts as they were attracted and drawn to her, so she became interested in penetrating with her own cold eyes the texture of the psychology of their hesitation, their shyness, their bewilderment, their jealousy.

She could not help but feel that when a woman falls in love and is captivated by the heart of another, especially in a situation in which the other party is a man, the woman becomes his subordinate both spiritually and physically. If a woman could make passionate love without losing her ego . . . if she could always be intoxicated with love while robbing the other party without being robbed by him . . . Haruko might have been cherishing such an illusion of love. Her having accepted Kokichi's love had not deprived Haruko of one iota of anything spiritual or physical. In a situation in which love is involved, the giving of love need not mean its loss. In short, up until that day of her twenty-six years of life, the truth was Haruko had not yet met anyone she could really love. Even though she might have moved the other party, she herself had not experienced being truly moved by a man.

There remained in Haruko's heart after she had seen Hiroshi Okumura a totally unexpected agitation. It was quite obvious she had been forced to feel on her own an unknown, strange, and sweet stirring of her heart by that childish handsome boy considerably younger than she was and no more than a student of the brush.

Until now, even though she could almost read at a glance the admiration of companions impressed with her beauty, be they male or female, she had never met anyone like Hiroshi, who expressed with his naked eyes the youth and freshness he felt. Those eyes were quite different from those of the childish and naive Kokichi. Haruko thought his eyes as pure and serene as a newborn infant's. These thoughts came considerably after this first event, the truth being that the moment Haruko's eyes joined Hiroshi's, she too, in blank surprise, had lost herself in some dazzling sensation of trembling, as if an electric current transmitted from Hiroshi had run vehemently and heatedly through her entire body. When she recovered her senses, she experienced a thirst to firmly seize and immoderately hold inside herself everything about that young man who looked like a beautiful girl. Until that day something like the sensation of a scorching throat or the itching of a cell had been unknown to the twenty-six-year-old Haruko.

There was one who grasped the significance of the moment of that destined encounter more sensitively and more correctly than the persons concerned. That person was Kokichi, who the instant Hiroshi came into the drawing room had in breathless suspense riveted her eyes on Haruko's expression. The following day Hiroshi received an unexpected letter, the envelope inscribed with the sender's name, Kokichi Otake:

An ominous premonition has attacked me and made me sad and afraid. And now I'm seized with a feeling of anxiety. I will probably have to spend the rest of my very uninteresting life with this feeling until once and for all my day of rest comes. And then several days later I will be reborn. But until that day I shall be lonely and tormented.

Hiratsuka has been asking for you to definitely come and stay with us. We are waiting. Please do.

—*Kokichi*

Hiroshi could not understand what it was all about. Because he had been so fascinated with Haruko, the only thing he could remember of Kokichi was that she was larger than a man, had a childish face, and had been in a playful mood. He thought she might be insane, but at least the words in the last part of her letter remained in his mind.

Hiroshi again visited Nankoin about three days later. He could not have imagined even in a dream that Kokichi's letter had been written in a fit of jealousy, in a frame of mind that wants to look at its fears as soon as possible, nor did he dream it had been sent secretly without Haruko's knowledge. Though he had had experiences in which he had been outrageously raped and wooed by the same sex, he could not even imagine the existence of women homosexuals.

Under the pretext of having been asked by Haruko on the day of their first meeting to make the cover design of *Seito* for its first-anniversary issue, Hiroshi came to bring her the picture he had drawn.

That day Yoshiko Yasumochi's new lover also happened to drop by. After dinner the five persons went out for a boat ride. When they returned from drifting along the Umairi River and enjoying the moon, Hiroshi discovered the last train had already left and he could not return to Fujisawa.

Although Kokichi had been excited all day long, at times playful, at times dejected, Hiroshi was in such a daze over his conversations with Haruko he had forgotten even the letter he had received from Kokichi. The outcome was, as Kokichi's letter had predicted, that he should stay with them, and he decided to spend the night at Nankoin. The cottage rented by Yoshiko deep in the wooded grounds of the hospital was vacated for Hiroshi's use. Yoshiko went into an empty room in the hospital, and Haruko left for the fisherman's detached cottage she had rented along the coast. Near midnight it suddenly thundered, a storm threatening. As Hiroshi was turning over in bed unable to sleep, he heard a woman's voice at the door. Haruko was standing at the entrance, a paper lantern in her hand, the fisherman's wife accompanying her.

"Since the thunder was so loud, I was afraid you might not be able to sleep, and somehow I became worried . . . and so I came to take you back with me . . ."

Although Hiroshi had never had any fear of thunder, he was, of course, glad to obey Haruko, who had come out to meet him in the dead of night. The moment he followed her from the house, after packing his painting equipment for his nature sketches, a tremendous clap of thunder surrounded them, flashes of lightning ripping the sky all over. But it was Haruko who shrieked and suddenly clung to him. In the childish timidity of Haruko, who until then had been so self-possessed she looked calm and sober enough to be the Mona Lisa, Hiroshi felt a tenderness for this woman who had abruptly rushed to him.

A brand-new fragrant green mosquito net was hanging in Haruko's room. That night Hiroshi was forced to wear her summer cotton kimono. When the tall Hiroshi put it on, he found it was much too short, and even though his face was beautiful like a girl's, his legs with their masculine growth of black glossy hair on his shins jutted out unexpectedly. Haruko laughed so hard at this image tears came to her eyes, and she put Hiroshi to bed as she would a child. Having been asked, he told her about his family and his past. Haruko, an expert listener, created a mood in which Hiroshi, though shy, could talk so freely about anything that he himself might have thought it strange. It was still thundering as if it had remembered to, but the two persons inside the green mosquito net were out of reach. Hiroshi could not feel Haruko was the woman he had met only a few days before. Her body, which smelled like cape jasmine and which lay where he could easily touch it if only he extended his hand sideways, was dazzling to him, and he felt his eyes and mind become tense.

"Oh, you can't sleep, can you?"

Haruko gently extended her hand and placed it on Hiroshi's brow, but suddenly after slipping out from under the mosquito net, she brought back with her a bottle of peppermints. Having kept his eyes closed, Hiroshi felt something soft on his tongue, and at that moment which so startled him, a soft tongue forcing his teeth to part slipped into his mouth, at the same time the fragrant peppermint flowed between his lips. Choking, Hiroshi coughed himself into a fit. Haruko's arms held him behind his back, her hot heavy body wrapping itself around him. The peppermint had completely washed down his throat, but Haruko's lips were still adhering to his like a butterfly clinging to a flower.

Hiroshi had no recollection of how he managed to slip away from under Haruko.

Inside the net she called gently to him, sitting and trembling outside it.

"Please come on under. I'll let you sleep quietly now. You really are a cute boy, aren't you?"

At that moment Kokichi, her face deathly pale, was sitting in the house in the midst of the woods Hiroshi had slipped out of. From the minute it had thundered, she had been tormented by a strange premonition and had become extremely restless. Tantalized by an illusion which continued to emerge no matter how often she warded it off, she had run in a daze to the center of the woods after stealing from her hospital bed. As she suspected, neither Hiroshi nor his possessions were there.

When with a reflex action she touched the bedding, she found even his body heat had not remained. The wild fancy which had distressed her had turned out to be true after all. Unable to sleep a wink that night, the whole time spent in agony, Kokichi could not even wait for dawn, and when she rushed to Haruko's house, she found the sliding doors locked. The fisherman's wife peeped out and, seeing Kokichi's strange face furious with rage, became nervous and uneasy. Merely the sight of that embarrassed and confused face enabled Kokichi to guess everything. Lined up inside the mosquito net in the room were two pillows, Hiroshi's painting equipment left as it was in a corner. Eyes welling with tears as she looked toward the seashore, Kokichi saw Haruko and Hiroshi wrapped in one woolen blanket and walking away from the shore while basking in the fresh morning sun.

A cluster of scarlet canna in the garden blazed up inside Kokichi's eyes, a red glass bell hanging from the eaves ringing with its cool sound. In that calm bright view of the sea everything had been wiped clean the morning after the summer storm.

The hand writing this letter is trembling so much that I can only stare at it. Please think of me sometimes, a me that is perpetually dreaming only of pleasant and sad things since *that* moment.

My child (Kokichi) keeps saying it is already time for her to receive a letter from you. Please be kind to my child. Please be sympathetic to her intensely jealous heart.

I remain here until the 30th. Before then I beg to have one of your paintings. Though I'd love to have your self-portrait, I have my doubts you will listen to this request. Send me something by the evening of the 30th. I will probably have to continue to think sad things all day long today too.

Here I enclose a souvenir photograph taken the other day in the compound of Benten Shrine at Nango. The man in the summer cotton kimono and bathing cap is the critic Choko Ikuta, and the woman standing quite properly at the extreme right edge of the photo is his wife. Snapped real cute like a boy is Kokichi. Someone said they photographed me like a Rossetti woman.

Waiting with all my heart to hear from you.

> August 27
> —*Haruko*

The day after Hiroshi returned to Fujisawa, this letter reached him, as if in pursuit. It was a love letter written by the chief editor of *Seito*, the popular magazine which had attracted widespread attention all over the country and which for good or bad was in journalism's spotlight. A woman respected and worshipped as a goddess by countless New Women throughout the nation who had been awakening to their own egos, an extraordinarily bold woman who had once seduced to the verge of death a man of literature with a wife and child, a strong-minded woman who had received the highest education available to her sex in Japan, who had been raised in a respectable family, who had endured in addition the severe austerities of meditation in Zen Buddhism and had seen through to her "real self," and who was also intellectual enough in a sufficiently manly way to discuss even Nietzsche—what a fresh love letter written by a twenty-six-year-old woman, as if it had been composed by a girl student! To Hiroshi, however, nothing in Haruko's past had anything to do with him. Though he had shrunk from her strange passion inside the green mosquito net that stormy night, she had been no more than a kindhearted elder sister with whom he had talked about love for the first time. To Hiroshi's eyes, a love letter from the girl who was his first sweetheart and recuperating from illness at Kamakura and this love letter from Haruko were about equal in content.

Hiroshi could not understand why Haruko was so protective of and so attached to such a repulsive woman as Kokichi. But because he could never imagine the two women were homosexual companions, he could not sympathize with Kokichi's feelings, and after bringing his self-portrait to the hospital and bidding Haruko farewell, he set out on a sketching trip to Miura Cape as he had previously planned.

Hiroshi stayed at the Koyokan Inn on Jogashima Island with an acquaintance, a member of the poetry magazine *Shiika*. He was Kan Niizuma, a young literature enthusiast. His eyes opened wide in astonishment to discover that a woman kept forwarding letters, food, and small parcels of books daily to Hiroshi, sometimes two letters arriving in succession the same day. And when Niizuma found out the sender was the famous Raicho Hiratsuka, his curiosity was even more strongly aroused. As he learned every item of the events at Chigasaki by coaxing and flattering Hiroshi, who was so naive and ignorant of the world that Niizuma himself felt impatient, the latter's heart was peevishly fretting to the full in interest and jealousy.

"You've gotten involved with an outrageous female.

You're such a complete child you'll end up in a real mess. You of all persons will be made the plaything of that minx, and in the end you'll only be tossed aside. Do you really know about that woman's history?"

Niizuma threatened Hiroshi in the friendly tone of a comrade and made him listen to all the scandals he knew about Haruko, embroidering and exaggerating them. He used exceedingly abusive language in referring to her homosexual relations with Kokichi. Though Hiroshi did not believe all his words, not one of the rumors about Haruko's past that he heard from Niizuma was pleasant to take. Of her homosexuality with Kokichi, Hiroshi was especially disapproving. At that very moment, driven by her morbid jealousy, Kokichi had sent in succession several absurdly threatening letters addressed to him at the Koyokan in which she said she would kill him or she would die if he did not give up Haruko.

"There! You see! I told you, didn't I? If you continue to concern yourself with these delinquent women, you'll only be hurt before you can advance in life. You'd better break off with her instantly."

Like someone elated over beheading an ogre, Niizuma agitated Hiroshi, who had become completely depressed by the unpleasantness of Kokichi's letters. Although Hiroshi's yearning for Haruko had not cooled, he could not bear the thought of the dirty association that bound her to Kokichi, and he finally came to think of breaking loose from this troublesome affair. Without a moment's delay Niizuma made the despondent Hiroshi pick up a pen to write a farewell letter.

Niizuma was intoxicated with the heroic excitement of a situation in which he was at least playing a part in the secrets of the nationally famous Raicho Hiratsuka and also in forcing Hiroshi to write a letter severing his relations with her. Feeling as if he were controlling the hero of this drama, Niizuma worked out the splendid phrases in the manner of a Cyrano. With a look of indifference on his face, Hiroshi made those words into characters as if he were performing an assigned duty:

It happened in a country in which the light of the setting sun was still lingering.

In a marsh by the seashore in this country lived two lovely mandarin ducks. There was perfect harmony between them, and not a time existed when they were not together, so might it not be said that the figure of the one was the shadow of the other? The elder sister mandarin talked about her young sister mandarin so much she called it "my child," as if that were her favorite expression. Many quiet days flowed by in such a happy state.

A day in summer. A handsome young swallow appeared from nowhere to visit the marsh. The young swallow had a crimson dream of yearning. A dream in which he wanted to be pure and beautiful forever and ever. To glance into his own dream was his greatest pleasure. The swallow was so young, and so truly handsome.

Then on the swallow's dream mirror was reflected out of nowhere a shadow. Even while he could not understand what this shadow was, he came to the marsh of the sister mandarins for several days that summer, amused himself with them, and then went back.

One day all of them went to the seaside, and finding it too late to return to his nest, the swallow decided to spend the night in the vicinity of the marsh.

That night various shadows were cast on the swallow's heart.

The shadows moved violently like a storm at sea. While the swallow could not sleep because the night was so violent with thunder and lightning, the elder sister mandarin came to fetch him saying, "Come stay in my nest." And then the swallow followed as he had been told and came to the nest of the elder sister mandarin. And the day dawned.

But the swallow could not well remember the events of that night. To remember them would have been too heavy a burden for the mind of the young swallow. The swallow flew away from the marsh once and for all. He migrated to a certain island. Letters and various books he received from the elder sister mandarin were the only consolations to his loneliness that autumn on the island.

Then one day, suddenly, unexpectedly, a totally misinformed letter came from the younger mandarin. It was a letter addressed to the swallow about breaking off the relationships. Once the swallow became angry. And once he was sad, but only for a short time. And finally he came to be able to think it over calmly. And many dark silent days followed.

With one thing and another it was already the middle of autumn.

The swallow, immersed only in silent reverie, was no longer the swallow he had been. He was getting too old to enjoy the "episodes" of those bygone days. But there were times when he thought, "Just how long will these leisurely days last? No, no, while I am lazily entangling myself in the troubles of this foolish affair, how can I follow my own interests? I'm a male. My own concerns are the most important. And especially if I myself withdraw from this affair, the sister ducks, who had become so odd, will again be restored as companions."

And he wrote a long letter about these matters and sent it to the sister mandarins, requesting the two to forget him.

He admitted his way of thinking was old-fashioned, but to a swallow who loved "himself" more than anything, there was nothing else to do if he was to break free from this whirlpool.

Not only during the present but at all times and seasons did he remember the mandarins, yet it is said that those flirtatious ducks finally forgot their affair with the swallow and eventually asked themselves, "Was there ever anywhere a bird called a swallow?"

17 September, on the day I am leaving the island

—*From H*

When Haruko received this letter severing their relationship, a letter written as a fable in literary prose, she was, as expected, truly worthy of herself by not running after Hiroshi. Since her love for him was the only active one she had experienced in her life, her self-respect was hurt, but without asking the reason, she wrote the following on the title page of a new collection of poems by Yugure Maeda entitled *Shadows*:

Look! Was that beautiful bird a swallow? If it really was the swallow I have known and loved, he will surely not forget, when the season comes again, to visit even on a whim the eaves of that saké shop along the street, will he not? Surely, surely, when the season comes.

And on the back of the page:

Merely because on occasion the mandarin ducks defile marsh water and merely because a murky whirlpool suddenly appears in the center of the marsh, why does that necessarily mean the lustrous wings of the young swallow will be polluted? Cannot the swallow draw his pure beautiful dream in the blue firmament forever and ever?

If that swallow is really the swallow I have known and loved, he cannot, you see, be that clever and logical.

She wrote only that much and sent the book to Hiroshi at Jagoshima. The more minutely she read the letter of farewell from him, the more doubtful it seemed to her. To have made up his mind about this serious undertaking and to have written it in the guise of a fable was much too artificial, and this style was on the whole too hypocritical, too flowery, too leisurely. She felt as if the Hiroshi of the fable were a different person from the Hiroshi of the letters up to that time, a Hiroshi who had been gentle, pure, quite unaffected. Very suspicious about the letter, Haruko even showed it to Kokichi. With incredulous eyes as if she were being let in on the tricks of a juggler, Kokichi read the letter again and again, her face disappointed by the overly easy manner in which Hiroshi had withdrawn.

When autumn came, Hiroshi and Haruko's short love affair and all its complications, which had ended much too soon, were circulated in full by Kokichi to the persons concerned with *Seito*. In the way rumors are usually transmitted, all the details of the affair, due to Kokichi's exaggerated prattle, were disclosed to outsiders as well, and not many days were required for the events to be subjected to victimization by the press.

Hiroshi's letter was so widely disseminated that before

anyone realized it, the words "young swallow" were being used as a synonym for young lover.

Even the fact that Kokichi had sent out several threatening letters could not, after all, be kept quiet, Kokichi herself conveying this information to Haruko and others. On the surface Haruko did not show the least agitation in her behavior, and with the coming of autumn devoted herself to *Seito*'s editing. However, it was Kokichi who knew that Haruko had tasted the pangs of unrequited love, the depth of the severe wound no ordinary one, as she had been forced to drink the bitter cup of betrayal by the only person she had loved in her life. Even though Hiroshi had gone away, Kokichi was plunged into despair over the fact that the pure love of old between Haruko and herself would never again return. Kokichi was quite aware that even though Haruko had kept her feelings to herself, she was in her innermost thoughts blaming her for her heedless conduct. Though all the members had been criticizing Kokichi before the summer and only Haruko had been defending Kokichi's rash actions and blind behavior so much that the others had been quite irritated about it, her eyes turned cold to Kokichi after the autumn came. Rather than say that, it might be more accurate to state she had become as impartial to Kokichi as the other members of the group had, but Kokichi could interpret Haruko's behavior as nothing but a rejection of their love.

Though Kokichi had recovered from her illness, her nerves were tremendously overwrought, and the disquieting atmosphere between Haruko and herself was felt by everyone. Unable to bear the strain, Kokichi took the advice of Yoshiko Yasumochi and withdrew from *Seito*. "After I Joined the Masses," which she wrote in the editor's postscript column to the November issue, became Kokichi's

last essay in the magazine. As usual, however, she personally visited Haruko's study and editorial office, and her
relations with the staff were maintained.

The participation of Noe Ito in *Seito*, if viewed from the
standpoint of time, took the form of filling the gap just
after Kokichi's departure. In the November issue carrying
Kokichi's farewell address, the aforementioned inept poem
of Noe's, "Eastern Strand," first appeared, its woodcut
drawn by Kokichi.

The family budget of Tsuji's home was even nearer rock
bottom of late. More than half a year had passed since he
had lost his job, and his translations and miscellaneous
writings did not result in as much money as he had
anticipated. Gone were almost all the articles to pawn and
the books he had intended to sell. Even his mother Mitsu,
who was quite easygoing and generous, sometimes complained to him with the remark, "What in the world are we
going to do?" but he merely replied with provoking
indifference, "Something will come along one of these
days," Tsuji never showing any indication of trying to earn
some money. The truth was that Jun Tsuji was grateful for
having the present time to himself, finally gained when he
was almost thirty years old, and the happiness of being able
to freely use twenty-four hours a day on only what was
completely of interest to him was, he thought, not something that could be bought with money or honor. His
translation of Lombroso's *The Man of Genius*, advancing a
little at a time, was all that occupied him at present.

As the family's wretched plight pressed nearer, Noe felt
inferior for being, after all, its cause, and she felt humiliated. Her mind, however, was too young to brood about it
all day long, her body too sound. Her small compact figure
was overflowing with youth and passion, and poverty did

not distress her in the least. Her thoughts were so animated by the abundance of knowledge she was absorbing from Tsuji she felt dizzy. Her mere questioning of Tsuji about anything she wanted to know or wished to be taught turned her seven inquiries into twelve answers. Furthermore, he was exceedingly gentle to her, and as he liberally poured his knowledge into her during the day, so he poured into her at night a ceaseless flow of love. In inverse proportion to the daily meagerness of food on the table was the greater fullness of Noe's body and soul, and she could forget her actual hunger and cold.

Haruko accepted Noe as one of the editorial staff in place of Kokichi and arranged to pay her a greater remuneration than she did the other members. Noe's editorial experience during her school days when she had put out the school paper all by herself and her own talents unexpectedly spoke for themselves. From the very first day she was favorably received by the senior staff as a useful member. To Noe, *Seito* was a paradise more comfortable than she had imagined.

Noe, who did her hair simply in foreign style, who remained indifferent to personal appearance and wore no makeup, was apt to be taken at a glance as two or three years older than she was, but she was actually the youngest of all the women gathered there. Her small compact body was overflowing with a vitality that had in it something rough and wild, both her movement and voice propelled in a lively way. As she became used to her surroundings, she talked so earnestly to everybody her nostrils expanded, her voice having more enthusiasm than that of any of the others, and she would come out with her brightest laugh no matter with whom she was speaking. She had a voracious appetite for knowledge and for improving herself, the black pupils of her eyes always intensely on the alert. Even while busily working with her hands or while reading, she was straining her ears lest she miss hearing someone speak. The mere fact of her presence radiated from her entire body a strange force as if in some way the very air around her had become animated.

Noe made a great effort to accustom herself to the atmosphere of *Seito* as soon as possible, to understand the complicated relationships involved in other persons' affairs, and to adjust to the group as if she were an old member. Almost every other day she went out to Haruko's study or to the editor's office at Mannenzan. With her departures bringing in some money, she felt justified in thinking herself free and unreserved in regard to her mother-in-law and Tsuji's sister. Always when Noe came back, she sat down by Tsuji, who would be at his desk, and like a dam bursting she would tell him with energy and haste every last detail of her experience that day.

"All the same, I like Miss Hiratsuka best in every respect, and she's talented, you see. A woman who has something great about her! Of course, they're a group with many kinds of women with strong personalities. And that's why all year-round we have some complicated psychological problems. But Miss Hiratsuka solves each one perfectly with a quiet and confident look."

"That's probably true."

"What's more, she's a very gentle person. Whenever it gets too late, she worries about my taking a jinrikisha or the streetcar and sees me off at the front door, telling me to be careful. Even though it's only a small thing, to be told that is very pleasant to me. It's something most people won't do."

"That's true."

"Anyway, it seems to me *Seito*'s now at a turning point, and the sweet, cheerful mood when they went on that spree with that wine of five colors and that trip to the Yoshiwara prostitution house has passed with Kokichi's leaving, and I feel, somehow or other, we have to begin now to strike out with something like distinct thought!"

"Did Raicho say that?"

"No. That's the feeling I got after listening to all of them. And there has been a great shift in our membership."

Tsuji amused himself with knowing from Noe's way of talking and its contents that at first she had been amazed by her seniors' too free and unrestrained speech and behavior; then the intimidated feeling of wondering if she could follow them had gradually led her to be accustomed to the atmosphere around these women and enter into it; and with that step she came to have confidence in herself, already mixing in among the senior members and feeling she had acquired her own chair no matter how small. Her way of talking was enthusiastic, and with the upper part of her nose wrinkled, the pupils of her eyes busily turning round and round, she spoke in a lively way, occasionally moistening her long thin lips. Tsuji always said to her merely "Hm" or "Is that so?" or inserted other short words at interludes.

Once Noe said to him, "Katsu-chan is really a very agreeable person. I like her best. She's thin, refined, and pretty, and all the fine points of the downtown Tokyo girls are brought together in her. Her butterfly hairdo really suits her, though you wouldn't think with the way she dresses and looks that her English would be so good!"

On that occasion Tsuji explained to Noe that Katsu's father was Kiyochika Kobayashi, the leading woodcut artist of the Meiji era who had succeeded in introducing light and shadow as a technique in woodcut prints, and after the remark Tsuji also told her about the history of woodcuts and the way to appreciate them. On Noe's informing him about Kiyoko Iwano's always coming to the office beautifully dressed, her hair styled in a round chignon, Tsuji related to her the literature and ideas of Homei Iwano, Kiyoko's husband.

"Although I feel I'm closest in thought to the idealists of the Subaru group of writers, I like Homei best among the naturalists. He's a good fellow."

"Have you ever met him?"

"No, I haven't. Generally I don't like to associate with writers and scholars."

Tsuji then informed her that at the time Homei and Kiyoko began living together, Kiyoko, even though she was bound to him spiritually, would not give herself physically, so they had put their two names, Iwano and Endo, side by side on the nameplate of the house and on the lantern hanging from the eaves, the world finding it quite amusing, all excited in the spirit of a mob as to whether the soul or the body would win. As if she were a piece of blotting paper, Noe absorbed rapidly and thoroughly everything she had been hearing from Tsuji. She seemed to feel bad if she forgot to tell him some trivial thing that had occurred outside, no matter how insignificant, and she would address him hastily even when she happened to wake at midnight. Though he gave no orders or made any promises, Tsuji came to clearly understand each and every part of Noe's behavior and psychological changes as if he were looking at something through glass.

The person who most surprised Noe was, after all, Kokichi. The latter was capricious and extravagant, her mind never settled in one spot for even a second, and what she had mentioned a moment ago she would reverse with the greatest ease an instant later. Though she was a terrible liar, she herself never dreamed her lies were such. Nevertheless, all the persons in *Seito*, including Haruko, could not help but take notice of Kokichi even after her withdrawal from the group. It was this very Kokichi who actively approached even Noe and sought her friendship. And when Kokichi did become friendly with her, whenever Kokichi talked, she abused and cursed Haruko. For all that, Kokichi could not even then abandon her love for Haruko, and she was troubled and irritated by the fact that her love for Haruko could not be returned in the least. Kokichi, who could only be thought of as a bundle of contradictions, had some strange charm about her, and Noe as well could not, after all, be indifferent to its appeal.

"Oh, I wonder what sort of woman she actually is. It's really odd. Everyone says she's a very talented person."

"All the same I guess she's a kind of artist. Real artists are more or less schizophrenic."

"Then are you schizophrenic too?"

"Of course, and besides, my schizophrenia's serious!"

That she was able to have this kind of conversation with Tsuji was to Noe an indication of her happy, dreamlike life.

Tsuji made Noe diligently attend the *Seito* study seminars which were held regularly every Wednesday and Friday afternoon beginning in October. Jiro Abe and Choko Ikuta had been invited as lecturers, the meetings to take place at the Mannenzan office, the topic an introduction and interpretation of Western literature, for example, an analysis of Dante's *Divine Comedy*. The participants addressed *Seito*'s readers and urged them to attend.

Since Noe had begun to help edit *Seito*, she not only left

the house often but became so engrossed in talking with her co-workers that by the time she was conscious of the hour, she discovered there were no more streetcars and every so often she could not return home. But usually no matter how late she came back, Tsuji was up waiting for her, not once complaining. Furthermore, he was careful not to let his mother find fault with Noe for her absence.

Occasionally when Noe returned, she happened to find Tsuji not yet back, and she would suggest she was leaving again despite the fact that it was already dark out. Mitsu would see her to the door with the kind words, "We're grateful for your help. It's cold out, so please be careful."

Staying up until midnight almost every night talking with Tsuji or reading books or writing manuscripts, Noe could not rise early in the morning. If she had been a typical young wife, she ought to have awakened earlier than her mother-in-law no matter how late the hour of retiring, but Tsuji apologized to Mitsu. "It's because I'm forcing her to study," and he made his mother accept Noe's late hours. Together she and Tsuji were always the last up in the family, their day begun with the two of them eating together the breakfast prepared by the mother-in-law. If only there had not been the economic poverty due to Tsuji's loss of his job, Noe would have had to admit that the happiness of their new married life was perfect.

In the December issue of *Seito*, the first Noe helped edit, Ichiko Kamichika, under the pen name of Yo Sakaki, published her translation of Maupassant's "In Corsica."

Like Noe, Ichiko Kamichika was born in Kyushu, but into a family of doctors in Sami village, Nagasaki prefecture. Born in 1888, she was two years younger than Haruko Hiratsuka and seven years older than Noe. Ichiko's father Yosai was a doctor of the Chinese school of medicine, but he was so progressive he thought medical science of the future should be based on Western principles, and he forced his children to follow the new disciplines in education. Ichiko, born during the advanced years of both her parents, was doted upon by her aged father, who was more like a grandfather, so she was brought up quite spoiled. After her father died of illness when she was four, her elder brother inherited his father's medical practice, and when her elder brother died young, the person who became her elder sister's husband established a practice as an oculist, so Ichiko was raised without knowing the pains of economic hardship. When she was a child, she was more mischievous than a boy, so wild in fact that once when she put on a new pair of wooden clogs she broke them immediately, but by the time she was twelve or thirteen, she was already to some extent a young lover of literature. She spent her time absorbed in reading old magazines, the works of the Kenyusha writers, and such famous novels as *Suikoden* and *Hakkenden*, all of which her dead brother had left behind, and when she went to upper primary school, she read anything she could lay her hands on, including Roka's *Nightingale*, Naoe Kinoshita's *A Pillar of Fire*, Toson's *Anthology of Young Leaves*, and the collected poems of Hakusei Hiraki, Kyukin Susukida, and Bansui Tsuchii.

She wished to study English, and the school she selected expressly for that purpose was Kassui Girls' High School, a mission school in Nagasaki, where she lived in a dormitory. From the time she attended this institution, her genius asserted itself, and after graduating she wished to further her education at Tsuda College. Because her second elder brother was to inherit the family medical practice, she was able to receive from him her school expenses. Her selection of Tsuda College was due to the fact that in those days it had a reputation for being difficult to enter, and if it was that difficult, she wanted to attempt the entrance examinations with something of the bravado of not failing. Self-confident, Ichiko skipped the tests for the preparatory course, abruptly took the regular course examinations, and succeeded superbly. Among the eight who tried, only two passed, but of the two, one failed during her first year, so Ichiko alone remained. In the regular course were many talented girls who had spent several years in the preparatory division before entering this course, but Ichiko obtained considerably fine results without being overwhelmed by them.

In the class a year ahead of hers was Kikue Yamakawa. Ichiko, who had thought of taking up literature as a career after leaving Tsuda, was absorbed in literary works as usual, so she did not fail to read *Modern Thought*, which was brought out by Sakae Osugi and Kanson Arahata, nor did she overlook *Seito*. Due to the fact that Ichiko's class happened to have many quiet, sedate girls in it, a student like herself was conspicuous, regarded as something of a rebel. At that time "Fragment of a Letter," an article written under Ichiko's real name, appeared in the September issue of *Seito*'s second volume, the school authorities finding out about it. What she had written was a protest against a man who had grown cold to the woman he had deflowered.

Tsuda College in those days had the kind of atmosphere in which a woman teacher, hearing that a student had gone to a *Seito* lecture, suddenly fell to her knees on the class platform and said as if praying, "Oh, dear God, please save this pitiful girl from the temptations of the Devil!" Ichiko was summoned by Professor Kenjiro Kumamoto.

The professor flung down on his desk in the teachers'

room the copy of *Seito* which carried Ichiko's work, and he sighed with the remark, "Haven't you had a marriage proposal from anyone yet?" He apparently thought that if only she married, all would reach an amicable end.

When she replied "I haven't," he smiled sardonically as if the situation were hopeless. That there was no inclination to expel her from school was due to the authorities' prizing Ichiko's talents. However, because they felt it dangerous to let her remain in Tokyo, they sent her away to teach at a girls' school in Hirosaki the moment she graduated. It was a clear-cut case of policy by banishment. The complications of this situation made Ichiko Kamichika use her pen name in the November issue.

After her work on Maupassant's story, she translated Havelock Ellis's essay on Whitman and continued publishing it until she graduated from Tsuda. She arrived at Hirosaki as a teacher, perhaps planning to study French in addition, but in less than a month at her new post she was discovered to be a *Seito* member and was dismissed. With reluctance Tsuda College called her back to Tokyo and used its influence to find her a position as an English teacher at a girls' commercial school in Kanda while also having her serve as secretary to Mrs. Bowles, wife of the headmaster at Friends' School for Girls.

Just at this time another of the three women of destiny who were to compete for the same man in the years to come made her appearance in *Seito*. She was Yasuko Hori, the wife of Sakae Osugi, her manuscript entitled "I Am an Old Woman" to be in the January issue of *Seito*'s third volume.

It was exactly on December 25, 1913, Christmas Day, that the final proofs for the New Year's issue of *Seito* were completed. The period of national mourning for the death of Emperor Meiji had been ushered out the previous July, and now with the Meiji era having come to an end, history was soon to make an enormous shift to the new era of Taisho.

Everyone was filled with profound emotion before the proof sheets of *Seito*'s fifteenth number. Ever since the magazine's birth, it had continued to suffer unjust denunciation from the public's faulty inferences and lack of understanding, so all the more was the staff feeling a self-confidence as well as a fighting spirit, a bracing of nerves for the struggle, which had been a thoroughly defensive one until then:

> Though no one knows when and where the words the "New Women" suddenly became fashionable, it seems of late these words are being warmly and attractively displayed in newspapers and magazines. The term is like a kind of toy balloon which some newsman first began to use and turned into a definite term. And the members of the Seito Society have been happily compared to these balloons and have been, it would seem, easily sent aloft in all directions. Now we have been seriously discussing in our editorial room the possibility of trying to print in the New Year's issue our opinions and impressions about this famous phenomenon of the "New Women." Quite apart from the views of journalists, we wish to think in all seriousness about the so-called "New Women" and women as they truly should be.

In line with these words written as a postscript to the December issue, the editorial policy of the New Year's number, which was full of enthusiasm as if firing a rocket as a signal, took up against the public's practical way of thinking a fighting attitude, an attitude which was far more active than *Seito* had shown hitherto. The January number had been explicitly designated as the "Special Issue on the Woman Question," and after making the intention of the editors quite clear, the staff was trying to dispel the aura of being merely the literary publication it had been until then.

The special supplement of the New Year's number entitled "About the New Women and the Woman Question" would itself create a sensation in arousing public opinion and would without fail cause more varied attacks than ever before to burst into flame. The mere thought of these reverberations excited Noe, as if her chest were being compressed.

This editorial expertise in *Seito* was neither dragging behind the times nor on the same level as that of other publications; rather it took the form of being ahead of the journalism of the period, and *Chuokoron*, perhaps stimulated by the December issue postscript, wanted for its own New Year's edition Raicho Hiratsuka's random remarks under the title of "The New Woman."

Having been urged by Haruko to write in the supplement of *Seito* her own essay entitled "The Way of the New Women," Noe had asked Haruko to let her read the manuscript for *Chuokoron*. Not only had Noe learned by heart all of Haruko's opening sentences, which as usual began on an exalted note,

I am a New Woman.

At least day by day I am endeavoring to really be a

New Woman. It is the sun that is truly and eternally new. I am the sun. At least day by day I wish to be and am endeavoring to be the sun . . .

but also Haruko's exclamatory words:

The New Woman is cursing "yesterday." The New Woman can no longer bear to walk silently and submissively along the road of the old-fashioned woman who has been a victim of tyranny.

The New Woman will never be satisfied with the existence of the old-fashioned woman who, through the egoism of man, has been made ignorant, turned into a slave, and transformed into a lump of flesh.

The New Woman wants to destroy the old morality and law provided only for the benefit of men.

The New Woman does not now desire the beautiful. She does not want the good. All she wants to shout is "Power! Power!" for the sake of creating a kingdom she has never known, for the sake of guiding her own divine mission in life!

Compared to these passages, how childish and faltering was Noe's own manuscript called "The Way of the New Women." Nevertheless, she was satisfied with it. She could take her place among the many senior members and could, at any rate, state her views in a dignified way. Had she ever thought the day would come when her own work would be published this soon and shown to the world? When she considered her ordeals of the previous summer, she felt as if she were existing in a dream.

In this New Year's edition, advance notice was given of the *Seito* lecture meeting, which was being tried for the

first time. It was scheduled for Saturday, February 15, at
Youth Hall at Mitoshirocho in Kanda, and the fee was
twenty sen. The official public notice emphatically declared, "Men are encouraged to attend along with women."

Noe had been requested by Haruko to deliver a speech
at the meeting. Though Noe had not yet made up her
mind one way or the other, she thought she would appear
on the platform.

No matter which page of this edition of *Seito* Noe
turned to, it made her heart throb. She felt that this very
issue would cause the staff to rise united to ward off the
sparks of reproach falling upon them. Under these circumstances she received a shock of a different order from the
contribution of Yasuko Hori, the wife of Sakae Osugi, the
famous anarchist. While even her apology that her article
was actually no more than what Osugi had written down
for her about what she had heard from others gave Noe a
strange feeling, the contents of the article were also
thoroughly satirical:

> I am an old-fashioned woman. I am an old-fashioned
> woman in every way from being raised in an old-
> fashioned family in old-fashioned circumstances to re-
> ceiving, in addition, an old-fashioned education at the
> introductory level.

The article which began so abruptly with these words
declared that if she were regarded as a New Woman, it was
because the man she was living with had new thoughts and
principles and she, as an old-fashioned woman, was doing
no more than submissively obeying his every wish, the
essay going on to state that even though *Seito*'s request for
her manuscript had been addressed to "Mrs. Osugi," she

had not been officially listed in the Osugi family register, the reason being as follows:

> When a woman marries a man, she sacrifices her surname as well as those ideas and feelings I have previously mentioned, and to have to terminate herself is the law for all of us old-fashioned women. Though I myself actually want to sacrifice my surname, my lover, at any rate, will not allow me to. And so he has told me I am still the former Yasuko Hori.
>
> I do not know whether or not surnames are this important. Nor has my lover told me that surnames are important. What he has such violent disgust for is some boorish and prosaic law that comes between the two of us. He keeps telling me the relationship between a man and a woman, from first to last, is not of a character that has to be sanctioned by law or even be mentioned by it.
>
> Once I was summoned to the courthouse as a witness about an incident concerning my lover, and I was subjected to a severe scolding by the official for not having had my name entered in a family register. In speaking to me about the matter, the judge asked me what I would do if I had a child. Because there was no avoiding a reply, I said I would probably register it as illegitimate. If a woman said this or did such a thing of her own free will with a purpose different from mine or a meaning different from that of many common-law wives in many places in society, it would seem to me that would be one of the things a New Woman would do.
>
> According to my lover, it would be ideal if a man and woman who loved each other could realize a life of living separately from one another and leading

independent lives, and if they happened to love someone else, they could love freely, and if their love cooled,
they could separate at any time. However, for an old-
fashioned woman like me, it is totally impossible to
agree to such a view. And even if I were told to, I never
could.

Nevertheless, according to my lover, such an ideal is
apparently impossible under our present social and
economic systems except for some few exceptions. And
so I am somewhat relieved.

These persons spoken of as the "New Women"
probably share my lover's view, do they not?

Noe told Tsuji that when she read this manuscript, she
felt as if she had been suddenly struck on the cheek. For her
benefit he commented on the article, "It was definitely
written by Osugi. He has a certain mischievous character.
Yasuko is his wife, a woman who's been living a poverty-
stricken life with her husband since they were married. I
think she's three or four years older than her husband, but
Osugi fell in love with her and married her. A famous
story's been passed around that although she was formerly
the sweetheart of Sho Fukao, a disciple of Kosen Sakai,
Osugi set the kimono he was wearing on fire, then wooed
her, and won her. I think she's the younger sister of Kosen
Sakai's wife."

"He's certainly an odd character, that Sakae Osugi."

"But I guess he's very favorably disposed toward *Seito*. If
not, he wouldn't have written this article expressly for the
magazine and sent it to you. Besides, there's some truth in
this essay."

"Well, under the circumstances, women are too miserable, aren't they? Even I can't bear it!"

Tsuji had already grown silent, grinning as he listened to Noe raging, her lips pouting.

Since Osugi had met neither Noe nor Ichiko, it can be surmised he never dreamed it likely these two *Seito* women who had read this article would act as his first partners in "man's ideal love," as referred to in the essay.

Yasuko's article became a topic of conversation even among the *Seito* staff, Haruko Hiratsuka having the greatest sympathy for Osugi's views.

"Though it's easy to misconstrue, I think the problem of entry into a family register gets to the heart of the matter. In the first place, to have any woman's name entered into a family register according to the regulations of a law she doesn't believe in is what we can't understand, isn't it?"

"But what about the children then?"

"The two parties can talk it over, and if they think entering the child's name is appropriate, they can place it in whichever register they find the more convenient. The concept 'illegitimate child' is something proscribed by present-day law. We don't have to be slaves to such a law."

When Noe thought about this point, she realized her own name had not yet been entered in Tsuji's family register. Though her name seemed to have been removed from Fukutaro's, she was not at the stage where she could easily ask her parents to remove her name from their own family register.

But Noe did not feel the least bit uneasy about this matter. Although she was not as clearly conscious about this question as Osugi and Haruko were, she had the feeling that having her name formally entered was of no consequence before the solid realization of her physical and spiritual connection to Tsuji.

It was Haruko who suggested having the year-end party take place in combination with the last day of the editing that year and with Christmas.

Everyone trooped out to the Maison de Konosu. Assembled there were Haruko, Noe, Katsu, Kiyoko Iwano, and Ikuko Araki, together with Toundo's publisher Yokichi Nishimura and Kokichi, who happened to drop in at the Konosu just then. The banquet and drinking party was held in a room on the second floor. For the first time Noe saw with her own eyes the reality of the New Women actually drinking saké, but she did not think it odd. Yet that evening Haruko became so conspicuously intimate with Yokichi Nishimura that a strange, uneasy atmosphere began to flow around them. Kokichi was the first to sense a new love affair starting to brew between Haruko and Yokichi, and it began to jar on her nerves. Katsu was seemingly ill-humored as well, as until only recently she had been in love with Yokichi but had begun to feel their love was flickering out because they were too timid and shy with each other.

During these past few months Noe had already been told in full about Haruko's former love affairs, yet she was surprised by the audacious spectacle of Haruko and Yokichi which she was seeing for the very first time with her own eyes. She was left in a tense frame of mind over a situation in which she could only feel Haruko was seducing the very man she herself knew was Katsu's lover. When Noe realized that Haruko, who had kept herself so aloof from the world, had the will to play with a man's heart as any ordinary woman might, she felt as if she herself had been betrayed. Noe for the first time found something shockingly coquettish overflowing in the figure of Haruko, a Haruko intoxicated with saké, her proper poise crumbling as she finally lay down then and there on the mats, her arms pillowing her head.

"After all, even Miss Hiratsuka is a woman. It may possibly be she's just an ordinary one," Noe thought.

Watching Haruko under these conditions, Noe could not help sympathizing with Kokichi and Katsu even though they had been harboring such obvious ill-feelings toward Haruko that night.

Kokichi was drowning her sorrows by alternately drinking whiskey and saké, and finally vomiting, she made a ridiculous figure of herself. Observing Kokichi under these circumstances, Noe came to feel Haruko was too cruel. However, when Noe received two days later a most considerate and gentle postcard, she felt herself rushing toward Haruko like a kite suddenly pulled by its string:

> I felt very sorry about sending you back alone so late last night. Did you reach home safely without catching cold? If you wish, I'll take full responsibility and beg your family's pardon a thousand times. Last night I was thoroughly drunk. So drunk I didn't even know Iwano-san had gone home. But today a reaction has set in and I'm exceedingly depressed. Yet my brain is so clear I feel I can accomplish anything. This morning I went to Araki's house and have only just returned. If tomorrow is convenient, please come see me. Though perhaps you're exhausted from any number of things, I'm asking you because I'm a little worried about you.

When Tsuji heard Noe's criticism of Haruko, he laughed saying, "She is, after all, a size larger than her colleagues!" And finally Noe found herself agreeing with his comment. Not only that, but she could not help feeling kindly disposed to Haruko, who kept an eye out for her and supported her position on every occasion.

The new year dawned, but Noe spent all day indoors with Tsuji. Even though she wanted to make some holiday calls, she had nothing to wear except her ordinary family clothes, so she could not go out.

Tsuji spent a minimum of time on his side jobs as private tutor and as teacher in a night school, but because he was prone to fling even these away, he was so utterly poor he could not even afford a nib.

There were signs, moreover, that Noe had apparently been pregnant since the end of last year.

"It can't be helped. A baby that's to be born will be born."

Although Noe did not know how far she could rely on any of the words of Tsuji, who took everything easy, she had, nevertheless, no one else to turn to. Confronted by the actuality of a pregnancy which was not yet accompanied by any of her own real feelings, she found herself floundering.

After January 7, when she had been invited to Kokichi's place, Noe happened to meet Ichiko Kamichika. Kokichi, who took kindly to everyone, was quite charmed by the clarity of mind of Ichiko, the most intellectual member of *Seito*, and recently Kokichi seemed to have been cultivating her friendship.

Although it was only the second time Noe had met Ichiko, the first being at a *Seito* study group, Noe could not bring herself to like her. Ichiko herself had no fondness for Noe, thanks to a first impression of Noe's being unrefined and impudent in making a fool of others, yet conscious of her charm in playing the unknowing innocent. Ichiko had come to think of Noe as a woman with a coquettish sexuality that seemed to strangely and forcefully assert itself, even though Noe did not show any concern about her face and hair and was indifferent to clothing.

The criticism of the New Year's issue of *Seito* on which they had placed their hopes was not too vehement. The fact that *Seito* had used to its own advantage the public's criticism and in a dignified way had decided on its own form of self-assertion had evidently given the entire nation curiosity, interest, and expectation. The advance notice of the February 15 lecture meeting was most focused on as a topic of conversation.

As might have been expected, Noe was completely caught up in tension and excitement on the morning of the appointed day. She had, after all, been selected as one of the lecturers at the meeting.

When Mitsu heard Noe was to appear on the platform to deliver a speech, she wondered, "Is the kind of clothing Noe wears all right for that?" and as if Mitsu herself were to be on the stage for a rehearsal as she had been in her younger days, the mother-in-law became quite nervous.

"Don't overdo it. Deliver your talk gently. After all, the point is that they're letting you on the stage because you're the youngest, Noe. It's better not to say anything too difficult."

Tsuji comforted Noe several times, encouraging her, and he was kind enough to read her manuscript entitled "My Thoughts of Late" and to listen to her practice it.

"You'll come hear me, won't you?"

"Well, I don't know."

"Please come! I'll really be depressed if you don't."

"Even if I did, you wouldn't be able to know where I was."

"You mean there'll be that many people?"

"I think so. Just the curiosity-seekers alone will arrive in considerable numbers. But I'm afraid the police may have to be dispatched."

Should Article V of the Maintenance of Public Peace Law be violated, any meeting, no matter what kind, would be risky. It was much more risky since the third Katsura cabinet, which had just come into power last spring with the overthrow of the Saionji cabinet, had hoisted as its banner "The Policy of Thought Suppression."

"I'm all right now. When I hear something like that, I get all stirred up! I'll really do it!"

Unyielding in spirit, Noe became even more enthusiastic, and she flexed her arms like a boy.

Though Tsuji had answered Noe in an ambiguous way, he left for Youth Hall at Mitoshirocho long before twelve. With his introspective and nervous temperament he felt he could not bear to look straight at the figure of his wife delivering a speech in front of an audience. Just picturing to himself the image of Noe on the platform made him feel as if his skin were crawling with embarrassment and shame. Nevertheless, he could not be that callous to desert Noe, who was giving a speech in public for the first time.

He could not bear to attend, nor could he endure the anxiety during the interval if he did not. He could only imagine as ludicrous the picture of himself mingling in that crowd and listening brazenly to his own wife's speech. On the other hand, it was even more comic for him to be overanxious at home, gulping down saké all day. With his mind bending first one way and then the other and after pondering any number of times the same thought of attending or returning home, Tsuji found himself being drawn toward Youth Hall.

When he arrived, he was surprised. He had thought it

would be wonderful if at most three hundred people assembled, but those present, who continued to enter in rapid succession, were swarming into the hall all the way from the entrance to the street, and there was such an uproar it did not seem as if the meeting could be brought to order. The words of the announcement had expressly stated that men should attend along with the women, and the audience was overwhelmingly male. When Tsuji entered the hall after being pushed and shoved from behind by that surging tide of humanity, well over a thousand persons had filled the room to overflowing.

About a third of the audience seemed composed of women. Tsuji tried to conceal himself, for if possible he did not want to meet any of his acquaintances, but here and there were faces he recognized. Students and literary enthusiasts predominated, but he saw Sanshiro Ishikawa and Sakae Osugi. He also detected the profile of Hideko Fukuda, whom he had recently met, having been asked to serve as her interpreter, her large, protruding eyes looking up at the platform. Near him was a group of Tsuda College students, including Kikue Yamakawa (née Aoyama), a gay and lively scene being created around him. Burying her graceful shoulders among the people about her was the wife of Toshihiko Sakai.

After the meeting began under the chairmanship of Yoshiko Yasumochi, Noe made her appearance on the platform as the opening speaker. Feeling his body shrinking in fear, Tsuji was intently watching her.

"Dear me! She's terribly small, isn't she?"

"Is even that a *Seito* woman?"

"She looks exactly like a high school student, doesn't she?"

"She's certainly not pretty."

"She's sort of cute."

These impudent whispers sprang up around him.

Noe stood respectfully like a high school student, and with a smile on her face and without losing her composure the way Tsuji in his anxiety had, she began reading her manuscript. Tsuji knew only too well the contents of her talk, which he had been forced to listen to many times. The interval of her speech, less than twenty minutes, was felt by Tsuji to be almost as long as an hour. When she bowed and the applause came, he felt relieved. The nape of his neck was extremely tight and hard. In brief, what she had said in her talk was as follows:

> The reason why women are unawakened is due to the unconscious long-lasting tyranny of men. In order for women to awaken, it is desirable for men to awaken first. Women, as they now exist, are falling into solitude in intellect and livelihood due to the nonawakening of men.

While Tsuji was listening to Noe's speech, thought by him neither good nor bad, he remembered the figure and voice with which, as student representative, she had read her congratulatory address in the auditorium of Ueno Girls' High School. Less than two years had passed since that event. And in that interval how she had matured!

Suddenly he felt so proud he wanted to shout to the thousand people in the audience that she was his very own wife. No matter how puerile the contents of her speech or how monotonous its tone, just the bravery and nerve in the way she was delivering her address with dignity in the midst of social conditions of thought suppression which even men were frightened by was deserving of praise. Now

Tsuji felt the actual vivid sensation of how carefully he had been raising Noe and how she had been growing by greedily depriving him of the compost of his own flesh and blood.

He found himself swallowing hard as he revived the touching memory of Noe on a recent beautiful night when she had pressed her face against his chest and with her entire body against him had suddenly whispered helplessly, "Is it possible for me to have a baby? What should I do?"

After Noe, Choko Ikuta came up to the platform and then Homei Iwano. Tsuji was listening with interest to Homei because Tsuji especially liked him among the writers, but in the middle of his speech a scene occurred in which Toranosuke Miyazaki interrupted him. The program did proceed as scheduled with Kocho Baba and Kiyoko Iwano, and finally the lectures came to an end with the closing words of Haruko Hiratsuka. Seeing Haruko mounting the stage amid shouts of joy ringing out, Tsuji quietly left the hall.

The following morning Noe, a newspaper in her hand, burst into tears after rushing to the side of Tsuji's bed, where he was still asleep.

"It's too much! Too cruel!"

The overly emotional Noe was apt to raise her voice and begin crying like a child for the most trivial thing. For that matter, once she wept for even a short while, she could usually stop suddenly.

Tsuji spread out the *Asahi* Noe thrust at him, only his neck showing from under the covers. The previous day's lecture meeting with a photograph inserted in the lower column of the society page was being ostentatiously reviewed:

GATHERING OF NEW WOMEN
Bombast Disgorged on Stage
by So-Called Awakened Women's Group

Because the ladies of literary talent of the Seito Society, who pose as New Women of the present generation, admitted they are not sufficiently awakened even after drinking wines of five colors and publishing a magazine, they decided to offer a public lecture at Kanda Youth Hall from one o'clock on the afternoon of the fifteenth.

Long before the appointed hour, high school girls who deliberately wanted to be thought new by wearing strange attire and wives of a new order who wished to profit as second Noras by awakening from this moment on began besieging the hall in rapid succession, but for those of us who have become accustomed these last few days to seeing boorish students at oratorical meetings on the protection of the Constitution and to hearing cries of "Down with Clannish Factions!" this meeting offered a kind of strange contrast.

First, a person looking like a fat schoolmistress but who writes under the pen name Hakuu delivered an opening address, and then a girl seventeen or eighteen years old called Noe Ito, so young that without even blushing and in a tone of voice that said, "It would appear Japanese women do not understand what solitude means," told us her recent impressions, but because the content was so very feminine and meager we felt it quite lamentable that this type supposedly thought herself one of the so-called New Women.

Choko Ikuta's "Discussion on the New Women" was reasonable in content and delivery, and it was one of the most pleasant speeches we have heard of late, but

"Demands Made by Men" by Mr. Homei Iwano, who appeared on stage after Choko Ikuta, though it had some momentary flashes of his inimitable philosophizing, too often tended to digress, and when he was about to discuss his favorite subject of the dissolution of marriage, Mr. Toranosuke Miyazaki, the self-professed savior of Marital Bliss, who happened to be in the audience, ran in a rage onto the platform and grabbing Mr. Homei barked at him, "Give us your explanation of your own divorce!" Thanks to the intervention of Mr. Choko Ikuta, the great hubbub this aroused gradually quieted down.

A short interlude of rest followed with a piano performance by Mr. Ryukichi Sawada. Then there was the usual pithy address of Mr. Kocho Baba on the topic "For the Cause of Women," and lastly Kiyoko Iwano, wife of Homei, climbed to the rostrum looking like a Japanese wife, her hair in a round chignon and her *haori* bearing the family crest, and waxed eloquent on the topic "Independence of Thought and Economic Independence," there being some places in which she made a few miscalculations on law and economics and caused all of us to be nervous, but in other spots the content was quite appropriate. Much more enlightening than the views of Mr. Homei were her remarks on the "Nora Thesis," in which she spoke quite vehemently for the New Women. And so it was at about five o'clock when the electric lights were aglow that the meeting adjourned with the closing remarks of Haruko Hiratsuka.

It was the criticism leveled at her that had made Noe cry.

"What's so bad about it? When we read the entire

article, we realize it was done half in fun, and they took it out on you only because you're so young. The audience admired you, saying how honest and alert you were."

"Oh? But you didn't say anything like that to me before this."

Noe's tears had already started to dry.

"You really are silly. I couldn't say such things in detail, being too shy to. I heard people comment you were sort of cute, something like that."

"Really? Well, how did *you* find listening to me? Oh, please, how was it?"

Since it was hardly possible for Tsuji to tell her he admired the contents of a speech he had become sick of listening to, he merely forced a smile without responding to her request.

"The long and short of it is the fact that a young girl's standing bravely on the platform on such an occasion will someday remain a historical event. Since I myself am a born coward, I could not have imitated you at all."

Tsuji's comforting words had already brightened Noe completely.

"Look. Please hide this newspaper so that your mother won't read it. I'll be so embarrassed."

As the days went by, the results of the lecture meeting became even more remarkable. The April number of *Chuokoron* published Sojinkan Sugimura's "Speaking Up for the New Women," its June publication a special issue devoted to "Regulations by the Authorities Against New Ideas in Women's Circles," Kazutami Ukita, Homei Iwano, Daikichiro Tagawa, Hogetsu Shimamura, and Isoo Abe called to the colors with essays in the journal. Furthermore, the special issue on the woman question was so successful the editors of *Chuokoron* decided to issue in July an unusual supplement entitled "Special Edition on the Woman Question":

> Scholars have declared the nineteenth century the era of the rise of the common man and the twentieth that of the awakening of women, so the day has passed in which one discussed the New Women merely as a curiosity and regarded the Women Question as a kind of temporary fad.
>
> We believe it of urgent necessity at the present moment to seriously and accurately make a minute and searching examination into many difficult problems ranging from the origin of the Woman Question to its present and future prospects and to find a fundamental solution to these problems. In publishing our "Special Edition on the Woman Question" this coming July 15, we sincerely beg the general public to read it.

Such was *Chuokoron*'s advance notice to the public, and journalism watched in earnest to see how the magazine would treat the subject.

Many articles on the woman question suddenly began appearing in other magazines and newspapers. The raising of the curtain on the new Taisho era gave one the impression the new age really began with this problem, and those responsible for pressing the buzzer for this opening curtain were none other than the New Women in *Seito* itself.

To further study this problem, *Seito* issued a sequel to its special number on the woman question. In the February issue the editors decided to publish for the first time an article by a socialist. It was Hideko Fukuda's "Solution to the Woman Question."

In those days Hideko Fukuda was living in Nakazato, Takinogawa, not far from Somei. And just at that time Tsuji was associating with the anarchist Seitaro Watanabe, having been asked by the latter to serve as his interpreter in English. A Chinese who had come to do research on the socialist movement in Japan after studying in France was eager to meet the veteran woman fighter Hideko Fukuda, the pioneer of women's liberation in Japan. Because this Chinese scholar did not understand Japanese but could speak English, Tsuji, out of respect for his close friendship and fondness for Watanabe, immediately accepted the request. It was due to this relationship that Tsuji once mentioned to Noe when they were about to retire, "It would be worthwhile just now for *Seito* to have an article appear by Hideko Fukuda, wouldn't it?"

Hearing this remark from Noe, Haruko immediately agreed to the suggestion. *Seito* was now going to go beyond being a mere literary magazine. Certainly it was just the right moment for the publication of a manuscript by Hideko Fukuda. Haruko herself expressly visited Hideko for this purpose and requested a contribution.

It seemed to Haruko that Hideko, who had large eyes of a hazy yellow and who eked out a living by peddling secondhand clothing, was a sort of dry, fierce, and disagreeable woman. Nevertheless, Hideko willingly complied, and the manuscript was soon forwarded. This was the only critical article by a socialist ever published in *Seito*.

Absolute liberation is not our absolute liberation as women but our liberation as "human beings." It is not the freedom of women but the realization of the freedom of "human beings" . . . Unless a thorough and exhaustive Communism is put into practice, a thorough and sufficient liberty cannot be put into practice . . . At the same moment in which the Communist system is set into operation, scientific knowledge and machinery will be utilized for the equal welfare of each and every person.

The February issue of *Seito*, which carried this thesis by Hideko, was immediately banned. At last the controlling arm of the government authorities was extended to *Seito*, whose embroiling itself in various disturbances had gained universal attention.

The curtain of real suffering was about to come down on Haruko, Noe, and *Seito* itself.

Chapter 4

JUST ABOUT THE TIME the *Seito* meeting ended, Noe found herself suffering from the first stages of morning sickness. Although both her mother-in-law and Tsuji's sister readily welcomed her pregnancy, the family economy, relying on Tsuji who as usual remained unemployed, had long reached rock bottom. It was utterly impossible to devise some means from the available funds to pay for the delivery and the rearing of the child afterwards. Noe felt she could not depend on Tsuji's optimistic remark that they would somehow manage, and as her bodily discomfort grew more intense, she became forlorn and hysterical.

Noe, who had been so healthy and whose appetite had increased so much she was ashamed of herself, now began vomiting all her food after a few bites, and suddenly finding herself desiring Tsuji's cigarettes, she would proceed to crush and crunch with her teeth the yellow particles of tobacco. Because she could not buy as many tangerines as she wanted, she would get some pickled plums from the kitchen and even hold on to their pits as if sucking a piece of toffee.

"Jun, a Buddhist service will be held the day after tomorrow at Kanda. You know about it? Can you manage something, just a little bit of money?"

"Oh, how many times are you going to repeat that to me? I do know about it."

"But if you're going to attend, you have to wrap up some money, don't you?"

"I told you I *know* about it."

Just hearing such a whispered conversation between her mother-in-law and Tsuji made Noe feel nauseous, and she was tormented with unpleasantness in her empty stomach, which had nothing to disgorge.

As her mother-in-law and sister-in-law did not blame her openly, adhering to Noe's nerves was the delusion that they were reproaching Tsuji for his incompetence in losing his job because of her.

When the married couple was alone, Tsuji found that Noe, who often cried and argued incessantly with increasing violence and hysterics, was more than he could handle, but he overlooked it, thinking it all due to her morning sickness. On the other hand, he had no intention of immediately scurrying out for a new job as his mother and Noe wished. It failed to strike home to him that their miserable family budget had been strained by the extra mouth Noe added. He felt optimistic that they could somehow manage enough just for a single baby. In the final analysis, it might be more proper to say that Tsuji, who had been more nervous than anybody else, had no courage to set his eyes squarely on the grave and fearful reality that a single life sharing his own flesh and blood was about to be born. To divert himself from his uneasiness, he clung to his desk all day long and devoted himself to translating *The Man of Genius*, from which he had no knowledge of any future remuneration. As for Noe, only when she met her *Seito* companions could she forget her physical discomfort and her anxiety about the family budget.

On the last day of February, about half a month after the lecture meeting had ended, Noe paid a call on Katsu at Kokichi's request, and on the way back she was asked by Kokichi to stop at the home of Sojin Kamiyama. Sojin had opened a shop dealing in eyebrow cosmetics, the Kakashiya on Hikagecho in Shiba, managed by his wife Uraji.

Having dissociated himself from the Literary Society, Sojin Kamiyama had established with Takashi Iba, Taro Akiba, and Toshio Sugimura the Modern Theatre Association and with its opening production the previous January of *Hedda Gabler* at the Yurakuza Theatre had scored a great success even at the box office. The performance by his wife Uraji, who played Hedda, had received an especially favorable response, the four-day run extended two more days, and they had just returned to Tokyo from a great success in Osaka, where their performance had created a sensation throughout the city. The company was already preparing for its second public offering. Noe had only briefly glanced at Sojin Kamiyama at the dinner party given in honor of the participants of the *Seito* lecture meeting, but because she was greatly interested in this talented actor with his unique face unlike that of an ordinary Japanese, she had accepted Kokichi's invitation to visit him. The more she kept company with Kokichi, the greater was Noe's surprise at the unlimited extent of her friend's connections.

"Mr. Kamiyama's group is worried because there are no actresses. The only one they can use is probably Uraji-san. I hear they found a real amateur for their next performance. They say she's a born actress."

"Where is she from?"

"Sojin happened to notice her when his group went to the Cafe Paulista. And he was told she always came to buy eyebrow pencil at his Kakashiya. They say it was all settled quite rapidly. They've already decided on her colorful stage name, Kujaku Kinugawa."

Since Kokichi was often versed in this kind of information, Noe was not at all surprised. She even felt a bit envious, thinking that if one had the right temperament and a little luck, it would not be bad to be an actress, a profession in which a person could become a star at a leap. No matter what the profession, it would do. Anyone would be satisfied if he could sufficiently draw out the potential of some talent lying dormant in himself and could live in a grand way by asserting himself. While these thoughts whirled inside her, Noe, taken by Kokichi, found herself at the Kakashiya. At the front entrance of the shop they unexpectedly happened to meet Uraji Kamiyama, who was just going to the Yurakuza Theatre, as it was almost curtain time. Having come out to see Uraji off, a girl seventeen or eighteen, her hair in Western style, pleasantly smiled at Kokichi. The beautiful girl of large build, her face round with animated pupils and a healthy complexion, was Kujaku Kinugawa, whom they had just been speaking about. Kokichi asked Kujaku to tend the shop, and she and Noe talked with Sojin in a room at the back of the house.

"She's quite nice, that girl. She has the makings of a great actress. She has no bad habits in speaking her lines, and she's extraordinarily quick-witted."

Talking proudly about Kujaku, who was tending the shop, Sojin expressed with self-confidence his aspiration to choose her to play Gretchen in *Faust*, their next production.

Kokichi grew vehement even to Sojin in her abuse of Raicho, whom she had derided all day to Noe and Katsu.

Kokichi was completely overwrought from having recently received Raicho's letter breaking off their relationship.

"Speaking of Raicho, Kokichi-san, do you know that the very same 'young swallow' has entered our theatrical troupe?"

"What? You mean Mr. Okumura? Really?"

Kokichi, her eyes opened wide, moved closer to Sojin.

"It's true. A singer by the name of Jun Harada brought him. Harada told me they were bosom friends living together along the coast at Chiba."

"How disgusting! You said the 'swallow' has become an actor?"

With an expression on her face as if she had already forgotten her abuse of Raicho, Kokichi was caught up in this new interest.

"That fellow Okumura," Sojin said, "is really a woman. Whatever way you look at him, he's the very image of a woman! I think I understand why that virago Raicho made such a pet of him."

"What! This is disgusting! I bet Miss Hiratsuka herself doesn't know anything about the news. It would serve her right! This is really something! I bet the two of them will be reunited! Basically Okumura's quiet and gentle. As for their affair, I'm sure Miss Hiratsuka seduced him. At any rate, since he's so clever, it's possible he may be able to imitate an actor!" Kokichi said.

"It's not a question of imitating. He's exactly right for the part of Siebel in *Faust.*"

"Oh, you mean the cellar scene at Auerbach!"

Completely fascinated by this fresh information, Kokichi was as excited as if suddenly informed her own lover was to appear on the stage.

"Please tell Mr. Okumura I send him my very best wishes!"

Noe could not resist the impulse to laugh as she sat to the side of Kokichi, who had no scruples about the impudence of her remarks. If Kokichi had genuinely been jealous of Okumura, had sent him threatening letters, and had forced him to break with Haruko, it was equally true that she was offering Okumura her best regards. She was fortunate in having a liberal-minded character that at any time or place could do a complete turnabout of her feelings and not think it unnatural or offer any resistance. By the following day the news that Hiroshi Okumura had joined Sojin Kamiyama's Modern Theatre Association became known to all the *Seito* members. It was, of course, Kokichi who distributed the information.

Haruko remained calm over the announcement, even her countenance unchanged. Noe suspected from Haruko's self-possession that her love affair with Yokichi Nishimura was progressing and that not even a trace remained in Haruko's memory of the "young swallow" Hiroshi. However, the rumor reached Noe that when *Faust* was performed at the Imperial Theatre from March 27 to March 31, Haruko in a front-row seat near the stage sat quite properly through the opening performance and productions of the days following.

"And not only that! Each day Miss Hiratsuka sends to her 'swallow's' dressing room a bouquet of roses. She's not so indifferent to him after all!"

This time as well Kokichi was quite busy furnishing such information.

It was said that Okumura's Siebel was neither good nor bad, the comely Okumura with his aptitude for painting allowed to do his own makeup as he wished, so a beautiful young man, too handsome for a mere student, appeared on the stage. Although the criticism of *Faust* did not contain a single word about the name or performance of the new face Hiroshi Okumura, the unknown nova Kujaku Kinugawa commanded such great esteem one felt she would become a future Sumako Matsui. All the drama critics unanimously gave her their attention and in splendid style offered congratulations on her future. *Faust* had a stunning success as entertainment, and the troupe set out for Osaka as it had done before to register even there its triumph to packed houses day after day. The fame of Kujaku Kinugawa as Gretchen reached greater heights. Already by this time, however, Sojin Kamiyama, the leader of the company, relaxed over his early and unexpected achievements and intoxicated with favorable reviews, brought about tremendous difficulties by creating a triangle with his wife Uraji, Kujaku Kinugawa, and himself. The triangle was the beginning of the dissolution of the company after its performance at Osaka, though the group had already anticipated that.

Hiroshi Okumura, who for the first time in his life had the experience of earning money through his own physical effort and who clutched in his hand his share of the performance fee, went on this occasion by himself to enjoy the spring in Kyoto and Nara at his own leisure. To be dragged into the maelstrom of the ugly strife between Sojin and his wife was unbearable to his delicate nerves, and irresistible had become the craving to grasp to his heart's content his painting brushes, which he had been separated from for a long time.

When Hiroshi returned to his solitary life after several months' absence and lingered in the fields of the ancient capital, the yellow rape flowers shimmering in a haze to the end of the horizon, he found himself with sudden and unexpected intensity remembering the beautiful pupils in Haruko's eyes. He could not help repenting his perverse stubbornness during the performances at the Imperial Theatre in Tokyo in deliberately pretending not to look toward Haruko's seat after having been badgered by his colleagues every day. He felt heaving inside himself a remorse that he ought to have sent his polite thanks to her for the flowers. The precious face of Haruko, which he had secretly peeped out at from the shadow of the theatre curtain and which was all the more graceful and elegant except for looking thinner than it had that summer, was emerging innumerable times in golden filaments of air above the fields of yellow rape. All the days he had been trying to forget since the previous summer suddenly seemed empty and discolored. Though he had set up his easel to face these golden fields, he did not paint a single stroke, continuing as he did to pursue the image of Haruko, his tender yearnings for her intensified as if he were a dam about to burst.

About the time the cherry blossoms were in bloom, the pain from Noe's morning sickness began to lessen of its own accord. As she recovered her health, she regained her natural liveliness and energetic behavior, and she enthusiastically began to take an active part in household matters, in the studies recommended by Tsuji, and in the editorial duties at *Seito*.

At that time the *Seito* office had moved to Sugamo, all the clerks and editorial staff members who had gathered almost every day in Haruko's room with its round window now having to commute there, so gradually they came less frequently to her office. The world's persecution and misunderstanding of *Seito* became even more severe, and it can safely be said that except for some of its writers it was frowned upon throughout society. Not only such scholars in the educational world as Jinzo Naruse, Gendo Miwada, and Jiro Shimada, plus Minister of Education Gijin Okuta and elder statesman of the press Aizan Yamaji, published their negative opinions and articles against the New Women, but even more violent arguments were heaped upon *Seito* by members of the female sex. They were led by Utako Shimoda and Haruko Hatoyama, with Mitsuko Miyazaki and Kimu Hyuga of the Real New Women's Association, which united with these leaders against *Seito* to level the most hostile and severe assaults. When Haruko, having remained unperturbed no matter what the misunderstanding or attack by society, was rebuked by her liberal father Teijiro, the father that until the February issue had been banned had sanctioned his daughter's freedom by closing his eyes to most of the things she had done, his admonition struck home to her. "If your magazine is one that has to publish socialist articles, you ought to abandon it at once. If you don't give it up, get out of my house this instant and do as you wish! I absolutely won't have socialists coming in and out of my house!" By telling him she had no connections to socialism, she pacified his anger for a while, but with the Home Ministry successively banning the April issue, in which her own "For the Women of the World" appeared, and her first book of collected essays *From the Round Window*, Haruko herself, heroine though she was, was severely shocked.

Even the Metropolitan Police Bureau came forward and, summoning in April Hatsu Nakano and Yoshiko Yasumochi as representatives of *Seito*, cautioned them, "You are disturbing the traditional virtues of Japanese women, so we are hereafter relying on the discretion of your staff." In the midst of this kind of pressure all the members strengthened their solidarity, endeavored not to degrade *Seito*'s quality, and planned another literary lecture meeting, but confronted first of all by the cold reality of being refused an assembly hall, they had to call it off.

Every day from morning till night Yoshiko walked to and fro trying to find a suitable place to meet. No matter where she went she was refused a lease. Some told her honestly that as individuals they were sympathetic to the idea, but if they accommodated her, they themselves would be subject to the criticism of society; others told her quite clearly they were refusing because the group's conduct was excessive. There were even some who avoided replying by saying they would respond to the request at a future time. What it boiled down to was no one would rent them a place anywhere for the meeting. Though they encouraged each other as much as possible and tried to elevate their sagging spirits, it was hardly to be expected that anyone could be cheerful under conditions of this kind.

On one such trying day Noe, who after a long absence had come to visit Haruko in the round-window room, happened during their talk to see Haruko unconsciously rubbing her long fingers over a picture postcard on her desk. Noticing Noe's eyes fixed on the card, Haruko let out a suppressed smile as if she could no longer hold it in. While still rubbing her fingers against the card, which seemed to Noe a view of Nara, Haruko said, "My 'swallow,' you see, has sent me tidings from Nara."

"Is he there?"

"Yes, he went to Osaka for the *Faust* performance. When I got his farewell letter previously, I still had a lingering attachment to him, so I wrote in the last book I gave him that if he was a 'swallow,' he would appear again when the season came. You see, he remembered those words."

Noe did not overlook the glow on Haruko's cheeks and in her eyes that betrayed the calm tone with which she spoke of Okumura as if talking about someone else's affair. Noe surmised Haruko was still very much attracted to him. It became all the more evident to her that Haruko's love affair with Yokichi Nishimura was a mere flirtation. Noe found herself unable to understand Haruko's feelings.

At that moment Haruko had already revived the exchange of letters with Hiroshi. She had not the slightest doubt that on his return from the Kansai district, he would head straight for her home to see her.

The love between Haruko and Hiroshi, who met again after a lapse of seven months, was instantaneously revived. Though she pretended to be quite calm, Haruko, covered with wounds to her very core by the recent oppression and misunderstanding of the world and also by the anger of her father, found herself clinging to Hiroshi involuntarily and wanting to be consoled by his pure childlike feelings unconnected to the world of *Seito*. When they spoke to one another, their misunderstanding of the previous summer melted away, and she came to realize who the real writer of the "swallow's" letter had been.

"I never thought you wrote it. A really sincere farewell letter couldn't have been written in such a calm empty manner in elegant prose marshaled with flowery flourishes, could it?"

Haruko dared to laugh liberally on hearing Hiroshi's confession. The truth was her pride would not yet let her tell him frankly about the unexpected shock that letter of the previous summer had given her. After this first visit, Hiroshi, like a willful child, came almost every day. He usually appeared, however, at the dinner hour exactly when her entire family was around the dining-room table. When the maid informed them of his visit, the face of Haruko's mother Tsuya suddenly became gloomy. The rumor last summer about Hiroshi and Haruko had been brought even to her attention. From her point of view Hiroshi was too young, too unreliable. That he visited them without any concern for the hour and that after he came he would talk at great length in Haruko's room without regard to time and without making a move to leave—all these points displeased Tsuya. If Haruko were to become capricious again, Tsuya wished that her daughter would at least cut short this silly love affair with a such a boyish-looking man.

But the colder the eyes of her mother and family became toward Hiroshi, the more overwhelming Haruko's feelings that she could not keep herself from protecting him. His naiveté, his purity, his innocence, which prevented him from understanding the motives of others, were to Haruko, who had been suffering these several months from the thrown stones of cruel abuse and calumny, the very qualities that made her think Hiroshi was a lucky find, uncommon and invaluable. While she enjoyed the paintings he brought and while she listened to his talk, which was never sharp or biting, she felt herself enveloped in a pleasant itchy sensation as if a hand were softly stroking the innumerable wounds of her heart.

Haruko, her mind rapidly inclining toward Hiroshi, was determined at this of all times to prevent him from escaping by keeping him eternally as a "swallow" that would never again take to the air. She expected to be able to vindicate the unreasonable humiliation she had received the previous summer by letting him vow his eternal love for her. Even as they met each other every day, the two came to exchange passionate love letters, and they finally planned to set out on a trip alone together without being plagued by others. It was for this reason that Haruko worked night and day to finish her *Seito* manuscripts and the articles requested by other magazines, and explaining to her family that she was starting out alone on a trip, she kept her rendezvous with Hiroshi at Tabata Station.

Dressed in a new summer kimono of *meisen* silk in a dark-blue pattern with white splashes, her undergarment neckband of light rose peeping out from her kimono, her *hakama* of olive cashmere, Haruko, lightly equipped with only a black leather portmanteau, arrived at the train station. The first to appear, waiting in high spirits like a child out on an excursion, had been Hiroshi in the guise of what suggested the artist: a red-embroidered Russian blouse, gray corduroy trousers, a homespun jacket and white beret, and a basket of food in his hand. That day the two lovers boarded the second-class section of the train for Maebashi and put up at an inn on Mount Akagi.

That night Hiroshi was no longer the cowardly young man who had fled from Haruko's embrace the previous summer. Since their reunion, his self-confidence, bolstered by Haruko's attitude and love letters, had conquered his innocence, and he was naturally endowed with the means to embrace Haruko in a manly way.

For a week the two lovers shared with each other the thick nectar of moments of love deep on Mount Akagi. They distinguished neither morning nor night, and although no time existed in which they tired of each other's caress, Hiroshi had planned to spend only four or five days there, so he had to return to Tokyo for a while. Haruko still had one more week left, and after disposing of some work she had to finish, she intended to go back to Tokyo.

While standing along a mountain path and seeing Hiroshi off, Haruko was seized by the uneasy feeling that she might not be able to spend one more week in these lonely mountains after this separation. Though it was only for a short while, the intensity of that period of several days of frantic lovemaking at Mount Akagi had never been experienced by her at any time during her twenty-six years of life.

With feelings of pity and compassion coiling round her as Hiroshi's figure receded in the distance even as he continued to look back several times while descending the path, Haruko was unexpectedly seized by the desire to run down toward the retreating figure.

In rapid succession from Hiroshi in Tokyo came a series of love letters, each more passionate than the previous one. Haruko repeatedly sent him letters with an intensity of passion not inferior to his own but with a much greater frequency of dispatch, to the extent that occasionally she forwarded him one after another three letters a day. A helpless and forlorn feeling enveloped the mind and spirit of Haruko, who remained alone, like a fish whose flesh had been sliced half off with a kitchen knife, and instead of going about her scheduled work, she did nothing but remember with all the cells of her being the moments she had spent with Hiroshi.

As she was thinking of winding up her program of work and returning to Tokyo in pursuit, a letter was forwarded to her inside a letter Hiroshi had sent. The minute she saw the characters of the sender's name, Kan Niizuma, her face became grim. She could not forget the name of the man who had forced Hiroshi to write the letter about the "swallow."

Niizuma's bulky communication was filled with the unexpected. He had known completely about her present trip to Akagi with Hiroshi. It was what could be called a threatening letter in which he noted he had, for certain reasons, completely read all the love letters that had come from Haruko to Hiroshi. Hiroshi had disregarded advice given in friendship and had carried out his secret trip to Akagi, but that Niizuma would not submit to an attitude which had trampled friendly advice underfoot was a menacing side thrust mixed with jealousy. As Haruko was reading the letter, she felt anger welling against Hiroshi for still associating with a man like Niizuma in spite of Hiroshi's former bitter experiences and for still heedlessly allowing such a man to read through all her love letters no matter what the circumstances. But her anger immediately shifted to Niizuma alone, and she came to feel all the trouble had been created by his sordid curiosity and jealousy, the entire wrongdoing singularly his. She realized the very unreliability of Hiroshi, who had been taken advantage of by this kind of man, was now stimulating her maternal affection for Hiroshi and was serving to make her feel she could not be easy unless she firmly held him under her wing. She became aware that rather than the youthful masculine passion he showed her in their lovemaking and rather than his innocent childlike purity which was so easily wounded, it was his infant-like helplessness with no precaution or defense against the malicious intentions of the world and its pitfalls which was the very thing she was most apprehensive about, the thing she could not take her eyes away from, the thing she was most attracted to.

After Haruko, still quite lost in reverie and relaxed in

body, heart, and mind over her intoxication during those intervals of sweet love with Hiroshi, found in her hands this threatening letter from Niizuma, her usual pride and fighting spirit were clearly revived for the first time in a long while. Having till then still entrusted herself to the mental process of being disposed toward Hiroshi with a naturalness like that of flowing water, she realized she had recently become exhausted by the pressuring assaults of society and had probably been thinking of her love for Hiroshi only as a way of healing her heart and soul for having been injured by the world. Not yet decided how far she would carry out her love for him, Haruko felt, on the contrary, she had been afforded, thanks to Niizuma's unexpected interference, an urgent opportunity to squarely confront the depths of her mind about him.

Such being the case, she had only to carry out her love for Hiroshi, the determination welling in her that if someone else intervened to endanger their love, she would simply fight on relentlessly and conquer. First of all to Hiroshi before anyone else, she would relate her strong resolve and urge him to wake up and realize his worth, and as she regained her former spirit after this great lapse of time, she confronted the letter paper before her.

Around that time an unexpected event happened in Noe's life in Tokyo to make her stand up against a severe ordeal.

The affair had begun on June 13, before Haruko had left for Akagi. That day, after Noe had gone as usual to the *Seito* office at Sugamo, she found a thick letter addressed to her from a man. With the impression that she somehow had a vague memory of Sota Kimura, the name of the sender, she casually began reading his letter:

My dear Lady:

Please forgive this letter from someone you do not even know. At any rate, I am the man who paid a visit to your editorial office on Friday in the middle of last month. To be perfectly frank, I had been wishing to become acquainted with you from about that time, and it was for this reason I had suddenly called on you . . .

The communication which began with these remarks was a confession spelling out in detail that Sota Kimura had read with pleasure Noe's impressions published in *Seito*, had been attracted by "an immaturity that had emerged from something which seemed considerably pure," and as he had gradually conjured up her image had come to cherish a feeling bordering on love for her. He was obsessed with the desire not only to see Noe in print but to actually see her as a living woman and verify her existence. He continued by explaining it was for that purpose he had abruptly called at her office:

I would be most happy if it were possible for me to meet you and if you could let me know the time and place most convenient for you. Possibly after meeting, we may find that your personality and mine are of such a nature we will repel each other. On the other hand, I feel that possibly you may all the more really begin to live in my heart. Or perhaps it may be that I will be able to talk with you quietly and pleasantly only as a friend. In any event, would you kindly express yourself frankly to me?

The letter in which these passages proposed an interview with her was clearly a kind of confession of love. No one had informed Noe that Sota Kimura had come to visit her, so this was the first time she had learned of it. Having finished reading, she was troubled, feeling at the same time somewhat abashed and embarrassed. She could not help sensing something ludicrous and pitiful in this love letter from a man completely in the dark about her cohabitation with Tsuji. In an instant she decided that Tsuji could not see the letter, but reconsidering, she thought she need not conceal this sort of thing from him. It could not be expected for her to remain silent about the event, due to her habit of feeling dissatisfied with herself unless she informed Tsuji in detail about all her experiences, even the most trifling. After eleven o'clock that night she showed Kimura's letter to Tsuji in his study.

"You see, I'm really worried, to be told something like this. Isn't it better to abandon the whole thing?"

Unconsciously her tone had become coquettish, and placing her hand on Tsuji's knee, she looked up at her husband who, without replying, was absorbed in reading this love letter come to his wife from another man. At that moment an unexpected pride and elation flashed into her mind. Noe had continued to cherish the idea that from the standpoint of learning and personal appearance Tsuji far surpassed her. The respect she had for him during the period when he was her teacher had increased to the extent of regarding him as the savior of her destiny, and even now when she was pregnant with Tsuji's child, she continued to harbor the sensation that she could not, after all, lift up her head to him. Furthermore, she was quite aware that during the years he had taught he had been the type of man girls easily fell in love with, and she could not suppress her jealousy toward those women in his past. Even while she was ostentatiously listening to Haruko sincerely offering words of praise about him, the Haruko who was so beautiful and so sagacious, Noe could not help being secretly obsessed by a kind of inferiority complex toward her husband. She had never thought her face and figure appealing to men. She had known how provincial and unrefined she was in comparison to anyone else in *Seito*. She was all the more bewildered because she had received a love letter from a man who seemed to be such a young literary enthusiast; at the same time she did not know what to do with this pride and elation welling out into the open, a feeling she was tasting for the first time in her life.

"Look here, you're not going to utterly ignore me, are you? What do you think?" she quibbled jokingly, a buoyancy in her as if she wanted to shake Tsuji by the knees. When he put down the letter after reading it, he said with a strangely sullen, sober, and melancholy glance, "I suppose it's better to reply since the letter's sincere."

"Well, to put it that way! It's not my fault, is it? It's the other party's fault, isn't it?"

Hiding the joy she felt at Tsuji's words, Noe deliberately pouted her lips.

"This man, Sota Kimura, is a member of the second *Shinshicho* magazine, which he published with Jun'ichiro Tanizaki and Shosen Onuki. Now he belongs to *Fusain*. You remember, don't you, when I once went out for a walk with you and this man's story had just come out in *Fusain*, which we read while standing inside a bookstore?"

"We did?"

"Kimura's father, the proprietor of the Iroha restaurant, was the first man to open a sukiyaki restaurant in Tokyo at the beginning of Meiji."

"Is he rich?"

202 • BEAUTY IN DISARRAY

"Yes. They say the Iroha has more than thirty branches. It's rumored each of these is run by one of the father's mistresses."

"What? Thirty persons? The father's mistresses?"

"As for his children, I guess they're countless."

"How disgusting! That makes me sick. And he's the son of that kind of man!"

Noe did not realize that her callous way of speaking about Sota Kimura was a kind of coquetry toward Tsuji. Strangely enough, he obstinately repeated his words that it was better for her to write a reply. Stimulated by the letter which she had received, Tsuji caressed Noe that night more passionately than he had in many a month, while Noe was also so intensely aroused she felt ashamed of herself, even as she realized the elasticity and freshness of her own body able to respond to any of Tsuji's vigorous maneuvers.

"Aren't you jealous, dear? Not even a bit?"

While holding firmly to Tsuji's back as he still remained inside her, his hard breathing continuing as if he were reluctant to withdraw, Noe had come out with those words in a coquettish voice.

"You fool!"

With only these words Tsuji increased his movement against Noe's beckoningly firm smooth skin moist with perspiration, his momentum and vigor once again suddenly reviving his powers.

Having slept later than usual the following morning, Noe saw Tsuji off, his features fresh and clear, his face brimming with happiness.

He worked as a private tutor as the very minimum side job he would take, but when he left home, he was usually certain to head toward a library where he could do his own studying. Unusual for Tsuji, he turned at the corner to suddenly look back toward Noe, who longer than usual remained standing by the door after sending him off, so he quickened his pace in confusion as if he were embarrassed. While feeling as if something adhesive were pulling between each of them in these morning sentiments which only a married couple can taste after sharing a night of satisfaction, Noe was in such high spirits she felt she wanted to whistle.

As Noe sat at Tsuji's desk, she leisurely began writing her reply to Sota, the same bright and sweet expression on her face. Due to the happiness in her she was not aware that even the characters and sentences in her letter had become more gentle, more tender, more charming than the occasion demanded:

> Having nothing that much to be hoped for, I believed it was preferable to wait, after all, for a chance to meet naturally before seeing one another, and I felt, somehow or other, it was better to avoid forcibly hastening our meeting.
>
> However, when I once more thought of your serious and sincere letter, I came to feel it was equally arrogant and uncivil, to be sure, to decline your kind suggestion. And so, even though I do not know what result will be derived from our meeting, I have come to the conclusion to leave the request up to you.

In this manner Noe accepted Sota Kimura's proposal, and when in detail she told him her schedule at the *Seito* office and her proofreading hours for the magazine at the

Bunshodo printers and finished the communication by informing him she would wait for him at his convenience, she carefully read her letter again and again.

Even so, what sort of man was Kimura really? To send such a fervent letter to a woman he had never seen, he must have been considerably passionate yet thoughtless. But at least he was a member of *Fusain*, so he must have been rather extraordinary. According to Yoshiko Yasumochi, though, he gave off a kind of childish impression with his white skin and smooth expressionless face.

While Noe lay sprawled out on the mats, her slovenly body seven months pregnant, she imagined this and that about the man she had not yet seen. She would first show her letter to Tsuji and then mail it. Inwardly, after all, Tsuji must have been quite concerned about it. And what should she do after Kimura saw her and seriously became fond of her? At any rate, as soon as they met, she would have to reveal to him her life with Tsuji. However, what if even after that Kimura became all the more passionate and pressing and urgent? When she reached this point in her thoughts, Noe felt a burning sensation throughout her body and quickly stood up. Once again she reread Kimura's letter. From between its lines she felt blowing against her a heated blast of air that gave off the odor of something masculine. In confusion after hurling the letter some distance away, she took out two brown paper bags hidden deep inside Tsuji's bookcase. Packed tightly in them were the love letters exchanged between her and Tsuji. The mere sight of a date enabled Noe to recollect in a flash Tsuji's words inside that particular envelope. These letters had been reread so often they had dissolved into her flesh and blood. Although almost all of them had been written with Somei as the sending or receiving center, there were also some that had been exchanged between them at this very same house they were in after the two lovers began living together. Though Tsuji did not talk half as much as Noe, his letters when he did write had a length and urgency not inferior to her own. Flashed through Noe's mind was this section from one of Tsuji's letters she liked best:

Parents and children and brothers of one's own flesh and blood, what are they really? Husbands and wives and friends, what can we say about them? Usually almost all of them live in worlds which are terribly separated from each other, don't they? All of them are living in an awful solitude, aren't they? You may possibly be a terrible enemy to me. But I will never be the least bit regretful in having an enemy like you. Rather, I feel I want to love you so much I will come to hate you. If I'm not lucky enough to qualify as your husband and if I hinder your development, it is better for you to abandon me at any time and fly off somewhere.

"Are you thinking I will go off somewhere? We love one another so very much, do we not? Do we not, my darling, understand one another so very much? These last few months I actually have felt I have been bound more closely to you than ever before. Oh no, I am not referring only to the matter of the world of sex. That is to say, I mean a perfect union from the standpoint of both body and soul. Dearest, you too have probably been thinking in this very same way, haven't you?"

While beginning in this manner to speak to Tsuji in her heart, Noe came to feel quite miserable about the existence of Kimura, who had in him something of the clown as he was about to encroach on the love between Tsuji and herself, a love so closely intertwined not even a drop of water could penetrate it.

From outside the veranda of the three-mat room, Noe's sister-in-law Tsune, holding her bedding in her arms, peeped inside. After Noe promptly thrust the letter to Kimura under her desk, she pretended to be racing her pen across her writing pad as if she had been doing that for some time. She always woke up several hours later than her mother-in-law and sister-in-law, and almost never doing any household chores, she would go out on her *Seito* business or lie around the house reading books or writing manuscripts. This situation, unusual for a young wife, had already become part of her daily routine before she realized it. What with Tsuji's silent powers of persuasion, his mother and sister formed the opinion from the very first that Noe was a woman who wrote about various things, and they abandoned all hope she would ever become an ordinary housewife.

Until Tsune went away after hanging up the bedding to air in the narrow garden, Noe continued to write words at random. While she repeatedly jotted down the characters for names like *Seito*, Jun Tsuji, Raicho, Katsu, and Kokichi, without any connection to one another, the words *Fusain* and Sota Kimura were mixed in with the rest before she was aware of it.

Noe had been waiting impatiently for Tsuji to return, and that evening she showed him her reply.

"Even though it's too long, I think it will be all right."

After skimming through it, he tossed it back to her without much ado. He looked as if he had completely forgotten Kimura's letter, but he had been irritated throughout the day by the fact that the print in the books he had been reading at the library had been transformed into the characters penned in Kimura's communication. When he thought about the fact that Noe, who had about her the flavor of a rustic girl, had so much charm she had been sent a love letter by another man, Tsuji's pride was agreeably tickled, but at the same time in recalling her cheeky glance when she showed him the letter, he also felt like storming at her for being so conceited about it. In short, by admitting to himself he was jealous, he jeered bitterly at himself. After supper a strangely buoyant Noe took Tsuji out for a walk and flung her letter to Kimura into the mailbox at the corner in front of a cigarette shop. Tsuji was observing Noe's short fat figure, her abdomen finally and conspicuously swollen and thrust out while she ran toward him as if she were still straining to catch the quiet sound of her falling letter, and for the first time he noticed how ugly her appearance was.

As for Sota Kimura, when he received Noe's reply, he was overjoyed by her unexpected positive response. He had forwarded his letter partly with the amused feeling of wanting to effect a liaison with one of the New Women, which some of his friends had done. Of course, it could not be denied that he had by then experienced many romantic attachments and love affairs. While resisting his father's extraordinary debauchery, Kimura had bought many women and had even promised to marry the daughter of an *utazawa* ballad master. Kimura had also become intimate with his half sister, his conduct proving much too embarrassing even to himself. Unable to manage well either his fiancée or his half sister, in his despair he had written to Noe. His heart leapt with joy on perceiving her letter in a handwriting that could not be expected of an eighteen or nineteen-year-old girl. He could not let the trapped fish escape. Immediately he began his second letter.

On the morning of the eighteenth, Noe, waking as usual later than anyone else in the family, was shocked to find in the mailbox a letter for her and a magazine bound with a thin band of paper. By the time she had retraced her steps from the front door to Tsuji's room, she had already finished reading the letter.

I am devoutly and sincerely waiting for the day when clasping the hands of Destiny I can meet you.

Still lingering before her eyes were these affected words that smacked of some young literary enthusiast. The afternoon of the twenty-sixth was to be the day for his visit to Bunshodo in Tsukiji. She had informed him in her previous reply she would be going there that day to do her *Seito* proofreading.

"It's come again."

Without even troubling to look at the letter she held out to him, Tsuji reached for the copy of *Fusain* sent to her. After seeing Tsuji off, Noe immediately immersed herself in reading Kimura's work in the magazine. She received a much deeper impression from his story "Trembling" than from his letter. The realization she was loved by a man who could write such a substantial story made her feel light-hearted.

Afterwards, four days later on June 23, a telephone call came in the afternoon for Noe, who with Katsu Kobayashi had been finishing her proofreading at Bunshodo.

"Is this Noe Ito-san? You must be Noe-san."

The low calm voice of a man began as if whispering. Noe immediately realized it was Kimura. He gave her his name and asked if he might come to see her then.

"Please. I'll be waiting for you."

Noe had also replied simply in a voice that suppressed her real feelings.

Kimura came so quickly she had not waited at all. When she met him for the first time in the drawing room on the second floor, a desk between them, she received only the impression of an ordinary man with a white round face. He had neatly smoothed down his hair, its pomade aglow. The stylish gold-rimmed spectacles he was wearing, rather than suggesting a youthful literary enthusiast, gave her the impression of a rich young gentleman. With his obi sprucely and tightly bound over his elegant unlined kimono of a Satsuma splashed pattern, he was holding his Panama hat in his hands. Even Noe, who was indifferent to her own personal appearance, knew Kimura's attire had cost a great deal. Casting a brief glance at herself looking as if she were a factory worker, her downy hair shimmering against her almost powderless face, her simple Western-style hairdo bundled against the nape of her neck, her blue cotton smock over her worn-out unlined *meisen*-silk kimono hiding her swollen stomach, Noe felt, on the contrary, her courage gathering inside her. Her eyeglasses with their nickel-plated frames were probably the only accessory which made her look somewhat intelligent. Hardly observing this unattractive Noe, Kimura with downcast eyes and subdued voice rapidly began telling her why he had written.

Examining a book in a corner of the room was Katsu, sitting with her back to them. She had heard about the situation from Noe, but she had not thought they were so intimate as to require her to leave the room. Though Noe was thinking she ought to tell him quickly that she had been living with Tsuji, she unintentionally missed the chance to because Kimura roamed from one topic to another. She could not refrain from speaking to him about the oppression of society and the pure fabrications of malicious gossip against *Seito*, and her voice was sharp during the discussion. When Kimura brought up the scandal about her and a certain man reported in the *Chuo* newspaper, Noe protested, saying disdainfully, "That's a complete distortion!" In a flash a bright expression spread over Kimura's face. Immediately after sending her his first love letter, he had heard from his friend Yutaka Nagao that Noe had been living with Jun Tsuji and that all her translations published in *Seito* had been his. With the intention of corroborating it himself, of verifying it with his own eyes, Kimura had moved up the date of his scheduled meeting and had suddenly come to visit her, and now he was quite impressed by her expression of childlike resentment and her determined tone of voice when he had mentioned the scandal. But the fact that even Haruko Hiratsuka had not noticed Noe's physical relationship with Tsuji, due to the impression Noe gave of a youthful freshness and simple outward appearance, made it understandable for Kimura at this moment to jump to the hasty yet hopeful conclusion that no man was connected to Noe. As for Noe herself, she immediately guessed this misunderstanding on Kimura's part from his tone of voice, but it became all the more difficult to bring up what she once missed the chance to say.

Meanwhile, Katsu joined them, and they passed the time in small talk, Kimura becoming quite jovial and before taking leave going as far as the Ginza with Noe and Katsu on their way back, as if he could not bear parting from them.

When Noe returned home, she discovered Tsuji had only just come back.

"Mr. Kimura came today."

"Oh, he did? How was it?"

Tsuji had blinked his narrow eyes a moment and blushing a little had asked this question while looking to the side.

"'How was it?' you say? Somehow he's a man who makes a very slight impression. There are faces we forget immediately, aren't there? He was that kind of person."

"What did you talk about?"

"What did we talk about? Well, let's see. Oh, just trivial things. Things any young literary enthusiast wants to discuss."

Actually, even though she tried to remember her entire conversation with Kimura, she felt there was nothing in particular she wanted to report to Tsuji. At the same time, for some reason or other, she did not feel inclined to tell him frankly about the unpleasant aftertaste she had experienced over missing the opportunity to inform Kimura of her living together with Tsuji.

The next morning immediately after Tsuji had left, Noe again received a letter from Kimura, his third, in which he passionately expressed his joy in having met her the day before. It was a letter in which Kimura's hot breath, trying to push his emotion further, was panting between the lines:

I love you, love you, love you. My ego lives in that love. The world lives in that love. To be perfectly honest, I had already loved you. Therefore, if you had violently betrayed that love of mine (since I am very much a person who makes choices on the basis of outward appearance), I thought I would be extremely unhappy today. And so I was trembling blindly in front of my fate.

But I have now gained the courage to believe more fully in my Destiny. Now I am truly happy.

Moved by the passionate ardor of Kimura's letter, Noe regretted her weakness the day before in not being able to confess her sharing Tsuji's bed and board. Feeling as if her chest were being compressed by a vague apprehension and unhappy premonition that a quite unexpected event was already happening to her, Noe confusedly sat at Tsuji's desk. Like someone in a daze, she dashed off a long letter at such breakneck speed that even her pen racing down the sheet seemed too slow and unsatisfactory. She minutely set down her history, from her birth up to her present situation, from her being joined to Tsuji to his losing his job because of her, so minutely, in fact, in such a confession-like way, that it might have been considered an indecent exposure of herself:

> That I have been living now with the man you referred to is indeed a fact. We have suffered terribly last year and this. Even now our hard times continue. But such circumstances have bound us together all the more firmly, and we are now unable to part from one another.

She had written this far at a gallop, but she had misgivings that expressing herself in this way might be taken by Kimura as boasting about a conquest. She even wrote she had shown Kimura's letter to Tsuji, and finally in reference to Kimura's question of the rumor published by Choko Ikuta about the Ellen Key translation, Noe set down the facts both in a frank tone and in a way that revealed she had strongly changed her earlier attitude:

And as for the question of my translation of Ellen Key, of course, with my poor ability in language, it was hardly to be expected I could complete it by myself. It was certainly due to Tsuji's ability that it was finished. I myself have been studying hard with the intention of being able to do things only by myself and not to have to depend on another person's gifts. I'll never hide the fact that I was helped and I'll never lie about it. While I am this deficient in ability, getting someone's help cannot be avoided. If someone tells me I must not get help in translating, I will not translate until I am able to translate alone by myself. I know that probably everyone realizes such a difficult translation could not have been done by me.

Since I have told you everything I had to tell, I beg your pardon for not reporting these things earlier; at the same time, I shall await your serious and earnest judgment on all these matters. June 24

By the time she had finished writing, so hard had she gripped her pen in continuing to dash off her letter at a stretch that her fingers had grown numb, and the pen could not immediately be released from her grip. As she leaned absent-mindedly against the desk, wondering if she ought to mail her letter after Tsuji looked it over for her, another communication from Kimura, his fourth, came as if in pursuit of her. It was a frank and specific letter courting her, though it was shorter than the former one, the reason for writing being his feeling that he had been deficient in fully conveying his intentions before. It had been composed the previous night.

When Noe finished reading this letter as well, she found

herself burning to her very depths, as if she had gulped down strong saké. She came to feel some outrageous oppression and even terror, as if she were being pressed downward into the arms of a madman. Unable to calm herself, she rushed from the house, her letters left as they were, scattered over her desk, as she set out for the *Seito* office. Even after trying to talk to Yoshiko Yasumochi, Noe could not calm herself in the least. Raicho, whom Noe had been relying on, had gone to Akagi and had not yet returned. Though Noe definitely loved Tsuji, why had her mind become so upset by a confession of love from a man she had met only once, a man whose love was so one-sided? She was so terrified she had to rivet her gaze directly onto her own heart which was this unreliable.

She walked about alone in the small grove Tsuji was so fond of and gradually she calmed herself, and when she came home, she found Tsuji had returned a moment earlier. As he looked back at her from his desk, she noticed he had on his face the gloomiest expression she had ever seen on it. When she realized his hand was holding her reply to Kimura written only a while ago, she snatched it instinctively and put her arms tightly around him. He averted his face from hers as she was trying to kiss him, and he continued his reading of the letter a second time. While coquettishly pressing her face against his chest and putting her arms around his body, she stole an upward glance at him. She realized that a nervous spasm was darting across his pale cheeks, that he was frantically biting his lips to prevent them from trembling. Even when he finished reading her letter, he did not say a word, and he neither tried to shake her away from him nor did he attempt to embrace her. All Noe could do was let her tears, the reason for which she did not know, trickle down sentimentally after they welled in her eyes, and while deliberately letting them soak into Tsuji's kimono, she finally wrote with her one free hand on a scratch pad on the desk.

"Are you angry?"

Tsuji immediately wrote beside it.

"I'm not angry. All Kimura's letters are pleasant. I only regret that your attitude yesterday was not clear."

Thinking she had better not go against Tsuji's will any further, she said, her tone coquettish, "Since this letter is too emotional and too confused, I want to rewrite it in the proper way."

"It's too long. Replies ought to be short and simple."

Without answering him on this point, Noe seized hold of Tsuji's hand and drew it to her breasts. They had filled out three times as large as when she was a young girl, and now they were so full it seemed the milk would spurt. That Tsuji had also been agitated almost as much as she had been by Kimura's letter had exposed Noe to a kind of terror and at the same time to a rather agreeable sensation.

On the following day, the twenty-fifth, just as Noe was preparing to go to Bunshodo, a letter from Kimura once again descended upon her, his fifth. Now in his letter she felt even a kind of violent coercion.

Because the previous day's communication had been composed too hastily and because he had not written her address on two of his letters and so they had probably not reached her, he was writing her again, expressing his same confession of love with more boldness than in his letter of the previous day. Noe was so agitated by his communication she had no energy to rewrite her letter to him.

Though she went to Bunshodo that day, she could not

remember what she had done the entire time. Katsu and Kiyoko Iwano had been there, but Noe had no idea what they had talked about.

Only Kimura's passion, with an indescribable intensity, enshrouded her like something oppressive, her thoughts so painful she could hardly breathe. Though she loved Tsuji, she could not help admitting she had definitely been moved by Kimura's passion. She perceived in her own mind that unconsciously she had been weighing and measuring the love of these two men, and she was startled. What an inconceivable thing! Could she be betraying Tsuji's love? Could she be thinking of her life without him? She continually kept exhorting herself that this very day when she returned home, she would write Kimura a short letter of rejection. Then she was surprised to discover an unexpected suffocating sorrow welling within her as if she were suddenly abandoning this precious love. When she got home, she found to her complete surprise that another letter, the sixth, had been placed on her desk. It had been written that morning.

> From the very first I have felt something was commanding me to love you.

What an exaggeration! While thinking it was, Noe found she was gradually becoming accustomed to these impassioned and heated love letters, four of which had been sent in succession in two days. The feeling bordering on fear and confusion after she had read the first letter had already disappeared before she realized it, and her eyes unconsciously and hurriedly searched around for the word "love."

If you and I are destined to love one another, I have no doubt that this love of mine will have the power to restore you to life as well. If not, and if this self of mine is doomed to have to love you by itself alone, even that will be equally all right with me. The love I am pouring upon you is quite sufficient to keep my soul alive.

Her face down against the letter, Noe was in agony exhaling her heated breath. Something hot was running through her entire body as if a raging flame driven from inside the letter had been transferred to her. Lifting her head, she opened her bloodshot eyes and like someone in a daze seized hold of her pen. She dashed off her letter as if hurling against the paper her agitation caused by the successive letters she had received:

I don't know yet what would be better. I sense such power in the words of each of your lines, of each of your sentences, that I feel as if I am going to faint. I thoroughly believe I am really happy to be told of this sincere and powerful love.

After she apologized for her late reply and revealed the agitation of her heart such as it was, Noe's pen did not know where to stop:

Oh, who could ever spurn your love? I love you with all my heart. Truly, truly, with all my heart—but I do not want to deceive myself.

Her pen honestly fused into the ink the heat of her feelings, and she set down her passionate sentences one after another. When she finished writing, she could not help but believe she now definitely loved Kimura. Fearful of rereading her letter, she put it in an envelope together with the long confession she had written the day before and inserted it in the bundle she usually took with her when she went to do her proofreading. She was not yet aware she would be carrying her first secret from Tsuji.

The following day, the twenty-sixth, on the way to Bunshodo, she resolutely posted the letter of the previous night. Due to that one night of sleep her violent emotions of the evening before had already faded, and she felt she could no longer delay her reply. She suddenly recalled the letters between her and Tsuji in those brown paper bags. Hers were twice as many as his. Those feelings she had when they were separated, feelings that even when she wrote and wrote she did not think she had written enough, all those feelings came back to her as if the time were but yesterday. From the moment they had begun living together, she thought that the intensity of her love for Tsuji had always been greater than his and that she alone felt desire for the other party. However, Kimura was different. It was the man who was kneeling before her, the man who indifferent to his own situation desired her love, the man who was in torment. It was she herself who had so much charm as to bewilder the male. This satisfaction from a vanity she was unable to hide made her elated even in the midst of her agony. On the way back from Bunshodo, she walked along Kagurazaka with Katsu, and when she reached home, thrust at her by Tsuji, who had returned before her, was another of Kimura's letters.

"How often he does write!"

In spite of herself Noe laughed. Even Tsuji forced a smile. This letter, dated midnight of the twenty-fifth, was

Kimura's third letter that day. His two or three letters composed in one day had been fired at her like arrows from a bow, and because she had already been forced to read five in succession in three days, she could not believe it was only a mere three days ago that she had met him. She felt as if it had been at least ten. His letter this time spoke quietly with a strangely subdued emotion:

> It is just past midnight. I feel my heart pouring into you in a dejected way. In front of me now is your figure with that desk between us. I am trying to write this letter as if I were talking to you. I do not know how to improve my lot except by writing to you in this way about the thoughts gushing out of my heart at the present moment. Moreover, I do not know how to expunge the hours of each day except by so doing.

In his letter which began with this passage, Noe also caught sight of a sentence that read, "I'm suffering from the premonition that you may leave me."

She could tell that Kimura, who had not yet received her reply, was beginning to feel wounded at the futility of fighting windmills and was gradually being driven away by uncertainty. Picking up the letter which Noe had flung down with a sigh, Tsuji was reading it carefully. While watching his profile, Noe was suddenly seized by fear, as if her chest were being tightly compressed. She suddenly had misgivings about the contents of the letter she had just sent off that morning without Tsuji's knowledge. When she thought what reactions that letter with its vibrant movement of wild emotions would create in Kimura, her regret in being too hasty was more than she could bear. Though she was urged by an almost irresistible impulse to immediately confess all to Tsuji, Noe's heart froze in fear when she thought how enraged he would be. Noe felt that Tsuji, who was so taciturn and calm and slow to react that she could not rely on him, was an adult whom she was after all unable to fathom, so this maturity in Tsuji was all the more irritating to her and at the same time all the more necessary for her.

"He must be a person with an enormous amount of spare time!"

Muttering these words as if vomiting them out, Tsuji flung Kimura's letter back at Noe.

"Twenty-four or five, I guess."

Tsuji's monologue continued. It concerned Kimura's age.

As for Sota Kimura, he had received at the same time Noe's two replies, which he had almost begun to despair of, and he was feeling relieved, emancipated. After those five letters he had written in four days as if he had been obsessed by a demon, the impression he had merely from Noe's letters which had finally reached him was extraordinary. Though he had not thought his five letters were fabrications, he was not prepared to state categorically that they were communications of pure love. And though he had, of course, to a considerable degree erotic and lascivious feelings should the opportunity for such present itself, he was unable to tell if there was not something sportive and histrionic in his emotions, as if he were a character in a play performing on a stage. In the first place, he had not only confessed his plan but had talked about and shown to his younger brother Shohachi and to his own literary comrades Noe's first letter and copies of his earlier communications. To attempt to shoot down one of the New Women had in those days sufficient value as a game of love among young men with literary inclinations. And the fact that the woman was perhaps already sharing someone else's bed was, contrary to what one might think, an even greater spur toward interest in the game. Even if such a young man did not trap his fish, he could still feel in a light vein that he was none the worse for the attempt. However, while Kimura had written and sent off his love letters one after the other, he had come to acquire the illusion that the stage mask of a lovesick hero was actually stuck to his face. Gradually his letters became full of ardor, and mixed into the feelings in which he had been waiting for Noe's reply was something oppressive and suffocating that he was unable to label mere curiosity. Even while he was conscious that he, as an ardent seducer merely for the fun of it, was now almost on the point of becoming the ardently seduced man himself, he had begun to slowly plan his pose at the moment he withdrew from the stage as the pure simple-hearted lover-hero. Though he had received from their first encounter the impression of Noe as youthful and intelligent, he had not yet felt for her the least bit of sexual attraction. All his past mistresses had been more beautiful, more erotic, than Noe, and they gave off an odor of gentle soft femininity. Since meeting her on the twenty-third, he had not even been sent a postcard thanking him for their interview, and Kimura's self-respect had been bruised. Only three days had elapsed since their first encounter, yet Kimura, possibly victimized by the delusion of the number of letters he had sent, felt ten days already had. It was at this very juncture that Noe's thick envelope containing two letters finally reached him. The letter he first read, though short, was divided into wild emotion and utter confusion, and after finishing it and being overjoyed at finding in it a kind of long confessional tone, Kimura was pleased more than anything else by the fact that his pride had been soothed. The feeling of relief that he was not an utter clown gave him the most reassurance. At any rate, not only did Noe's earnestness and sincerity overflow in the text of her letter, but a passion impossible to suppress was spurting out from the lines.

Kimura was quietly thinking how he could proceed from the climax of this play and bring it to its gorgeous finale. He taxed his ingenuity to compose a beautiful farewell letter in the most quiet and funereal style possible. When he closed with the typical hackneyed expression of a letter of farewell, "I pray for your happiness," he felt relieved, felt some indescribable emancipation. Without a hitch he had finished performing his literary role as the blighted hero, and the curtain fell. He felt as if he heard applause all around him. While he was intoxicated by this illusory applause, he found himself wanting, like some great actor responding with an encore, to once again write a farewell letter.

The following day, the twenty-seventh, Noe received Kimura's first letter of farewell. That letter, without a line of bitterness and with a prompt and reasonable indignation, was so orderly and so beautiful it made her feel a kind of pathos. And while she experienced relief, an indescribable violence of passion immediately thrust upward from below that sensation of security. When she thought of how oppressed the letters of that man had made her these last four days from the twenty-fourth to the present moment, she was jolted by feelings of insecurity and instability, as if her hands had suddenly been released at the apex of some violent emotion. Beneath her indignation toward this too selfish man was an overlapping malaise that he was much too simple. Could such a passionate courtship be so cheaply overturned? Noe's mind was disturbed by the panic of a woman who before she realizes it is about to be deserted by a man. They had to come to some understanding by meeting one another. With an exasperation as if she wanted to strike with her fist the chest of this man who was thinking that with such a farewell letter everything was settled and finished, Noe suddenly spread out her stationery:

I am extremely sad to be separating from you in this way. After meeting you, I feel my peace of mind has totally collapsed. Now I can no longer remain idle. I want to meet you once more no matter what.

Noe was unable to understand what dangerous words she had written, how improper they were for a married woman. As if being urged onward, she mailed the letter immediately after writing it. Then fatigue from the wild emotions of these last four days suddenly made itself felt, and like a top she collapsed into a deep sleep until evening. The *Seito* proofreading was at last finished, and from that day she had no need to go out. On Tsuji's return in the evening, Noe showed him Kimura's letter, and he merely nodded without expression. At any rate, relief that the event was over infiltrated even the scant movement in his eyes. He said in good-humored tones while handing Noe three concert tickets he had received at the place he had gone out to, "Let's meet there tomorrow. Invite anyone else you wish."

Once again Noe missed the chance to tell him about her letter of the previous day. Tormented by an ominous premonition that something extraordinary was about to occur, Noe saw in the new day after having hardly any sleep. As she thought of her terror when that confused letter she had sent in secret to Kimura was discovered by Tsuji, she became extremely restless.

Once again the following day a letter from Kimura descended upon her. It was not his answer to her letter, but his second communication dated the twenty-sixth and written as an encore to the ecstasy of the deliciousness of farewell. This time, even a letter politely addressed to Tsuji was enclosed. This farewell letter to her was twice as long as the first, and in it Kimura's serious reference to the bittersweetness of resignation was able to gratify and soothe Noe's self-respect. The letter to Tsuji was merely a formal apology and appreciation, but from its concise and pithy passages Noe conjured up the vision of a medieval knight. A lingering attachment and regret, as if she had let some precious bowl drop, remained from this love affair which had ended before it had begun.

That evening, even when she met Tsuji at the concert, Noe continued to assume a sullen disposition. Since her pregnancy she had become quite capricious, so Tsuji was accustomed to these changes and took no notice of them. This indifference made Noe all the more impatient and irritable. She was under the illusion that the new love she had cast aside for this man was of unparalleled value. Her daily dissatisfaction with Tsuji, who was shiftless and irresolute, welled up inside her. Realizing she was possessed by this feeling of something like enmity toward Tsuji, she became confused. Kimura, whom she would no longer meet, was remembered with pain and sorrow as if he had been her companion in love. When Tsuji came near her, she even felt conscious of a sensual disgust. Noe was shocked and terrified by this image of herself.

"By the way, a letter came for you from Mr. Kimura," she said on their way home.

"What? For me? Let me see it."

"It's at the house."

When he finished the two letters from Kimura, Tsuji grew sullen and rebuked her.

"You sent him a letter you didn't show me, didn't you?"

"Yes."

"Why? What did you say in it?"

"I've forgotten. Just some nonsense. I merely added a postscript, that's all."

While studying Tsuji's face, she dawdled and managed to evade a reply, the upshot being she was able to smooth over the question of this last letter.

The following day was Sunday. From exactly the time that this event with Kimura had cropped up, Noe's mother-in-law Mitsu had not been at home, the visit to a relative caused by a trivial quarrel with Tsuji and his wife. It was fortunate for Noe that they had at home only her sister-in-law Tsune, who was more easygoing and carefree than the mother. Early that morning, Tsuji, most unusual for him, had brought out the bag of their love letters and was arranging them by date. Up to then, whenever Noe had taken them out, he had become embarrassed and ill-tempered, and after ordering her to stop looking at them, he would turn aside. While Noe would usually have been prone to take pride in such a change in Tsuji, she was secretly waiting for Kimura's letter. She was firmly convinced there would be a reply to that agitated letter of hers. Strangely enough, however, no news came from Kimura that day.

The following afternoon, the thirtieth, Noe suddenly received a telegram:

PLEASE COME TODAY BY ALL MEANS KIMURA

With the telegram still in her hand she felt dizzy, as if she were being dragged down to the depths of the earth. Yet she could not help but go. The die had been cast by herself.

Kimura, who after sending out his two farewell letters had received Noe's passionate reply written as if the woman were shouting, was for the first time since starting on this venture overflowing with happiness as if he wanted to leap for joy. At last the victory was his! This letter revealed Noe's complete confusion! He had moved a woman to these passages of incoherence, to these shouts, and the heart of a married woman at that, and merely by the power of his pen! The cocky conceit of the male welled in his breast. Having reported ever since the affair began his own step-by-step progress to his friends, he wondered if there could ever be an honor greater than this success. Subduing his heart, which was dancing for joy, Kimura with bated breath was anticipating that Noe would jump at this very moment into his trap. However, she did not put in the slightest appearance. Although he had written to tell her he would wait at home on the twenty-ninth and thirtieth, he suddenly became alarmed over her complete failure to turn up. Unable to contain himself, he had dashed off a telegram, and no longer able to wait, he had gone to visit her at her home.

Having passed him on the way, Noe found herself at Kimura's house at last. Her own shabby appearance made her miserable when she saw the magnificence of his residence at Kojimachi. Treated politely by the maid, Noe was conducted to Kimura's room. As soon as tea and cakes were brought in for her, another housemaid came in with the note Kimura had left. It concerned his wish for her to wait for him should their paths cross and she happen to arrive. Realizing he had gone to visit her at her home, Noe became desperate.

It was already the hour of Tsuji's return. Rising to go yet unable to and still not knowing what to do, she found the time steadily moving ahead. All too soon she became aware that the lights were being switched on and that it was completely dark outside. At that moment Kimura rushed into the room, his footsteps flurried.

"Just as I thought! You've come as I asked!" he said as if flushed with victory, the blood rushing to his cheeks, his eyes aglow.

It was for the two an encounter after only a week, but that week in which they had been under extreme tension had a weight and stress as though it had been almost half a year. Noe was absolutely dumbfounded by Kimura's restless excited tones in which he began talking so fretfully the moment he sat down.

Could this be the same person who had composed those numerous love letters which were so passionate, so beautiful, so desolate, so self-possessed? Noe finally came to the realization that from those love letters she had definitely created the illusion of another man disguised as Sota Kimura. The more Kimura talked, the more chilly she became, as if cold water were being poured down her back. Without hesitation Kimura went so far as to inform her he had met Tsuji that day and had suffered from his surly and morose treatment. Noe was repelled by Kimura's tone of voice in which he seemed to take it for granted she was now quite naturally more on his side than on Tsuji's. Obstinately she remained silent, her glance downward as she continued to listen to him. This she had not bargained for. She had not expected this type of man.

No matter how hard she searched, the image of the

Kimura she had drawn in her heart from his letters was not to be gained from the man in front of her eyes. Kimura confided to her even his past love affairs and his complicated family situation. At the same time he pulled from his desk drawer a bundle of letters of encouragement and advice from his friends about their love affair and showed them to her. Taking them and rapidly glancing through them, Noe shuddered.

She felt enraged by the fact that this private love affair between Kimura and herself had been gossiped about among the young literary enthusiasts, as if it were a public event. It was impossible for her to understand why Kimura had with one letter after another put their love affair on display to his friends.

"Are you still attached to him?" Kimura said as though urging her to choose between the two men.

"Yes."

Noe had immediately responded. But she could not bring herself to explain to him her feelings for Tsuji. It was past twelve when she returned that night. The moment she entered their room, she was petrified by the threatening expression on Tsuji's face as he looked back at her. With his face twisted in hatred, he declared, "What are those? I mean those glasses! What you still wearing them for?"

In her vexation Noe shuddered convulsively. Having thought she could win him over by honestly confessing her disillusionment with Kimura, she found her heart crushed by Tsuji's words. In no mood to apologize, she immediately crawled into bed. Tsuji seemed more hurt by this attitude than by her unchastity, and out of habit he wrote something on a piece of paper and flung it at her.

"Your behavior is impure. I'm displeased. Assume a definite, clear attitude."

Noe avoided replying, maintaining only the point that she was tired, and she continued to lie there indifferently. Tsuji lay down beside her as if he had finally abandoned his demand.

While Noe was annoyed by his sighing and turning and twisting in bed, she was suddenly seized by the arm.

"If you're so distraught, let's separate. That would be better."

The moment she heard these low brooding words of Tsuji's, Noe was assailed by a fit of wild irrational passion.

"No, no, no!" she cried out, violently flinging herself against his breast.

It was on the following day that Noe had to give both Tsuji and Kimura a definite answer. Her nervous exhaustion these last several days became too powerful for her to endure, and just to rise from bed gave her pain. The heat and dullness from her pregnancy seemed to lie heavily upon her, and she felt like an invalid. She idled away the entire day, merely writing letters to her father and to Raicho at Akagi. Tsuji came back with an expression more sullen than the previous day's, but Noe felt no inclination even to speak to him. As she was about to go out silently to send off her letters, Tsuji suddenly caught her by the scruff of the neck and pulled her back.

"What are you doing?"

"Show them to me! What are you sending out?"

Embarrassed and miserable in the presence of Tsune, Noe felt the blood rushing to her head. She became hysterical, her eyes turning upward, her breathing seemingly coming to a halt. While Tsuji in confusion comforted her under these conditions, he suddenly said, "I hate this mess! I can't stand it. Look, let's go to Kimura's now. Let's settle it!"

As bewildered as she was, Noe pleaded with him to at least wait until the following day. He threw over to her a lengthy letter he had apparently written the night before. The agony he had been tormented by, both from jealousy and wild fancy during those four hours Noe had been at Kimura's the previous night, was endlessly written about.

As she reached the middle of the letter she was reading, Noe suddenly burst into tears.

Tsuji took another hard look at himself as a result of this incident. At the bottom of his heart in which he had behaved as the good husband, recommending Noe write a reply to Kimura and going out of his way to explain to her Kimura's situation, he could not help but admit that from the very first he had secretly resented the man for meddling with another person's wife. The helpless vanity characteristic of the native Tokyoite who tends to feel it unrefined to openly and frankly bare such human emotions as love, hate, joy, and sadness was known to Tsuji at his own personal cost. He had to perceive once again that in Noe's wild passion, with which she had hurled herself so forcefully at him at the beginning of their love affair, was a flow of blood unusually sensitive, fragile, and ardent toward the enticements of others. Tsuji had never dreamed he could be this jealous of her. He was forced to admit that even in his own heart that talked so pompously about such things as the cultivation of his wife's talent, the observation of her development, and the defense of women's rights were nesting the instinct and egotism of the male who persists in binding his wife to himself alone and who wishes to confine her to the home.

Furthermore, the hated one in this present situation was Kimura alone, and Tsuji had to admit that the more agitated Noe became, the more lovely he found her, a feeling of love welling inside him that he could never abandon her. However, the moment she might begin worrying that her growth would be hindered by such matters as housework and childrearing, what should he do? When he had thought this far, Tsuji felt afraid to try to promote Noe's development and awakening any further.

When Noe finished reading Tsuji's stark confession, she became obedient for the first time and apologized for her behavior the previous night. From her explanation Tsuji realized nothing physical had taken place between her and Kimura. He believed they had not even clasped hands, to say nothing of kissing, and while he felt relieved, he was filled with self-scorn. In short, when he became aware that all his agony of the previous day was hanging only on this one particular point, he found his pettiness all the more impossible to bear. But still superimposed on this self-disgust was the thought that he must not let the opportunity slip away. He could not feel at ease until he had made Noe promise she would go to Kimura's the next morning.

Receiving without warning Tsuji and Noe at his home the following morning, Kimura instantly surmised the situation. Everything was now clear to him when he saw Tsuji so composed and transformed from his behavior of the previous day. This interview was from start to finish a crushing defeat for Kimura.

Kimura insisted that if he had at least not seen Noe's last two letters, he would not have become this active toward her. It was those two letters that Tsuji wanted to read. But Kimura said they had been left at the house of his younger brother Shohachi. Noe's anger came surging up inside her. Just this point alone told her how their love affair was being treated as a source of amusement by Kimura's set.

The three of them immediately went on foot to the editorial room of *Fusain* on Hitotsugi in Akasaka. The *Fusain* had changed its name to *Life*. Kimura brought down the two letters from upstairs. Apparently egged on by his friends gathered there, Kimura openly assumed an unmistakably sullen look of indignation. He had become alert to his own self-hatred for his role as a buffoon. When on the spot Tsuji finished reading the letters, he said, "Were those your real feelings?" and calmly stared back at Noe.

"Yes. I was quite sincere about them at the time," she said nonchalantly without blushing, glancing at the letters by Tsuji's side.

Unable to contain himself any longer, Kimura shouted, "I'm thoroughly disgusted! You have my utter contempt! If that's the kind of person you are, I take it on myself to absolutely cast you aside!"

At Kimura's suggestion they decided each party should write about the affair to block out any irresponsible scandalmongering by the world.

Under the titles "Agitation" in *Seito* and "Fascination" in *Life*, each party in the affair published an article in the August issues. Newspapers and magazines joyously snatched at these confessional notes, the journalistic world in an uproar over them. The New Women had once again provided a topic for conversation. It was rumored that the magazine *Shin-Kodan* would even bring out an article entitled "New Type Love with Letter as Go-Between." Educators and psychologists jumped into the debate to argue over the event. In no time at all the name Noe Ito became famous.

The most comical aspect was Kimura's being so blinded by love that to the very last he had not noticed Noe's seven months of pregnancy. Raicho censured Noe for this affair by pointing out that Noe herself seemed unaware of her own pregnancy and had not once reflected on her attitude about the birth of the child.

All things considered, thanks to Kimura's clownish antics, this episode was settled with Noe and Tsuji's conjugal ties all the more firmly bound.

At just about this time Raicho's love affair began to burn even more furiously than the extreme heat of August, Raicho having returned from Akagi. Although Hiroshi met her as innocently and as easily as before, she could not be content, once they were physically bound, with the same conditions as before the summer. The great distance between Hiroshi's lodgings and her own residence was more painful to Haruko than anything else. Her family's dislike of Hiroshi became all the more undisguised. Moreover, he continued to live with Jun Harada.

> I can't bear carrying on our own individual lives separated from you in this way! I want much more free time to be with you.
>
> I can no longer remain a "dreamer." I cannot exist on "illusion" only. To speak frankly about myself at present, I cannot be satisfied unless I can have you equally day and night. What to me is day without its night? What also to me is night without its day? When I think that Harada is living with you under the very same roof, I cannot bear the envy I feel. But I haven't the slightest idea how such a confession of mine will affect you.
>
> It is hardly necessary to say that I love you very, very much. I have never before experienced such deep feelings.

While she was writing to Hiroshi, the purity of her love and the depth of her passion made her eyes overflow with tears before she realized it. Although he was a lover she could never rely on, he was so charming it was more than she could bear. When she thought of the perfection of her love for him, she felt she could never regret it should that love nullify her entire past. It was for the sake of this love that a courage was surging within her in which she would tamely submit to any persecution, any sacrifice. But not to meet Hiroshi for a single day was at present a torment she could not endure:

Can I exist without seeing you until the evening of the day after tomorrow?

While jotting down words sweet as those of a high school girl, Haruko had turned her beautiful brow into a series of lines. To build a life for the two of them by urging on Hiroshi, who was so unreliable, had been this heavy a load even before their actual life together could begin. When Haruko thought of their future, the pupils of her eyes could not help but be cloudy. More than anything else, she had to carry out the resolution she had firmly made at Akagi. And that was to publish an open letter to Kan Niizuma, that is to say, to publicly announce to the world her love affair with Hiroshi. And it was as clear as day that with this announcement the censure and assault of the world would arise once again. Because of the mere fact that Noe's "Agitation" happened to be published and was stirring the public to such furor, for Haruko to do the same would mean to again be pouring oil on fire. But when she wondered how even the less than twenty-year-old Noe had shown this much courage to frankly expose herself to shame and inconsistency before the public, Haruko also came to feel encouraged to announce her own love affair, thinking it was not the groundless shallow affair Noe's had been. What made Haruko hesitate and waver in this grave resolution was only Hiroshi's inner feelings. The old wound of his sudden betrayal and her humiliation of last summer struck home all the more deeply because she had kept it in the background. At the moment she stood up forcefully and eagerly, alone against her enemies all over the world for the sake of their love, at the cost of any difficulty or sacrifice. Should Hiroshi dodge again like the "swallow" that had flown away with the coming of fall, she would have to play out the farce by herself. Before she put her plan into execution, she had to make certain of Hiroshi's resolve by firmly demanding it once again this time.

On the first line of her writing pad she jotted down, "1. Please vow to me your fidelity once again."

When she examined what she had written, she felt those words were too abstract and too literary. Haruko found herself wanting to make everything doubly certain from Hiroshi by putting down something much more concrete. When she ran a line through these words, she again began to write:

1. No matter what hardships and complications may occur in our love hereafter, can you thoroughly bear up with me under these trials? No matter what external pressures may befall the two of us, can you promise not to leave me as long as the fidelity of our love does not disappear?
2. Supposing I demand you marry me, what would be your reply to that?

3. If I maintain to the very end no desire of marrying you and, rather, hate this relationship of men and women through marriage (especially as constituted as an institution today), what attitude would you take toward this point of view?

4. If I do not want to marry but wish to live with you, what is your reaction?

5. If I wish neither to marry nor to live with you and if I wish to live separately to the last and have a suitable number of days and nights with you, what would you say about that?

6. What ideas do you have concerning children? If I love you and have sexual desire for you but no desire for reproduction, what would your reaction be to that?

7. Do you really intend to move from your present boardinghouse? Or are you not really serious about moving? Might you move any day if it's only a question of money?

8. What prospects do you have for a livelihood hereafter?

Although she could not but sympathize with Hiroshi's shock in having these items she had set down in a rush thrust at him, she could not pacify her troubled heart if she did not behave in this way. If only she could fully understand and captivate Hiroshi's heart, she felt she could stand up for the sake of the successful completion of this love even if the entire world became her enemy.

As if a dagger were being held against him, Hiroshi was quite startled by Haruko's letter with its searching inquiry. At the same time the delicate nerves of Hiroshi the dreamer and idealist were also injured not a little. Haruko was exasperated by his disinclination to write an immediate reply, and she showered upon him letter after letter in rapid succession:

Be it tomorrow or not, please search for a house in the vicinity of Sugamo or Somei. I will immediately begin to find a way for the moving expenses.

That was how impatient she was. An area she could walk to from her father's house, surroundings in which they had sufficient time to love one another freely—these were all Haruko desired. And after these were achieved, she could declare triumphantly to Niizuma and the world her love for Hiroshi. A gardener's detached house or a second-floor flat with no one next door—such rooms were sketched in her fanciful flights of imagination. Though she had misgivings about the unreliable Hiroshi's weak will, they might somehow be able to get along if they seriously cooperated with each other. After a short period of strengthening the foundation of their lives, she would become independent of her parents by leaving their home at the convenient moment. That was Haruko's conception of their future love.

Three letters a day from Haruko reached Hiroshi's lodging, all asking him to make his decision and reply. He felt himself completely fanned by Haruko's passion and besieged by her flames. As she had feared, a scandalous article on her trip to Akagi, Niizuma having spread the news, was already appearing in the papers. She came to feel all the more impatient.

While thinking deeply that no man in any age or

country had ever had thrust under his nose a letter of such rigid and demanding inquiry from a sweetheart, Hiroshi at any rate picked up his pen to reply for the sake of mollifying Haruko, who was becoming hysterical:

1. You can be sure.
2. Let's.
3. Whatever the present institution may be makes no difference to me because it was originally created by man. If marriage is distasteful to you, let's remain as we are.
4. I don't know what you mean. Isn't the situation of two people who love one another cohabiting the real meaning of marriage? What you want to say is you do not wish to marry legally because you cannot approve of today's institution of marriage, but you wish to cohabit—that is what you mean, isn't it? If this is your meaning, my feelings of fastidiousness do not approve very much, but even so let's do as you wish.
5. This answer is similar to 3, but when I think about the present situation, I somehow feel it is impossible.

While writing his replies this seriously, Hiroshi felt himself foolish. He was quite fond of children. Even while walking along the street, he found himself unconsciously driven to speaking when he happened to meet them. As for the children, they took kindly to him. Just imagining the child Haruko might have caused him to smile. But she would probably not be so willing to bear a child. Even while he thought of the mess he would be in, he could not help feeling strongly attracted to Haruko all the same. That the inner Haruko, whom he had formerly viewed as being noble and intellectual as a celestial goddess, was so stuffed with female foolishness and feminine tenderness brought Hiroshi self-confidence. The more impatient and agitated Haruko became, the more calm and assurance Hiroshi had.

As soon as she read Hiroshi's reply, Haruko turned her attention toward searching for lodgings. She discovered a room in the home of a middle-aged widow living with her daughter, and Haruko made Hiroshi move there.

And then in the September issue of *Seito*, she published an open letter entitled "To Mr. N from Akagi." This sensational article, which followed Noe's "Agitation" of the previous month, was even more trumpeted about by journalism. Raicho's open letter was filled with fighting spirit as it condemned Niizuma's jealousy and interference in her love affair with Hiroshi:

> I am clearly declaring anew that H is my darling younger brother and I his elder sister.
> If ever anyone inflicts injury on my love for H, I will mercilessly conquer the intruder.

This open letter in which Raicho vigorously proclaimed her love for Hiroshi resulted in her exposing by herself her own private affairs. In the eyes of the world it appeared that *Seito*, which seemed dyed red in thought, gave rise to a pinkish haze in which the mood of love was enveloped. Many times each day Haruko visited Hiroshi at his lodging to bring him food and carry him books. A life of this kind that resembled playing at housekeeping threw Haruko into raptures. But before long they were asked to vacate the room. The stimulation from the life of unreserved lovemaking by these two people was too much for a widow with a child to raise.

"You see, I still have a daughter to educate."

No words could be found with which to respond to the widow's mild-mannered objection.

Again with extraordinary zeal Haruko located a place. A two-story house for rent along an alley where a Togenuki Jizo deity stood in Sugamo village near the *Seito* office was their new nest of love. At the Maison de Konosu on Christmas Eve, the lovers toasted one another, pledging the future to each other and strengthening their promise to enter a new life. That it was unnatural for them to live separately any longer was Haruko's absolute conviction. At the beginning of the new year, she left her parents' home to plunge into a life with Hiroshi. Another open letter, this time entitled "To My Parents at This Moment of Independence," was published in *Seito*'s fourth volume, the February issue in the third year of Taisho.

The manuscript, dated January 10, 1914, was written in such a thoroughly appealing way as to be unusual for Raicho, its sentences overflowing with gentle emotion. She wrote in a touching confessional manner about the difference in her and her parents' ways of thinking, which were basically contradictory even though they loved and understood one another; about the inconsistencies, mental struggles, and bitter feelings that she and her parents, having their own separate worlds to live in and different dimensions to live by, were existing with despite the fact that they were dwelling together under the same roof; and then about her sadness and her determination that she had to be independent of her sympathetic parents, rebelling against them and making them unhappy.

After her former open letter to Niizuma, Raicho now dared to frankly reveal her attachment to Hiroshi:

There is something particular I must say to you, my parents. What I want to say is different from merely asking you to let me leave home to live by myself, as I have often said in the past, for I am going to begin a life as free and simple as possible with a man whom you have known from early summer last year, a man who visited me constantly at our house, a young man called H, who is five years my junior and whom I have called my "young swallow" and my younger brother, a young man who paints.

Even though I had made up my mind several times to leave, I believe what strengthened my unshakable resolve at the last for me, having been deficient in the courage to boldly carry out that resolution, and what made me accomplish my independence was the power of my love for H. As a rule I have the feeling I want to be gentle and affectionate to people younger than I am— be they men or women. Probably this tendency is connected to my having no younger sisters or brothers, and especially these last few years has that tendency become quite evident to me. Persons my age or older have hardly ever caught my eye, and always those who have come into view as objects of my affection have almost all been my juniors . . . Among those younger persons was the quiet and shy H, who attracted my attention and moved me more than anyone else. H, who is five parts child, three parts woman, and two parts man, became for me increasingly irresistible and charming. And my kisses as his elder sister or as his mother changed, before I realized it, into the kisses of a lover. On the other hand, H was at first full of apprehension as if he were terrified of me, but recently he has become quite dear to me and has behaved toward me as if he were my lover. Having known for the first time what love is, thanks to me, he really loves me with his pure heart. He protects me so much I find it amusing . . . Our love is so deep that if we do not see one another for even a single day, we feel uneasy and cannot settle down to do our work. Since these feelings have come to us for the first time, they mean all the more to us, especially to him.

She explained how in order to eliminate time wasted in visiting each other under uncertain conditions, the only alternative had been to hasten into a life of cohabitation, but afraid that such a life might even deprive her of the power to work, she had thought over the possibility that if it proved unpalatable once she tried it, they could again live separately. She candidly revealed that Hiroshi's economic competence was completely nil and that even the money sent by her parents had come to a halt, and she asserted that if by chance she realized their cohabitation was a failure after the lovers had put it into operation, she would take all the responsibility upon herself and would never bother her parents. Her pen even touched on the subject of a child, which her mother was so anxious about, and clearly laid before the public were Raicho's long-cherished views on the system of marriage:

Since I am dissatisfied with the present system, I do not want to marry under that system or any other sanctioned by law. I have such antipathy toward the institution of marriage I cannot even bear the names husband and wife . . . Nothing is more natural than for a man and woman in love to live under one roof, and I believe the formal wedding ceremony is of no concern if only the two parties agree. Not to marry is all the more natural since marriage prescribes unfavorable claims and duties to the woman. Not only that, but long-established custom and morality carried out in the name of contemporary society contain many inconveniences, including such various irrational burdens as being unnaturally and sacrificially forced to regard the husband's parents as her own, so I do not want of my own free will to place myself under such conditions. Because H understands these reasons quite well, he does not desire to marry.

Not only does logic not permit us to marry, but merely from the matter of our tastes the institution of marriage is offensive. I do not even like to think of H as my husband since it very much dampens my enthusiasm, so when the two of us are out for a walk, H himself hates to have us addressed as Mr. and Mrs. He says it is better for us to forever remain an elder sister and younger brother.

As for a child in the future, we are not in our present situation thinking of conceiving (though how it will be as we move ahead I do not know). I feel I want you to understand that those who place value on themselves and who live for their work do not so rashly give birth to children. Actually, I have almost no desire under the present circumstances to become a mother, and because H is not even independent yet, he is not, from the viewpoint of the world in general, qualified to conceive a child.

When these comments appeared in *Seito*, the two lovers were already immersed in their new life on the second floor of the detached house of a gardener.

That fall in September, the second year of Taisho, in which a worried Raicho was absorbed in bringing to fruition her love affair, Noe had successfully given birth to a boy on schedule. The child, Makoto by name, was treated with love and affection by Noe's mother-in-law Mitsu. The young mother, fully eighteen years old, who had an easy delivery and was doing well after her confinement, had plenty of her own milk.

Impatient during the period of convalescence after the birth, Noe began writing a novel on the subject of her past, and in no time at all she was back with her colleagues at *Seito*. At the very same moment she was blessed by her fated encounter with Emma Goldman.

Though this chance encounter provided Noe with the opportunity to publish in *Seito* Emma's *The Tragedy of Woman's Emancipation*, which Noe as usual had asked Tsuji to translate for her, Noe felt her heart leaping with joy. After she had come in contact with the life and thought of this tragic woman revolutionary and anarchist, it was as if she had at long last discovered the ideal figure of the woman she had been seeking. She was jolted to the depths of her being by Hippolyte Havel's biographical sketch of Emma, which had been especially recommended by Tsuji and which she read with his help.

Noe was captivated by the indomitable way of life in which Emma Goldman, born into a middle-class Jewish family in czarist Russia, had already determined at sixteen that she would devote her life to the liberation of the people, had since then dodged the storms of poverty, persecution, and oppression, had withstood the repeated ordeals of imprisonment and exile, had immersed herself in the propagation of anarchist thought, and lighting the fires of revolution with oil from her own flesh had become with that flame the leader of the workingman. Emma had not merely been a thinker, and the fact that she "lived" to translate theory into action by offering up her own life made Noe's active and passionate blood boil.

"I feel much closer to Emma Goldman than to Ellen Key."

With her eyes glittering in excitement from the impressions she had received in reading Emma Goldman, Noe could not help conveying them to Tsuji.

"That's probably so. Ellen Key's too refined for you. Raicho's happening to come across Ellen Key exactly suits her nature and temperament. In the same way, you and Emma are a good combination. You're both wild, passionate, and active."

Tsuji had clearly perceived that Noe had reached a crucial point at which for good or bad she should unite her easily swayed sensitive nerves to some outside stimulus and supply her thought with something that would serve as backbone. The beautiful and highly cultured Ellen Key, born in Sweden into an aristocratic family, was better suited in personal history and outlook to Raicho. The ideas of Ellen Key, who advocated the equality of the sexes without sacrificing her gentle softness as a woman even as she cried out for the emancipation of women, offered just the right enduring sensibility of taste and nobility to Raicho. In the same way, Tsuji felt that it had been preordained that Emma and Noe were persons born under the same fated star and destined to meet. Tsuji had probably calculated that as Noe's notoriety of a sort increased in society, many temptations would beset her, so for her own safety Noe, who would never be able to firmly defend herself against these temptations, ought to link herself to Emma. Tsuji felt nothing was more productive for Noe than to read even in Japanese Emma's thoughts and biography which he, rather than to say helped her on, practically translated for her in their entirety. As might be expected, Noe digested Emma's thought and life in her own way and passed these into her own flesh and blood:

Emancipation does not mean changing one's hairdo. Nor does it mean walking dressed in a cape. Much less drinking something called "a wine of five colors." However, those people who consider themselves noble and refined by abusing women who dress in the latest fashions and drink, abusing them as if they were committing some terrible sin, those people seem all the more unable to understand what emancipation means. Dress is an expression of taste to those persons who have individuality; to the masses dress means popular fashions. Drinking is no more than one's own personal preference. Neither dress nor drink has any real connection to true emancipation.

Noe cited these familiar examples and went on to explain Emma's opinion of liberation:

Emancipation must make women human in the truest sense. Each and every aspect of the inner woman earnestly desirous of affirmation and activity must obtain its perfect expression in this emancipation. All artificial barriers must be broken. The footprints of obedience and slavery which for centuries have been lying along the thoroughfares leading to great freedom must be swept away.

At the same time, Noe encouraged herself by noting

how lukewarm the suffering of the *Seito* group had been, how simple their agony and oppression when compared to Emma's battles. Noe kept her heart aflame, hoping to make Emma's courage, passion, self-confidence, freedom, everything her own. This essay of Noe's on Emma, together with the translation of Ellen Key's *Love and Ethics*, were published as a single book by Toundo in March of the third year of Taisho. This maiden publication, priced at sixty sen in a purple-covered pocket edition, was Noe's achievement at the age of nineteen, and neither Tsuji nor Noe could have foreseen that in a sense the event would have more significance for her destiny than the birth of Makoto.

Sakae Osugi found Noe's book appealing, and immediately taking it up in the May issue of *Modern Thought*, which he himself published and circulated, he extolled it together with *Seito*. That was in a way the beginning of the fateful encounter between Osugi and Noe.

Sakae Osugi, a year younger than Jun Tsuji, was born in the eighteenth year of Meiji in Marugame in the district of Sanuki. His father Azuma Osugi, a professional soldier, was so conscientious that even in the army he was called a man of virtue. Sakae Osugi himself entered a military preparatory school but was expelled for some violent incident. Although cheerful and optimistic by nature, he had a tendency to stammer, and due to his complex about this deficiency there were times when some strangely violent actions emerged. When he was nineteen by the Japanese way of counting, he went up to Tokyo and entered the fifth-year class of Junten Middle School. That same year he attended Danjo Ebina's Hongo Church and was baptized. At his boardinghouse on Yaraicho as he was studying for the entrance examinations to the Foreign

Language School, he saw some of the university boarders holding large paper lanterns as they went boisterously outside to demonstrate, their banners lettered "Great Oratorical Meeting on the Mine Pollution Problem in Yanaka Village," and he began to take an interest in social problems. At the same time that he was allowed to enter the Foreign Language School, Shusui Kotoku and Kosen Sakai resigned from the *Manchoho* newspaper, founded a weekly, the *Heimin Shinbun*, and advocated as their slogan "Socialism and Pacifism." Sakae Osugi was at that time so inclined toward socialism he could not help running off immediately to join them. With the same zeal with which he had once gone to receive baptism, his hair deliberately cropped short to immerse his head as fully as possible in the sacramental waters, he visited the Sukiyabashi office of Heiminsha one cold snowy night and joined its social study group. It was the close of the thirty-sixth year of Meiji.

"Since I was born into a military family, was raised among soldiers, was taught at a military school, and was quite deeply impressed by the falsehood and stupidity of army life, I want to devote my life to socialism."

With this greeting he joined the group and became such an enthusiastic comrade that afterwards he dropped in at the Heiminsha office almost daily on his way back from school.

The young, handsome, and dignified Osugi was also sexually precocious. By the time he had graduated from the Foreign Language School, he had already lived with a woman twenty years his senior. When he was involved in the Tramcar Anti-Fare-Raising Incident and was cast into prison for the first time, he mastered Esperanto in his cell, and each time he was imprisoned thereafter, he formed the habit of "one offense, one language," and so learned

another foreign tongue. In this year of his first imprisonment, he once again separated from a woman and forced
Yasuko Hori, who already had a lover, to marry him. In the
fortieth year of Meiji, having twice in succession been
thrown into prison for two articles he had written in the
Heimin Shinbun, he was already a full-fledged socialist.
The following year, in the forty-first year of Meiji, he was
again imprisoned for the Red Flag Incident and sentenced
to two years and six months at hard labor. It was this
imprisonment that apparently saved him from dangerous
involvement in the Case of High Treason. Since his
release from prison Osugi had done hack work for
Toshihiko Sakai's Baibunsha, and already he was famous as
a social anarchist who had suffered hardships with his
comrades.

One month after the first edition of *Seito* came out, he
published with Kanson Arahata a monthly periodical
called *Modern Thought*. Masked as a journal of literature
and ideas, it was published to hoodwink the sharp and
coercive eyes of the government authorities and to keep
alive the roots of the socialist movement which had been
completely crushed after the Case of High Treason. Osugi
printed a criticism each month in *Modern Thought*, made
wide appeals to subscribers from various circles, and
created a new trend in the traditional literary magazine.
Such critical essays by Osugi as "Enlargement of Life" and
"Creative Progress" and such essays on current events as
"All of Us Are Hungry" and "What's New?" along with
the works of Kanson Arahata were favorably received by
the literary world. Such ideas and expressions as "the
establishment of self" and "freedom and emancipation"
had become current notions or slogans of a sort. However,
both Osugi and Kanson Arahata became dissatisfied with

putting out a magazine this lukewarm. For the lead article in the May issue of *Modern Thought,* which contained the criticism of Noe's article on Emma Goldman, Osugi wrote an editorial entitled "Intellectual Masturbation." The meaning behind those words was that publishing this unnatural magazine had already become as disagreeable to them as self-pollution. Instead of deceiving themselves by discussion of vague abstract arguments for young bourgeois, they were inclined to advance concrete arguments for laborers, their real comrades. In short, the editorial was an advance notice of Osugi and Arahata's plan to cease issuing *Modern Thought* and to reestablish *Heimin Shinbun.*

Jun Tsuji had regularly been reading the latter since its inception by Shusui Kotoku and had also subscribed to *Modern Thought* from the start. Though he was by nature shy and timid like an urbanite and unable to act, for example, to turn toward the practical activities of socialism, Tsuji had correctly grasped the direction in which the world was moving. At the same time, under the influence of Stirner's *The Ego and His Own,* which he had read with pleasure as if it were his Bible, he had clearly perceived that Osugi had also received Stirner's baptism and that Osugi's thought might be called "Stirneristic anarchism." That Osugi had taken up at this time Noe's work, which was no more than a book Tsuji had translated almost in its entirety, and that Osugi had praised Noe in the highest terms gave Tsuji a kind of titillation.

At the end of her introduction Noe had deliberately specified Tsuji's help:

I must not forget that this work of mine was also brought to completion by T. If T had not been beside me, it could never have been finished, with my poor linguistic ability. Of this fact I want to give particularly clear notice.

Though Tsuji had told her to omit this passage because it would seem artificial, Noe would not hear of it. Her pretext was that everyone knew it anyway. Osugi's high praise had not included a single word about the translation, but was bestowed on Noe for her own thoughts in the preface:

> I am not praising Noe merely because she was strongly influenced by Emma Goldman, who is a socialist, the same as we are. It may seem quite rude, but for a woman so young and born among women who have been raised in ignorance for such a long period, I honestly cannot withhold my admiration at how she could have attained such lucid writing and thought. A man older than I am might be able to say the same thing of Miss Raicho, but her ideas are already vague and muddled, and her outlook is already fixed and immovable. It seems to me the future of Miss Noe is far more worthy of attention . . . If Miss Noe were a little older and wiser, I would expound on her diagnostic misrepresentations and errors, but since she is young and honest, I will remain silent and wait for her noble mind to ferment.

Osugi could not help telling his friends about his interest in Noe and his expectations. He even spoke about her to Kosen Sakai, who dropped in for a visit one day.

"A real woman's finally emerged even in *Seito*. She says she's still leading a life completely unrelated to society, but if she's really the kind of woman she says she is, she'll no doubt fly from that kind of environment before long. It seems she's very strong-willed."

Sakai had also read Noe's book. "Yes, her writing is really quite forceful. I simply can't believe she's nineteen or twenty. Few men can write as powerfully as she can."

"Still, there's a lot of talk her husband helped her a good deal."

"Oh, her poor husband! He's doomed to being thrown away one of these days like a pair of worn-out sandals."

Sakai laughed out loud. Greskofskaya, who was nick-named "the Old Woman of the Revolution" and had joined the movement after abandoning her husband, had been written about by her comrades as "the woman who threw away her husband as if he were a pair of worn-out sandals," so these words had become fashionable among Sakai's comrades. From the very first Osugi had attached no importance to Tsuji. The man was apparently capable in English, but Osugi had heard Tsuji had hardly any academic career and that he was a laggard who had long been unemployed.

"That's probably so. Sooner or later she'll fall in love with someone in our group, or if not she'll separate from that kind of man."

"Oh dear, it's dangerous, dangerous, Yasuko-san. You'd better take care of your husband!" And Sakai laughed.

While laughing, he had mentioned this as a joke to Osugi's wife, who was sitting next to him. Yasuko, a gentle person, her eyes with an unusual glare in them, said ill-temperedly, "You really are hopeless. In no time at all you're always speaking in that way. I heard the two of them were passionately in love and married, weren't they? Can they so easily leave one another?"

But she commented immediately afterward, "Even so, I can't know what my husband will do because of the way he is, can I?" While smiling, Yasuko nevertheless remained with her eyes strangely glaring.

"Don't say such silly things about me," Osugi said to her.

"No, it's really true. Be careful, Yasuko-san. Osugi's sweet on the fair sex."

Though Sakai again laughed it away, he did not trust Osugi, who so easily fell in love with women. From appearance alone Osugi struck one as a great man. In addition to a magnificent physique, he had in some way that beauty of feature which suggests the foreigner, his large distinctive eyes brimming with strange amiability and gentleness. He was so careful about his appearance that he cultivated a stylish mustache, which became him quite well, and he was scrupulously tidy in his clothing. Women found all these things appealing, and Osugi himself did not keep secret his sexual appetite for the opposite sex. Free love had long been his pet theory, and he cherished the idea that if only he loved a certain woman, he could have as many other connections as he wished. From the mere fact that he had been passionate enough to forcibly make Yasuko his own, Yasuko who had had a lover, it was obvious Osugi was a man tender and gentle toward women; in fact, he was quite compassionate to Yasuko, who was in delicate health. Having lived together for eight years already, the married couple was happy, Yasuko devoting herself to Osugi for his affection to her.

From the powerful tone of voice with which Osugi praised Noe, his companions soon suspected a relationship would develop between the two, the members of the group beginning to gossip about it. At the outset of almost every love affair, rumor proceeds at a much faster rate than the realization of the parties concerned, and as fire is generated by the smoke underneath, so in Osugi's case that precedent was not omitted. Since Osugi had seen the naive and schoolgirlish Noe at the *Seito* lecture meeting, he could not restrain his curiosity about her precocious talent. Not to have a girl like her in his group was a loss to socialism. Yes, she would become a superb fighting comrade if she were properly educated. She could be trained as the Emma of Japan. If he cultivated her, it could be possible. As he justified these thoughts in his mind, he admitted to himself that feelings bordering on love for Noe had already sprouted in him.

About two months after his criticism appeared in *Modern Thought*, Osugi, taken by his comrade Masataro Watanabe, visited Tsuji at the home he had recently moved into on Takebayacho. Watanabe had first met Tsuji at Hideko Fukuda's and since then there had been such great affinity between him and Tsuji that Watanabe had become a constant caller. Having started his career as an apprentice to a barber, Watanabe had been awakened to socialism after listening to a speech by Sen Katayama, and after the Kotoku Incident, Watanabe had turned into an ardent anarchist. While working as a barber and a street vendor of wheat gluten, he endeavored to propagandize his isms. It was his joke that if he did so with a razor against a customer's throat, everyone would nod in approval, but because he had been born a Christian and was living along a slope leading to Hakusan on Yubigadani-machi in Koishikawa and because his personal character was so beloved and respected by most everyone, he had been nicknamed Saint Hakusan. Walking around the tenement quarters outside the business center, he did itinerant hair-cutting at one sen a head, children his main clients, his newspaper for the enlightenment of farmers called *Glimmer of Light* continuing to be published in the midst of extreme poverty. Even though he was a barber, he let his own hair and beard grow as long as he wished, and he always appeared in a worn-out kimono, his *haori* cords made of paper, but his thin cheeks and tired eyes weak from tuberculosis were brimming with a Christlike love and benevolence that made everyone admire him. It was unusual for Tsuji with his fear of strangers to become devoted to Watanabe at first sight. On the other hand, Watanabe himself became a friend on finding Tsuji had a surprising amount of knowledge about socialism and, through Stirner's writings, competent opinions on anarchism. Watanabe often visited as if he were an old chum, and because he was fond of children, he was as attached to Makoto as if the infant were his own, and he would want to hold the baby. Badgered by Osugi, Watanabe had accompanied him to Tsuji's.

Appearing unexpectedly at the entrance was Noe holding her baby. Osugi was astonished that the schoolgirlish Noe, who was now every inch a housewife, had become voluptuous.

"How good of you to come! I've been wanting to meet you for a long time. I really have wanted to."

Osugi watched with pleasure as Noe's eyes sparkled amiably, her beautiful teeth seen broadly between her lips, a mixture of innocence and voluptuousness. The more closely he observed the unpretentious Noe, the more youthful and fresh she looked, and he found something charming in the animated movement of her face. Because Tsuji was not at home, Noe deliberately kept Makoto by her on her lap, and while giving the child her breast as if it were quite natural to, she courteously welcomed her guests. Before long, the baby was handed over to Watanabe, as usual.

"I'm surprised you're in such good health. I did hear you were sick and weak, and Mr. Sakai in his essay in *Modern Thought* entitled 'Osugi and Arahata' wrote you had a pale complexion and were quite tall. And so I could only imagine you were a much thinner and paler person."

"Ha, ha, ha, ha. You're disappointed, aren't you? Because I'm such a dark and solid giant!"

Osugi was quite pleased with Noe's frank and easy and friendly reception, which seemed to suggest she might throw herself against his bosom at any moment. It brought pleasure to Osugi's eyes to see that Noe, who wrote dignified articles that would make any male blanch and who with her fighting spirit could snarl at anyone, was merely a fresh youthful woman of twenty or so and, moreover, abundantly overflowing with the pure refined beauty and voluptuousness all women have after child-birth. The turn of her mind could easily be seen by the speed with which she responded to his talk. That she had much more knowledge about socialism than he had expected surprised him.

"If we compare *Seito* to your *Modern Thought*, ours is really like a child's toy. I'm so ashamed."

He had never imagined that Noe, who spoke in this way, had read almost all he had written in his magazine.

Tsuji's mother, dressed plainly but neatly, brought in tea.

When Osugi was about to leave, Noe detained him. "Tsuji will be back very soon. He very much wants to meet you." And he did return a few moments later.

The minute Tsuji entered the front door, he heard Noe's bright laughing voice. Floating before his eyes was the expression on Noe's face at the moment she sat opposite someone, a face filled with liveliness as if from its inner parts a radiant light had emerged. When he came into the room in which the guests were seated, Noe turned her head to look back at him. With cheeks flushed with excitement and a smile spreading across her face suggesting her happiness, she glanced up at Tsuji and as if singing said, "Oh, I didn't notice you'd returned. Dear, Mr. Osugi's here to see you."

Osugi was still focusing on Noe's radiant face. For a moment Tsuji felt estranged, as if he had entered the wrong house.

Osugi did not receive the slightest impression from this small timid-looking man. Even when he began speaking to Tsuji out of politeness, there was no real response, only short noncommittal replies. As had been rumored, Tsuji was, he found, mediocre and worthless. Noe was too good for the likes of such a type. While Osugi made these observations to himself, he felt it was only a matter of time before Noe abandoned this man.

After Osugi and his friend left, Noe said, traces of excitement still on her face, "Oh, was I surprised! I had no idea Mr. Osugi was so strong and powerful. But he's a gentle person."

"Yes."

"He said I had a much more promising future than Miss Hiratsuka. He said he found something interesting in me which he couldn't define."

"He did?"

"As for Miss Hiratsuka's recent declaration of independence, he told me it was interesting that even a person like her had, after all, to use leaving her parents' home as a springboard to realize her love, and so that shows the limits of women today."

"Hm."

"What's wrong with you? Are you sick?"

"I have some translating I have to do by tomorrow. So be quiet for a while."

Noe was offended and left his side. For the first time she became irritated by his unsociable narrow-mindedness, extreme in his likes and dislikes toward her guests. While delicately conscious of Noe's expression behind him, Tsuji himself was wondering why he could not feel that much attraction to Osugi, for whom he had been cherishing so much goodwill. What in the world had Osugi's aim been in visiting them? It was obvious, wasn't it? Tsuji heard a voice inside him saying it was only because of Osugi's interest in Noe.

The everyday life of Raicho, who had dared to live with Hiroshi Okumura, was much more miserable than she had expected. Even though her simple hope for the two lovers to share their days and nights had been realized, the economic means to support it failed to accompany them. They had presumed upon the kindness of friends and acquaintances in asking them to form an association to pay five yen for each of Hiroshi's paintings, but only three or four persons had become members. In addition to those earnings, all they had for living expenses came from Raicho's occasional income from her manuscripts. Rent was seven yen, and no matter how hard they tried to economize, thirty or forty yen besides the rent was vanishing each month. Furthermore, that *Seito* was finally losing its novelty was reflected in the severity of the world's criticism, the magazine's sales gradually dwindling. Although at her parents' home she could, indifferent to almost every household care, use her entire day for her own inner enrichment as she wished, she now had three meals a day and even the laundry to do, all the troublesome duties of editing *Seito* also falling on her shoulders as usual. Though she had written in her open letter as if Hiroshi had made the demand that they live together, it had been Raicho herself who had proposed it. As she had declared in her public letter, it was her responsibility alone to eliminate the pains and contradictions of their new existence and to conquer them. She even learned how to frequent pawnshops, and for the first time she herself went out to solicit ads and collect bills, tasks she was unfamiliar with. Even though she tried to do so, the results were generally ineffective because she had not been trained for such things.

Not surprisingly, their cohabitation was severely censured by society. In spite of their theorizing about it in every possible way, the general consensus was that theirs was nothing but an illicit alliance overwhelmed by sexual desire, even the inner circle of *Seito* not always welcoming their life together.

From the start the *Seito* coterie had worshipped the beautiful Raicho, a kind of implicit homosexual adoration toward her serving to form the underlying tone of their union, so its members had received a shock as if they had been betrayed, keenly disappointed as they were by the fact that Raicho was completely beside herself over the young effeminate Hiroshi. This led to a distrust of Raicho and a cooling in their affection and enthusiasm for *Seito*. In order to gain the love of this one person Hiroshi, Raicho had to sacrifice innumerable friendships. Bitter complaints were heard among the members even about *Seito*'s advertisements of Hiroshi's drawings.

Several months after they were living together, Raicho, completely exhausted physically and spiritually, looked as if her entire body were covered with wounds. Suddenly one summer day a large parcel was sent to her from Mitsukoshi Department Store. When she found a new linen mosquito net inside, tears spontaneously ran down Raicho's cheeks. The heart of Raicho, who with nerves on edge had held her shoulders firm against the world ever since her cohabitation began, was filled with her mother's silent generosity, the tears Raicho had resisted for so long flowing all at once.

Unable to look on with indifference at Raicho's bungling way of life, Noe suggested, "To prepare meals for one or two more people is all the same to us. I can't stand watching you waste your talent on that kind of triviality. Why don't the two of you come to our house and eat with us?"

Raicho was grateful for this proposal, and in no time at all they moved near Myogi Shrine at Kami-Komagome in Noe's neighborhood. At this period the home of Yaeko and Toyoichiro Nogami was just behind Tsuji's, separated only by a fence, and Noe often rushed into Yaeko's house to borrow soy sauce or bean paste and rapidly became friendly with her. With the fence between them as they stood talking to each other, they discussed the biography of Sonya Kovalesky that Yaeko was translating, and they also talked about Wedekind's *The Awakening of Spring*. Yaeko, ten years Noe's senior, had studied under Soseki and had already won recognition in literary circles. She had married her fellow-student Toyoichiro and, with children already, was carrying on a happy intellectual family life. Superior in her powers of reasoning, Yaeko dispassionately criticized *Seito* for its showiness and its emptiness of substance, yet she went about publishing her work in it from the point of view of not wanting to blindly echo *Seito*'s principles. In the same way that Raicho was attracted to Noe, Yaeko loved the young girl for her enthusiasm and single-minded aspiration, exactly the opposite of her own character. Before Yaeko realized it, even she was cherishing her sincere friendship with Noe, who like the directness with which bread absorbs milk had taken into herself all the knowledge she received from the other.

"To put it quite frankly, *Seito* is very low-keyed and dull of late. As Tsuji himself mentioned, your translation of Sonya is its only real highlight."

With a deep sigh Noe made Yaeko, who had nothing to do with the editing of *Seito*, listen to her complaints about the fact that ever since Raicho had begun living with Hiroshi, the editor had not gotten along well with the coterie and had found the magazine difficult to manage. Yaeko had no sympathy whatever for Raicho and Hiroshi's living together. In Yaeko's view, Raicho's opinions on the system of marriage were unquestionably from the very start the empty, puerile, and ridiculous theories of a spoiled daughter.

At about this time Waka Yamada, who had just returned from America, also began to contribute to *Seito*. Her husband Kakichi was well versed on the woman question abroad, a legend having spread that he had picked his wife out of a group of prostitutes and had built her up as a reputable female critic, but no one knew how authentic the story was. As Raicho was deeply impressed by Mr. and Mrs. Yamada's breadth of learning, she decided to attend at the Yamada home on Minami-Igacho in Yotsuya lectures on Ward's *Pure Sociology*, asking Hiroshi and Noe to come. With her baby on her back Noe enthusiastically participated in these meetings, but the Yamadas' plodding regularity and her own wild rusticity did not wear well together, and gradually she stayed away.

Raicho and Hiroshi established the pattern of every day at mealtime setting forth to eat at Tsuji's house, but in less than a month Hiroshi held up his hands in despair. Though he was a vegetarian, Noe always prepared only fried chopped meat in sizzling oil for something that was supposed to be curried rice or stew, so he was unable to bear the situation. Moreover, because of Noe's outrageous manner of cooking, for example, making sukiyaki in a washbasin instead of a pot and chopping onions on the back of a mirror, Hiroshi's nerves could not stand it. In almost no time at all, their communal culinary program was withdrawn at Raicho and her lover's request.

What with economic considerations and Raicho's physical and spiritual exhaustion piling up, *Seito*, for the first time since its inception, missed putting out a number, its September issue. When Raicho thought of the heat of that brilliant summer three years ago, she could not believe the gloom of this year's summer. The moment she published the October issue with its inscription as the third-anniversary number, Raicho, as if escaping, set off for a rest with Hiroshi to the seaside at Onjuku in Chiba prefecture. All of *Seito*'s affairs during her absence were entrusted to Noe.

The month following the publication of this third-anniversary edition, the first number of *Heimin Shinbun* under Sakae Osugi and Kanson Arahata was issued. Those who knew the names of these men regarded as inspiring and heroic the fact that *Heimin Shinbun*, which was to Osugi and Arahata the native soil of their hearts and the very womb of their movement, was appearing in the regenerative light of day in this winter of darkness of still severe oppression since the Case of High Treason. At the same time, the publication of this "newspaper" was watched in breathless anticipation by the socialists as a test case on the future of their movement.

No sooner had the first issue come out than its sale was banned the same day. It had not been unanticipated but the shock was still great.

Noe was burning with indignation in her innermost depths over this event. Since Osugi had suddenly visited her a while back, he had dropped in a few more times. He was usually accompanied by Watanabe or Sukeo Miyajima, another of Tsuji's acquaintances. With Tsuji always at home, Osugi gradually came to be more sociable toward him. From some expression in Osugi's large eyes or some nuance in their conversation, Noe sensed he was favorably disposed toward her. Though glad to talk to Tsuji about anything, no matter how trivial, Noe could not bring herself to confess this certain kind of "feeling."

"Don't you think Mr. Osugi's taken a slight fancy to me?"

"Don't be so conceited."

Noe was seized by a kind of premonition that she could not dismiss the matter with such a light remark.

In the November issue of *Seito*, for whose editing she was entirely responsible for the first time, Noe resolutely gave vent to what she had been thinking about the *Heimin Shinbun* incident:

No sooner had the *Heimin Shinbun* of Messieurs Osugi

and Arahata appeared than its sale was banned. When I think of how the precious items in those ten pages have gone to waste, I cannot help spilling tears. I am one of those who have a secret feeling of esteem for both these men with their powerful and congenial spirit and their profound fervor. Luckily I was able to read the issue.

I distinctly felt that the great ardor and power of both these gentlemen were vibrating through the entire space of that newspaper. What they had written had mainly to do with the awakening of the workingman. However, I feel the logic behind what they wrote does not apply merely to laborers but to all people. I cannot help but be suspicious as to why this newspaper should incur the displeasure of the authorities when it limited its remarks only to the workingman. Why is it not permissible to say and teach what is reasonable and just? I had wanted to introduce here some part of their newspaper if it had been possible, but since I heard that the entire ten pages had offended the authorities and if I reproduced any section I would suffer a by-blow in a crime of my own in printing it, I will refrain because all my hard work will have come to naught. But from the depth of my heart I do sympathize with Messieurs Osugi and Arahata. It may sound somewhat empty and transparent and strange, but I cannot find any other words at present.

When Osugi read Noe's article, he was jubilant. Could there have been any better love letter to appeal so directly to his heart? He felt as if he could detect in Noe's simple indignation a compassion and love for himself alone.

"What do you think of this! While each and every one

nervously puts on an ignorant face, only *Seito* has taken up the subject. It looks hopeless, doesn't it?"

With this ironical remark Osugi showed Noe's article to Arahata and tried to get him to reprint it in its entirety in the second number of *Heimin Shinbun*. Because Arahata from the first had held the New Women in contempt and because he was most sensitive to Osugi's rapid attraction to Noe of late, he was not as transported with joy as Osugi and did no more than briefly report it in three lines.

Just as they were about to publish their second number, they saw from inside the printer's office more than ten alerted police investigators surrounding the building and preparing to seize the newspaper the moment it was published. Though Osugi and Arahata broke through this iron ring by car, there was hardly any place to hide the newspapers they carried out with them. The copies Masataro Watanabe had received in trust had been taken to a confectioner's shop in Kanda. But an assistant police inspector was discovered lodging on the second floor. When Watanabe, highly perplexed at Tsuji's house, asked what countermeasures they might consider, Noe sprang to her feet and said, "Leave it to me."

At such moments something about Noe suggested no one would be able to stop her. After she rode alone in a taxi to the confectioner's shop and loaded all the papers deposited there into the car, she quickly left and came back home.

Having heard about this episode from Watanabe, Osugi was all the more captivated by Noe's resolution and power of execution. In Noe, who was about twenty and undeniably small and lively, Osugi could not help but feel an affection which had a more intimate trust in it than that of his comrades.

In *Seito* that month, as she had done in the previous number, Noe again indignantly assailed the banning of the sale of *Heimin Shinbun*:

> I am not a socialist, nor am I an anarchist. But I have an interest in these movements. I even have sympathy for them. It is natural for me to have sympathy for them because their doctrines are truthful. It is quite natural to have such an interest.
>
> I feel that these persons in present-day Japan are not so dangerous. No matter how hard they strive, their ideas cannot be grasped quickly by our people. It seems to me that the oppression inflicted on these men has been too severe. In this densely populated country of ours, the people regarded as socialists are, I hear, fewer than three thousand. And I have heard that just about all of them are afraid of being oppressed. I believe their situation is hopeless. Only a few would truly sacrifice themselves for their principles. The disaster of twice banning the sale of the twice-published H newspaper will expose the excessive timidity of our government.

When she had written that much, Noe was reminded of the cowardice and lethargy of her own group, which Osugi had once told her looked only to its own safety. While Noe impatiently drove her pen along, she even abused her colleagues who with their weak spirit had not tried to help Osugi and his friends. And swallowing whole the complaints Osugi had at one time made to her about his dissatisfaction with his wife, Noe declared:

> Especially from a woman's point of view do I hope the

wives of these men of principle will be more assimilated to their husbands. If these wives thought how much that fusion with their comrades would help the movement, they would desire to become a little more generous. The behavior and attitude of these wives, which I have heard about directly and indirectly, have been quite vexing.

Even while Osugi regarded Noe's article as too simple, outspoken, and immature, when he considered her youth he came to think how lovely it was that she could be this earnest and courageous, unafraid of the censure of the world or the opposition of the authorities. As for those around him, they disposed of the matter either by laughing it off or showing their ill will toward Noe. They surmised that Osugi had probably courted her by disparaging Yasuko. The truth was that their wives—Yasuko, Tameko, who was the former's elder sister and the wife of Sakai, and Yayo, Watanabe's wife—had not only adapted themselves to their husbands, but as wives of men of principle had calmly assisted them in their work despite the anxiety of not knowing whether they would be deprived of their husbands at any moment, all the while silently maintaining their families and to the last firmly bearing poverty and oppression.

Osugi's colleagues unremittingly derided Noe merely for trying to befriend them, blaming her immature smattering of knowledge as the cause of her absurd remarks. They felt it ludicrous for Osugi to announce to them his intention of putting Noe to use as a comrade in some practical way and for failing to admit to himself his own amorous impulses.

Tsuji did not show any particular opposition to or approval of Noe's utterances. Seeing that her assertions were at least correct, he felt he could not but admit that Noe's courage was quite beyond his own. In no small degree was he surprised at her ability to be so deeply and instantaneously impressed by his casual words to her or by the impressions Osugi and Watanabe had carelessly expressed, an ability that could digest these comments by interpreting them in her own way and could then eject them as rapidly as bullets from a machine gun.

"That too is one of her talents, I guess."

Although Noe's stories were not the least bit interesting and differed by not so much as a hair's breadth from a composition, Tsuji had to admit that the high-spirited descriptions of her impressions, supported by her self-confidence and vitality, had for about a year become more and more animated.

At this time an unexpected stroke of good fortune befell Tsuji and Noe. The translation of Lombroso's *The Man of Genius,* which Tsuji had worked on hard and steadily ever since his loss of employment, had been making an endless journey among publishers for almost two years, the house that had first promised to bring it out having gone bankrupt. Noe was quite vexed about it, and instead of the passive Tsuji, she herself endeavored to make the rounds with whatever letters of introduction she had received to try to sell the translation. But no matter where she went, no one would consent to a book by Lombroso, who was not well known in Japan, not to mention the fact that the translator himself was unrecognized. However, a member of Sotaikai, Saburo Ogura, who happened to have read Noe's "Agitation" and was attempting a sexual analysis of the heroine's dilemma, introduced Noe to Uetake Shoin.

This publishing house, which was to later bring out *War and Peace* and *Une Vie*, had just issued Artzybashev's *Sanine* and was willing to immediately publish Tsuji's translation.

The bright tidings were like a dream to Tsuji. When he reflected on the fate of his translation, which had continually been handed around to others ever since its completion and had received all kinds of contempt and maltreatment, its acceptance was an unbelievable joy. In the long run Tsuji could not but feel thankful to Noe for this good fortune brought about by her reckless strategy and endeavor against impossible odds.

Tsuji was seized with love for Noe as he watched her openly pleased, skipping about the room like a child and saying, "Oh, it's wonderful! Now I can be puffed out with pride toward that crowd which so maliciously said you were a laggard and a fool even though they knew nothing about you! 'See here, amuse yourselves by looking at my husband's real ability!'" Tsuji was filled with tenderness for her, feeling she was after all his one and only better half in this world. The memory of their numerous hardships and humiliations contained in this translation and recollected at a bound moved Tsuji, off guard, to tears.

"Now I can tell you this because they are going to publish it. I was obsessed and regretful about this translation because I was always missing the chance to get it published. I thought I couldn't die in peace if it wasn't published, and often I woke up at night shuddering."

It was rare for him to vent such a frank confession.

The translation was scheduled to be published without fail by the end of December, and Tsuji was busily engaged in correcting the final galley proofs.

Meanwhile, Noe was equally blessed with a great turning point in her life. Instead of Raicho, she had brought out almost by herself two issues of *Seito*, the October and November numbers, and a certain self-confidence and ambition had begun to stir in her. It was a self-confidence with which she herself might possibly put out the magazine, a dream that without having to be restrained by Raicho or any of the other senior members, she might obtain a much more remarkable result if she were allowed to freely put the entire volume to practical use on her own responsibility.

What urged that dream on was the deep impression she received from the courage with which Osugi and his friend had issued *Heimin Shinbun*. In the midst of a social situation in which they had to suffer oppression just for printing a mere ten-page newspaper, the dream swelled inside her that she had to make *Seito*, with its many more pages and a market, into a much more significant, valuable, and useful magazine.

Having gone to Onjuku, Raicho for the first time in ten months of cohabitation could dismiss from her mind the curious eyes of the world and immerse herself in her life of love with Hiroshi. Was it a mere dream to ask Raicho, who had no intention of returning for some time, to transfer *Seito* from her shoulders to Noe's own round ones? As soon as the idea occurred to Noe, her innate tendency to act began without a moment's delay.

Chapter 5

AT THE BEGINNING of November, Noe sent a long letter to Raicho at Onjuku with a copy of the November issue of *Seito*. To be more exact, it was to sound Raicho out on the possibility of transferring *Seito* to Noe, the expectation being that Raicho was no longer interested in running the magazine:

> I'd like the job to have a little closer connection to my personal life, but since the work at present is hanging in midair, it's rather difficult to. If you leave all of the responsibility in our hands, we will once again be resolute, and we will try to do as much as we possibly can.

At the outset Raicho had not thought it possible to leave the edition of *Seito* only to Noe, who was still very young. From the first Raicho had relied on Tsuji, her opinion of his erudition and character high. After Raicho and Hiroshi had come to live nearby and the families had begun associating, she found that Hiroshi, who was shy among strangers, was getting along well with Tsuji, often exchanging views on literature and art with him, so that all the more she came to have feelings of goodwill and trust

toward Tsuji. When she left for Onjuku, she had thought
Tsuji would take charge of the editing with Noe, so Raicho
had entrusted *Seito* to her. And because Noe had known
about Raicho's attitude, she had from the very start proposed that Raicho leave the editing to the two of them. At
the conclusion of this tedious contradictory letter, Noe
first modestly humbling herself as incompetent and then
immediately exposing her self-confidence, was the radical
proposal of asking Raicho to withdraw to let Noe assume
the editorship.

As might have been expected, Raicho thought the
matter serious, so after receiving Noe's letter on November 7, she went back to Tokyo on the thirteenth to discuss
the question directly with her. Noe's second letter, which
passed Raicho on the way, was forwarded to her. In this
second letter Noe's aggressive feelings were enumerated
even more openly:

> We will work with all our might, and even though it will
> be quite difficult for you to live entirely on it, we will
> send you about twenty yen at the beginning, and, of
> course, when we are able to send more, we will . . . What
> do you think? If you agree, we want to thoroughly
> change our lifestyle and to devote ourselves as much as
> possible to *Seito*, and then we think we can do the editing
> in a much simpler way and in a much shorter period;
> moreover, we can try to do other things too. Would you
> be so kind as to entrust everything to us? However, I
> think it better that you remain on the magazine as its
> senior representative. We will, of course, assume any
> and all responsibilities. We have absolutely no intention
> of causing any trouble to our senior representative, so I
> pray that you put your trust in us.

Raicho felt a ludicrousness and repulsiveness toward Noe, who with her concrete dream had already resolved to completely take over the magazine. Raicho even came to feel angry about Noe's arrogance in saying so rudely and authoritatively that they would send her twenty yen and that Raicho's name would still remain on the magazine. Because *Seito* was the magazine to which she had devoted innumerable thoughts, both pleasant and painful, Raicho felt she ought to discontinue publishing it once and for all. At the same time, however, she felt regret when she reflected that if she stopped publishing *Seito*, which up to now had been saturated with her own hardships and pains, it would mean she had succumbed to the world's suppression. If such were the case, should she not hand it over to Noe, who was so eager to try to do it? At the end of all Raicho's doubts and perplexities, she was gradually drawn toward Noe's proposal.

Visiting her on the morning of the fifteenth, Raicho saw a Noe radiant in lively anticipation and hope. Noe revealed without hesitation or reserve an enthusiasm in wanting to take immediate charge of the magazine. When Raicho realized that all of her colleagues had left her and that it was this youngest of the *Seito* members who trusted in her and stood by her to the very end, she felt quite sympathetic to Noe in spite of herself. Raicho came to think it might be better to stake her destiny on the daredevil vitality of Noe, who was always busy and who even in the midst of that busyness and under extreme tension had discovered her real self. Even Katsu Kobayashi, to whom Raicho had been so attached, had now fled to the camp of Kokichi and Ichiko Kamichika and as if pitting herself against *Seito* had become a member of their women's magazine *Saffron*. Should Raicho transfer *Seito* to this one and only loyal

274 • BEAUTY IN DISARRAY

confidante who had remained by her? Although she felt
Noe was the exact opposite in character to her, Raicho had
come to cherish a familiarity and trust she could approve of
in Tsuji's practical way of thinking. At the same time she
had clearly perceived the self-interest Noe had been driven
to in trying to make the magazine the basis of her own
livelihood by bringing *Seito* to prosperity. Raicho even
conjectured that because her own way of managing the
magazine was that of an unsophisticated ignorant girl
belonging to a bourgeois family, she had gone into the red,
and so Noe was secretly thinking that if she were asked to
run it for Raicho, she would succeed in making a real profit
out of it. While talking with Noe, Raicho found welling up
in herself the desire to sunder as soon as possible her
practical contacts with the bothersome world, confine
herself to the pastoral life of romance only with Hiroshi,
and more and more gauge the fullness of her own inner
life. After Raicho returned home that day, she forwarded
on a postcard her determination to hand over all the
business to Noe.

In high spirits brimming with hope, self-confidence,
and courage, Noe visited Raicho on the seventeenth.
Raicho turned over everything to her except *Seito*'s back
numbers, which she wanted to keep as mementos, and on
that same day Raicho shut up her home. If she was washing
her hands of *Seito*, she would also move from the house she
had used as her office, and she intended to begin a
thoroughly private life with Hiroshi in completely new
surroundings. It was in this way that Noe fully carried on
her own twenty-year-old shoulders the heavy responsibility of being both in name and fact the manager as well as
chief editor of *Seito*.

As might have been expected, the world was startled by

this event. Because Noe's youthfulness and recklessness due to her ignorance of the world had made her snap indiscriminately and scathingly in *Seito* at all her opponents and even at celebrities who offered opinions she did not like, bawling and yelping at them like a pup, journalism itself had half-in-fun overlooked her conduct, never thinking it possible for the twenty-year-old Noe to carry on her shoulders alone the weight of *Seito*. At any rate, the press had to admit Raicho's personality had cut a brilliant figure among the female critics. Not only the difference in age between Raicho and Noe was felt, but their status as personalities could not bear comparison. Rather than regarding Raicho's transfer of the magazine as unselfish, they were dumbfounded by her recklessness and all the more open-mouthed in amazement at Noe's foolhardiness in undertaking the task. With the thought that Noe would not be able to put out even two issues of the magazine, the world heaped ridicule upon her.

In fact, Noe had not been able to procure even a single advertisement no matter where she went. Tsuji was solely taken up with his Lombroso, and at best he could only advise her while talking in bed about where to gather manuscripts and the like.

"Ultimately a magazine of this type must be carried out by the editor's own decisions. Raicho was too good-natured, so she paid too much respect to other people and failed. That she used the system of consulting others was, I think, the cause of her lack of success with *Seito*. She ought to have carried everything out under her own personality. The flash of genius peculiar to her was completely demolished and dulled by that system of mutuality. Your *Seito* should be carried out by your devil-may-care vitality! That's the only way."

Though he gave her this advice, he did not help her in any practical way. After having to solicit ads all by herself, to go out to negotiate with paper dealers and printers, proofread, send replies to readers, do household chores, rear her baby, and perform other tasks, Noe realized for the first time that what she had wrested from Raicho by force was a heavier burden than she had imagined. When she went out, she found ridicule and contempt waiting for her instead of encouragement. Every letter from *Seito*'s readers was the more keenly expressive of regret about Raicho, though it was no use now because it was too late, and all of them expressed only misgivings about Noe's talents. In her room beside the entrance which she used as her editorial office, she felt as if she were being heavily pushed and overpowered by anxieties and responsibilities about her future. At such moments her innate and unyielding will to win gushed up within her. Resistance and anger against the world's cold scorn blazed up in her to provide a form of energy for her work. With her hands she knocked down her own faintheartedness and nerved herself for the struggle.

One such day Osugi came to call on her. With the remark "It's my thanks for the other day," he held out to her Kropotkin's *The Conquest of Bread*, and he gazed at her as if he were going to envelop her with his large eyes. What he had meant was her having hid in her home copies of the second number of *Heimin Shinbun*. Tsuji was also present, and the three talked together as if they were old friends. Noe was even more impressed than before by the courage and fortitude with which Osugi so passionately wanted to bring out his newspaper in spite of its being banned no matter how often it was published. As it was the period in which she had stood in the midst of ridicule and had tasted the bitterness of loneliness after taking over *Seito*, Noe was moved by the promise of Osugi's self-confident attitude, a vitality in his large body and a cheerfulness in his expression as if nothing had happened despite the unreasonable oppression against him. He encouraged Noe in her future endeavors with *Seito*.

"Although it's long been one of my pet theories, Raicho's era is already over. Even though the things she said seemed new, she was in the long run only a petty bourgeois by nature, a person who could see only herself. The other day I happened to come across something she published in some magazine, and in it she wrote that she had nothing to do with the world, that it was actually annoying for her to have any connection to it. And while she said this and that about the substantiality of her inner life, what in the world was this splendid inner life which had such enormous significance for her? What a huge joke! Is it possible for anyone to do any kind of progressive work in this generation of ours by turning his back on the world! At any rate, *you* have courage. I have a much better opinion of that unknown quality in you than in Raicho. I say, isn't that so, Mr. Tsuji?"

Oppressed by Osugi's enthusiastic turn of phrase, Tsuji merely smiled, remaining silent. As if to change the subject, he whispered to Noe, "That reminds me of the old copies of *Heimin Shinbun* in the house. We have to hide them somewhere."

Hearing that Tsuji had kept all the numbers of *Heimin Shinbun* since the days of Shusui Kotoku, Osugi was surprised. He felt he had to take another look at this irresolute little man.

"Is that anything to be so concerned about?" said Noe, regarding it as a mere trifle.

At that moment Noe suggested on impulse, "Oh, what with its being so frequently banned, just the waste of paper must be unbearable! Should I send some of *Seito*'s paper to you? Since we have to buy it every month anyway, we won't mind at all." That Noe, who had only just acquired *Seito* from Raicho, should make such a bold offer surprised Osugi. Though he was by no means so simple as to immediately accept her generosity, he fastened her kind remark deep in his heart. To Noe, who had been suffering from the world's misgivings and ridicule and who had been troubled by feelings of solitude, Osugi's sudden visit and his open and frank encouragement made her so happy she shed tears. She felt anew the courage welling inside her.

With the two articles "*Seito* and I" by Raicho and Noe's "On Taking Over *Seito*" appearing side by side in the January number, volume five, in the fourth year of Taisho, Noe clearly revealed her attitude to the world. Raicho made public a part of Noe's letter which had been sent to her at Onjuku, clarified the process by which she had arrived at her decision, and concluded:

I have handed over to Noe-san not only my participation, but all the possessions from my work.

Hinted at between the lines was Noe's audacity, which might be construed as having deprived Raicho of her rights by force. Raicho, on the other hand, emerged as a magnanimous, impartial, and generous figure for the way she had withdrawn.

Ignoring these matters, Noe wrote:

Little by little I gradually came to feel from that time a change in the direction of my thought. It seemed to me that up to the present there had been quite a gap between society and me.

To become a socialist then was considered by me to be rather unnatural and forced. But before I realized it, I did not think being socialistic was so contradictory. Even if I jumped right into the middle of the socialist movement now, I have come to feel there would not be any special contradiction or pain.

At any rate, from now on I am taking all the work of *Seito* into my own hands. I will rely on my own powers only. I want no help from anyone. So I am stopping the membership system, and I wish to work for the greater emancipation of all women . . . First, I am removing all the bylaws of the Seito Society we have followed until now.

Henceforth, *Seito* has no regulations, no policies, no causes, no isms. Those who desire isms and cannot do without regulations had better make their way by themselves.

The only thing I am providing for all women is a magazine without isms, without policies, without regulations . . . Those who wish to use *Seito* as a springboard for rising in the world are free to do so, and those who wish to publish their thoughts are asked to please do so. In order for the magazine to be helpful to those who wish to use it, I will let it have no significance whatsoever in itself. I only ask that the selection of manuscripts be left entirely to me . . . I don't mind being a mere laborer for management and editorship.

It was a radical bill of reform full of daring self-confidence for a twenty-year-old chief editor.

In her practical daily life Noe had much less time than

before to pay attention to domestic duties, and when she came home after spending the entire day bustling about from one place to another and was forced to listen to Mitsu's complaint, "Since Makoto went over to where you hang your everyday clothes and cried remembering you, I was at my wits' end," Noe felt her heart contract. Nevertheless, now that things had come to this pass, her unyielding spirit stirred within her to continue the magazine at any cost. When she finished editing the January number, she felt as if the courageous excitement of a knight's breathing were seething within her as she vowed frankly toward the phantoms of all her supposed enemies:

> I want you to watch and see whether or not I am strong enough to continue this magazine. As long as I have breath, never will I release my grip on *Seito!*

On December 11, the day Noe, as if possessed, was putting the finishing touches on the editing of the January issue, Lombroso's *The Man of Genius* was finally published by Uetake Shoin as one of its books in the Uetake Library Series. Its favorable response was greater than expected, the reaction that its sales would call for some twenty or so successive reprintings unforeseen.

For the first time since Noe began living with Tsuji, the chance offered itself for him to bring to his family a large sum of money. After an interval of many years Mitsu and Tsune could put on bright expressions and welcome in a new year that really looked like one. When Tsuji remembered those New Year holidays on which he had not enough left over to buy even a single nib for his pen, he was as happy as if he were in a dream.

Though it might be said that from one point of view

Noe had never experienced a time in which she was this calm and happy since beginning to live with Tsuji, she could not help but feel the piling up of a vague dissatisfaction with him.

Now that Tsuji was contributing money to the house, Mitsu, who until this time had controlled herself as much as possible, was no longer able to restrain her discontent toward Noe. Having grown impatient over Tsuji's shiftlessness ever since he had lost his job, the mother had to hesitate in saying what she wanted, even to Noe, despite realizing that the cause of Tsuji's unemployment was her. The very fact that the scant amount of money Noe brought into the family was the only definite source of funds to support their meager budget made Mitsu feel she had been forced to keep her mouth shut about Noe's continually going out to *Seito*, returning late at night, and even occasionally staying away overnight even though she was a woman with a family. Originally Mitsu had liked her. Fond of the bright and cheerful, Mitsu had believed the existence in her home of the young and lively Noe would brighten it. That she was hardly able to do any housework, that Tsuji did not want her to be taught how and so she had never been like a real daughter-in-law, and that she had not been half as useful as Tsune, all these things had not troubled Mitsu very much. But the way Noe had become engrossed in *Seito* ever since she had formally taken over the magazine smacked of insanity. Whenever Noe went out, Makoto was thrust upon Mitsu, the child's mother on the move from one place to the next the entire day. And when Noe was at home, she merely confined herself to her room just beside the entrance and busied herself putting manuscripts in order. Such conduct was all right during the time Tsuji had no income, but now that he was able to bring some money into the house, why should Noe not settle down to turning her thoughts to housework and childrearing? Mitsu would often complain and reveal such attitudes. Though Noe did not like housework and was poor at it, the fact remained she could do these things if she tried, all of which proved quite provoking to Mitsu.

Mitsu was apt to complain with some insinuating remark. "In the middle of taking care of a child, a woman has no time to read books." The situation was much worse when Mitsu was told that even though Noe had taken charge of *Seito*, not only might she need more money than before but might run the risk of losing money if she was not careful, so Noe's activities seemed to Mitsu a useless diversion. She was likely to start a quarrel with Tsuji by saying, "Can you scold your wife with just one word as a husband should?" even while she tried to work on Noe's sympathies with the comment, "Jun is really to be pitied, isn't he? If you were an ordinary wife, he'd be looked after in all ways. If I die, what would he do?"

As for Noe, she felt that for a woman to occupy herself only with housework and childrearing meant her position as a woman would never be improved, and she herself at least wanted to grow more and more as a human being, not merely to be a wife and mother. Although she thought it would be better if Tsuji defended her by standing between herself and Mitsu, he almost never had any inclination to. From Noe's point of view, all things considered, he had real affection for his luxury-loving parent no matter what remarks he might make to his mother, and though there were times when he abused her if the occasion demanded, his blood ties were so strong that just the three of them, the mother and her two children, often became perfectly united. On those occasions Noe felt as if she had been cast out by herself, Tsuji seemingly far removed from her. From the moment she had come to live in this house, her not being treated as a young wife would seem to have been due to Tsuji's ideas, so she did not comprehend that her position in this family was a much greater blessing than that of most wives in society. The very fact that she had a mother-in-law and a sister-in-law who bore her share of the housework and the raising of her child tended to make Noe forget how much she could occupy herself with *Seitō* and her other activities, and she magnified her reactions to the emotional tangle and harassments she felt.

One January day Noe heard for the first time from Mr. and Mrs. Masataro Watanabe, who dropped in for a short visit, the news about Yanaka village. Due to the fact that this village, located along the shores of the Watarase River in Tochigi prefecture, received its water supply from the same source as the Ashio copper mine, pollution from the mine had been flowing into the river, the farmlands and fisheries throughout the downstream areas heavily damaged as a result. All the victims had combined forces under the leadership of Shozo Tanaka and fought tenaciously, culminating in the famous Incident of the Direct Appeal to the Emperor by old Mr. Tanaka, and for a while an agreement had been reached between the mine owners and victims, with the government acting as intermediary. However, even after the compromise the mine-pollution problem revived each time a flood occurred, so the government established plans to prevent the river from inundating by making the entire village area a reservoir. Even since the fortieth year of Meiji, from the moment the government began purchasing the land around Yanaka village, the inhabitants had mounted a campaign against the plan and had stubbornly tried to resist.

Meanwhile, purchase of the land by the government was made compulsory, but the die-hards who stayed on to the last persistently refused to sell. Finally, the government, having reached the boiling point over the entire affair, determined to evacuate the area by force and rapidly began demolishing the homes of the insurgents one after another.

This problem, which had been smoldering for thirty years, was common knowledge to the informed, but it was a revelation to the young Noe. As Watanabe was burning even more with indignation because he was explaining it all very simply to the unenlightened and easily moved Noe, she was so upset herself she was immediately reduced to tears. Those who had fought on even when their homes were destroyed after they were ordered to evacuate the area ten years previously and were remaining in shacks had been driven into a desperate situation because with the completed reservoir surrounding them, water was overflowing from the river as the spring thaw set in, and if they remained, they would sink to the river bottom along with their makeshift shelters. Watanabe suggested going to see these conditions while there was still time.

"Why in heaven's name would the world abandon them?" asked Noe, red from surprise and anger, as if closing in on Watanabe.

"You've only just heard about it, so you're startled, but, you see, it's already thirty years since the struggle began. People merely have the feeling, 'Dear me! Are they still at it?' At any rate, now that it's so late, they don't know how to solve it."

Noe was unconvinced by this explanation alone and still asked many questions.

Though Tsuji kept silent as he listened to their talk, he

felt inwardly that Noe's way of getting excited was comical. He could understand how the easily moved and easily agitated Noe could become aroused on hearing about this conflict for the first time, and he could also understand the feelings of Masataro Watanabe, practical activist and idealist to the core, in wanting to take the trouble to inspect the situation. However, for Noe, unable to pay even the slightest attention to her own child, to say nothing about doing housework, to be stirred like a savior toward some miserable affair of the entire nation was from Tsuji's point of view quite droll.

For the past few days the gap between his mother and Noe had turned critical, and having been forced to listen to complaints from both parties, Tsuji had come to feel quite disgusted. Noe burned with indignation as she said Tsuji had completely failed to understand her point of view and had not shielded her from her mother-in-law. Though he felt his mother's complaints were those held by all mothers-in-law in society, he doubted, to do his parent justice, if a young wife who had acquired the amount of freedom Noe had was the common order of the day. From the very beginning he had made his mother and sister agree to give Noe enough time to allow her to study, and it was for this reason that Tsuji himself had not expected Noe to do the work of an ordinary housewife. Fortunately both his mother and sister were quite good at domestic chores, and because the two of them worked, everything inside the house ran smoothly, there being almost no tasks for Noe. That was the very reason why Noe could freely visit *Seito* and why she had been given ample time to read her books and write her manuscripts.

The trouble occurred after they had the baby. Noe found that just the baby alone was too much for her, that it

286 · BEAUTY IN DISARRAY

was completely beyond her control. She had thought that if she only tried she could accomplish anything, including doing her housework and raising her child, tasks possible for any woman, yet Noe discovered all she actually did was parade around with a small red lump of flesh, her arms carrying a baby who merely screamed and could not speak. In order to catch the desire behind the child's crying voice, she would have had to spend twenty-four hours a day with it. This small tyrant screamed out even in the middle of the night and had to be fed. Whenever Noe did not know how to handle the shrieking child, her mother-in-law would take it in her arms, and instantly the crying would cease. Without realizing it was due to her own inexperience and her immaturity in childrearing, Noe concluded that the crying resulted from her mother-in-law's pampering the baby by perpetually holding it during her absence. She could certainly not ask her mother-in-law to wash diapers, much less give it her breast. The mere birth of a child made Noe's everyday schedule hopeless. Even though she sometimes attended meetings with the child strapped to her back, she could not be at ease. And when she went out alone after entrusting the child to her mother-in-law, she felt refreshed, and wondering why she had been so careless as to have given birth to a child, she felt remorse.

Though she appealed to Tsuji about her opposition to her mother-in-law's opinions on the raising of a child, he hardly ever gave Noe anything that could even be called a reply. As for the housework and childrearing, Tsuji had absolute trust in his mother's abilities, and he had, more than anyone else, witnessed Noe's clumsiness. He felt rather more contempt for Noe, who had been swept off her feet by such a matter-of-fact dispute between a bride and her mother-in-law, so common in society. Having expected from the first that Noe would realize she was not an ordinary housewife, Tsuji had believed she would cast away all household chores and childrearing and with much more dignity entrust all these matters to her mother-in-law by cajoling her, it being much better for Noe to pursue her own studies.

Noe challenged Tsuji's views on these matters by saying, "You're her own flesh and blood but it can't be like that between me and your mother!"

Finding the conventions, falsehoods, and deceptions of society which she was in the habit of talking against nesting deeply rooted in the very center of Noe's own sentiments, Tsuji felt like forcing a smile. But to explain to her each of these contradictions and to make her even more excited would have been quite troublesome. Rather, he wanted to appropriate time of this sort, even a minute of it, to his own reading.

One should face one's difficulties by oneself and by suffering grow from them and solve them. Noe was no exception.

While casting a side glance at Noe writhing in an agony of pain, he watched her with the hope that she would immerse herself in her work as the person responsible for *Seito* and would find some way out of her difficulties and into her inherent good qualities.

Even after the Watanabes left, Noe was unable to release herself from the shock she had received in the conversation about Yanaka village. She wanted to talk more about it with someone. While breast-feeding Makoto, she probed into her mind, which was seething with excitement. Gradually the face of a man clearly flashed before her—his prominent nose, a mustache just below. Osugi would listen to her much more carefully, wouldn't he?

Without knowing why, Noe had absolutely no desire to speak to Tsuji, who was just beside her. Probably because he had hardly put in a word edgewise during her talk with Watanabe, and when he finally did, she had felt he was indifferent to this problem by saying to Watanabe that no matter what they tried to do, the situation was hopelessly beyond saving.

"What are you brooding so much about?" Tsuji asked, looking back at her from his desk.

Noe finally separated her breast from Makoto, who even while sleeping had the nipple in his mouth, and as if angry, she said, "About Yanaka village that we were discussing just a while ago."

"Oh. That insignificant thing! You'd better stare at your own feet rather than think about that!"

Noe was offended. She realized Tsuji was alluding to the unpleasant situation of the last few days with her mother-in-law.

"To make a long story short, no matter how hard they struggle, it's useless. To keep struggling over something so obviously useless is ridiculous. Would those people go to their death by drowning? Their resistance comes only from spite. Your getting all stirred up is much too senti-mental."

Turning around in bed, Noe made her back stone-rigid as if to protect herself from Tsuji's voice.

A few days later Noe ruined several sheets of stationery trying to write to Osugi. She was dying to talk to him, after all, about the problem of Yanaka village, which had been smoldering in her heart ever since the time of the Watanabe visit. Why did her confidant have to be Osugi? The fact was Noe did not penetrate deeply into her own feelings at the time. She did not realize that ever since the moment

Osugi had appeared before her, his referring each time openly and enthusiastically and frankly to her boldness, her determination, and the unknown potentiality of her talent had all the more pampered and titillated her pride and vanity. Tsuji was in his third year of living with her, so he had come to have nothing more to say about her talent and charm. What with their living in the same house, he had even forgotten his sweet custom of writing love letters to her. Even though his unchanged love remained aglow within him, he thought, with that shyness and bashfulness characteristic of the native Tokyoite, it was the height of the prosaic and inelegant for a husband to mouth his affection for his wife after so long a time together.

It was Noe herself who was too accustomed to his affection and was almost overlooking Tsuji's merits to the extent that she felt his taciturnity and brusqueness came from his indifference to her and his lack of love for her. Even more than the average woman did Noe herself have the most conventional characteristic of a woman, that which usually takes delight in the male's look of admiration and word of praise, though of this characteristic in herself she did not have the slightest realization. She had already forgotten the vanity and frailty stirred in her by the short-lived courtship of Sota Kimura, whom she had not loved at all.

On the surface Noe's object in writing a letter to Osugi was to express her gratitude for his having sent her a photograph of Rosa Luxemburg. In no time at all, however, Noe's pen had gone beyond the limits of a conventional letter of thanks:

Though I have had up to now and will have from now on as well great interest in your ideas, I feel this interest of mine has been gradually changing into something beyond mere interest.

The night before last I heard of the miserable situation at Yanaka village, and I could not help but feel quite agitated about it. Even now I am continually absorbed in thinking about it. It seems that Tsuji has been secretly laughing at this attitude of mine. We discussed this event for a fairly long time that night. I believe, after all, that I cannot calmly and serenely pursue just my own affairs. I believe, after all, that I am by nature someone discovering in herself the desire to work in surroundings in which others share her own sympathies. In this respect Tsuji is quite different from me. If the two of us walk in different directions as each one wishes, I feel we will become quite incompatible. While looking hard at this nature of mine, I am wondering in what way it will develop. Though I am not endeavoring to walk in the direction of your members, I expect the time will come when I will have to walk by myself. I have written some very bold things. Please forgive me.

Noe did not realize the seriousness of what she was then writing. Though she thought the intensity of her enthusiasm was due to her moral indignation over the problem of Yanaka village, it was mixed with her excitement from her feelings of love for Sakae Osugi, which were beginning to stir beneath her consciousness.

At the end of her letter, moreover, she added in a postscript that she wanted to insert a copy of *Heimin Shinbun* for her readers when she sent out the February issue of *Seito*, so she asked Osugi to forward to her thirty or forty copies of his newspaper. Of course, it never occurred to Noe even in her remotest dreams that beneath her action lay a subconscious coquetry toward Osugi in which she was eager to reveal herself already beginning to step toward him and his followers by this practical act of cooperation, a cooperation that might possibly be dangerous and fatal for her.

No matter how many times Osugi began writing to her, it did not go well. When he finally threw down his pen, he flung himself over on his back. Noe's letter could be regarded only as her love letter to him. Having interpreted its contents as her confidential disclosure that she was informing only him about the grave secrets of her heart which she had not even revealed to her husband, he noticed as he was trying to write his own impressions of the Yanaka village incident that his letter was beginning to recount his own fervent love for her. His reply was full of ardent words and phrases with which he was prepared to destroy her life with Tsuji and to welcome the woman who, at any moment, was about to fly to his own bosom.

Tsuji's fainthearted nervous expression flashed across Osugi's mind. As he had met Tsuji a few times, Osugi's understanding of and affection toward him as a man had deepened of late. When they talked about Stirner's philosophy, Osugi was surprised by the fact that Tsuji knew Stirner in more detail than he himself did. The thought that Tsuji was not only a man who had shown much concern about *Heimin Shinbun* but had also greatly cultivated Noe up to the present moment made Osugi begin to feel friendly toward him. But these emotions and the emotions of love were quite different matters. The conviction that from this time hence Tsuji was no longer the person to lend a hand to Noe's growth and development and that he himself was had already sprouted in him. This expectation had been his from the very start. At the same time Osugi, who for almost ten years since his love affair with Yasuko had formed no other relationship and had devoted himself to his social struggles, wanted to stay away from these troublesome human complications which any love affair inevitably entailed. While more disturbed by the violence of his emotions than he had thought possible from Noe's letter, Osugi did not send her a reply even after more than ten days had passed.

Noe was inwardly hurt by not having had any kind of response from him. When she wondered if he had finally disregarded her seriousness as childish sentimentality, humiliation and shame welled within her. After a while he dropped in for a visit a few times without warning, always spoke in a lively way on many topics with her and Tsuji, and then simply got up and left. Not a single look would he expose about that letter. Noe also behaved as if she had completely forgotten it, and with feigned innocence she would break into the conversation between Tsuji and Osugi, her laughing voice scattered among their words.

In addition to the February issue of *Heimin Shinbun* being once again banned, the printers declined to put out the paper. No matter which house Osugi contacted, it would not confront the danger of printing a newspaper that was certain to be repressed the very day it was released.

When Noe heard Osugi reveal this situation during his visit to Tsuji, she said, "Then I'll ask our printing firm. The foreman there won't be afraid to do it."

On the spot Noe wrote out a letter of introduction, and her printer gladly agreed to undertake the task when he received it. However, the publication of the sixth issue of *Heimin Shinbun* was also banned the very day it appeared.

No longer was it possible for Osugi to publish his paper. Critical voices were heard even among his followers that he ought to include only those articles which would be allowed. Osugi could find no significance in putting out anything if his principles had to be compromised. Though he was of a firm character, he was attacked by the feeling that his limbs were being torn from him. Many manuscripts that had been paid for were waiting to be finished. He was about to go off to complete these at his favorite inn at Hayama, but he wanted to meet Noe first, if only to glance at her. Stealing into him toward her were tender sentiments which had been unnaturally suppressed into an emptiness that came from his agitation and frustration. When he thought about it, he could not help admitting he had always visited Noe while inwardly hoping Tsuji would not be present. Osugi wanted to meet her with only the two of them together, even once being sufficient. His reply to the previous letter had weighed on his mind, and he had missed his chance to thank her for the introduction to her printers. He could provide any number of reasons for a meeting. In short, he wanted to see her. Realizing it was just about nearing the final proofreading for the next *Seito* issue, Osugi without advance notice dropped in at the printing office. He was told Noe would not be there that day but would come at about two the following day. The next day he again visited the office after preparing for his trip to Hayama. He waited from two to three and even to four, but Noe did not turn up. Spreading over him was the suffocating feeling that he could not set out for Hayama unless he caught a glimpse of her. Had he finally fallen in love with her? A passion was flaring within him that should Noe appear at that instant, he would without a word tightly embrace her small plump figure.

Weary of waiting, he left a letter behind, but even after he departed, his feelings were pulled by possibilities, and at the streetcar stop he let two or three cars pass. Noe did not, after all, step down from any which came from the direction of her home.

Even after he reached Hayama, an irritable dissatisfaction, like that of someone deeply in love who had been neglected in the promise of a rendezvous, goaded him. He had fallen in love finally . . . and even though he had disciplined himself not to.

Unable to go about his work, he passed his days with eyes gazing only upon this new love he had awakened to. The cold he had apparently caught while waiting for Noe at the printing office grew worse, and it even reached the fever stage. He left Hayama without delay.

When Noe heard Osugi had waited for her no less than two hours, the simple note he had left behind received as evidence, she was so seized with joy she almost shouted aloud. As she had been deeply hurt by feelings of humiliation that he had ignored her letter, she felt her self-respect had finally been restored. Moreover, the following day Noe read Osugi's article published in *Shincho* magazine entitled "Virgins, Chastity, and Dishonor," subtitled "Praises for Noe-san and Abuse-ass for Kazan":

Noe-san:

I have not become familiar enough with you even outwardly to be able to call you my friend. Nor can I say clearly how friendly I have become inwardly. However, among the women I am associating with at present, the one I have felt most friendly toward is, after all, you. And that is the reason at this time when I am discussing the question of chastity, my heart is most exhilarated . . .

Just reading these opening remarks made Noe feel as if she were receiving Osugi's public letter of love. As if dazzling her, each character vividly leaped inside her. Osugi's discussion on chastity had been developed out of the article Noe had published in the February issue of *Seito*, "Miscellaneous Thoughts on Chastity." Her essay revealed her ideas on the subject, which had been debated in *Seito* these last several months, that is to say, her views in opposition to Satsuki Harada's "Though I Die of Starvation, I Want to Make the Best Use of Myself," itself written to refute the major point behind Hanayo Ikuta's argument that chastity is of secondary importance when we confront the necessity for bread. Citing as an example Raicho's critical article on these debates, Osugi had furthermore stated his cherished theory that "women's chastity has been invented in order to enslave women under the system of private property."

Osugi attacked Noe's weak points. On the one hand she said if we asked why virginity is so precious, we cannot but reply that virginity has been considered so sacred that it should never be violated. On the other hand she said, "If we assume that women could earn bread by sacrificing their virginity, I would rather send virginity packing without regret!" and also "How sad it is that widows in our society are only solaced by a vain and conventional morality, being enslaved by insignificant feelings of chastity while they pass tasteless, lonely, and empty days. What a miserable life that is! Yes! The abolition of convention! There is no other way for women to be saved except by that abolition!" Noe's ignorance was also pointed out when he noted that unless we broadened the biological cause of women's chastity and shame into a social cause, there could be no real self-awakening for them.

Noe, however, received the impression that under the guise of his discussion on chastity, which had become an issue of late only accidentally, his article was a confession of his dormant feelings of love for her. A too ardent and fresh breathing was heard in this address by a married man to a young woman with a husband and child. In short, Osugi was enjoying his deceptive teasing in which he addressed the married woman he was in love with by enveloping within the abstract point of his argument the sensual topic of chastity, which could easily have been treated in any concrete way whatsoever. Although Tsuji must have read this article, he had not, contrary to his usual habit, said a single word about his impressions.

Unable to restrain her natural urge to write, Noe immediately began her second letter to Osugi. With the strokes of her brush spontaneously overflowing as she wrote in full about such items as having read his article in *Shincho*, her still being caught up in the Yanaka village problem, and her gathering material on it with the thought of making it the subject of a maiden work which would have real significance for her someday, she filled her letter with feelings of affection for him.

If you really think it's all right, please come to see me. I will also pay a visit to you.

Noe could not help writing she was confiding only to him what was once more a secret from Tsuji, her inclination to prepare a novel based on the Yanaka village affair. In her letter she was totally unaware of the gravity behind the significance of sharing with another man a secret kept from her own husband. She was not even conscious that to a man her way of writing might just as easily have been

taken as coquetry. After reading her letter, Osugi accepted
as fact that the love between Noe and himself had already
advanced too much to be confined by the framework of the
hasty premonitions of his friends.

What narrowly applied the brakes to Osugi's passion
was only his deference to and consideration for Yasuko,
the wife who had actually endured with him dire poverty
since he had married her. Though Osugi could assert any
kind of extreme remark from a theoretical point of view,
one side of him was uncommonly weak and sentimental in
its tenderness toward his own immediate family. Yasuko,
who was sickly, tubercular, and chaste, had become so
much a part of him she was like his own flesh and blood
rather than his wife.

On the other hand, since the "Agitation" episode with
Sota Kimura, Noe had developed sufficiently to see herself
more objectively, so unlike the time of her experience with
Kimura, she had become more cautious about allowing
herself to precipitately incline toward Osugi's affection,
which she was being so overly moved by. With some fixed
distance between them, their friendship as the "dearest of
friends" had been kept up, a kind of impatience concealed
between the two.

At that time an unexpected event occurred to sweep
Noe off her feet. When she became aware of it, she could
hardly believe how the situation had happened. Tsuji had
secretly been unfaithful to her. Moreover, the other party
was, of all persons, her cousin Chiyoko. Chiyoko had also
married and at that time had come up to Tokyo to live, but
during her visits to Noe's family after the birth of Makoto,
she was startled to see Noe so engrossed in *Seito* she was
hardly paying any attention to her husband and child.
Furthermore, after having created such a sensation among

her friends and acquaintances and after having dared to flee at all costs to the safety of Tsuji's bosom, Noe had told Chiyoko her marriage seemed a failure. Quite dissatisfied with her own commonplace and only too upright husband who had adopted her family name, Chiyoko was charmed by the aura of Tsuji's sensibility and wisdom. The awe and respect she had for her former teacher still remained. The figure of Tsuji totally disregarded by his wife seemed to Chiyoko, who had been strictly brought up in family discipline, that of the most ill-fated and miserable husband in the world.

"You're so generous Noe-chan has really become elated, hasn't she?"

Talking to Tsuji in his study was Chiyoko, who happened to drop by during the absence of Mitsu and Tsune, both having gone with Makoto to a relative's anniversary.

"No matter how important her work is, she has the duty of taking care of her husband, hasn't she? It's too much for her to be going out at night."

"She always does."

"What! 'Always,' you say?"

"Noe's a woman who can't stay quietly at home. Moreover, she's gradually come to feel disenchanted with me, I think."

An unexpected weight had entered into these words which had been said as a joke.

"What in the world! She's been allowed to have everything her own way!"

Unable to let the rip in the upper part of Tsuji's kimono sleeve pass unnoticed, Chiyoko went to get a needle. "Just remain as you are. I'll fix it right away. Don't move for a moment."

While conscious of Chiyoko's hair smelling of pomade

near the nape of his neck Tsuji, his kimono on, had the tear in his sleeve sewn. When he heard the sound of the thread snapped by her eyeteeth, her cool hair grazed the nape of his neck. His arms suddenly around her, Chiyoko gave way without offering any resistance.

"You poor dear man."

Chiyoko's trembling voice swept aside Tsuji's hesitation.

Noe had been totally unaware of the incident until Mitsu had broached the subject with something that sounded like an oblique hint. When she ferreted out the real meaning behind Mitsu's remark that while it might be all right for Noe to gad about, she had better do so after she had steered her own husband's oar, Noe was as furiously confused as if she were insane.

"Do you like her? More than me?"

"It was the whim of a moment."

"'The whim of a moment'! Since Chiyoko has a husband, it's adultery, isn't it?"

"You talk so unlike your pet theory on chastity which you've been parading around."

"What did you say? How dare you talk so impudently while you're the one who betrayed me!"

"Get control of yourself, at least for my sake. You don't have to make that much of a fuss about it, do you? All Chiyoko-san did was sympathize with me. I was overcome by her kindness, and I was temporarily infatuated with her and forgot myself. That's all there was to it. Neither of us is thinking about breaking up our families. It's all over now."

"Has there ever been such selfish justification?"

Noe flung at him anything she could get her hands on, a book, a bottle of ink, a vase, as she screamed out in tears that either she would kill him or she herself would die. She was so indignant with rage over Tsuji's betrayal she was herself startled by the extent of her love for him.

"I really am surprised. To be perfectly frank, I never dreamed you still had so much affection for me. From around January your attitude has been that of a wife whose love for her husband had cooled completely, and I felt you were remaining with me merely because there was nothing you could do about it. The truth is I was quite lonely and completely lost track of your intentions."

"You never told me any such thing, did you?"

"And can you say that recently there's been in yourself any suggestion of wanting to talk seriously to me?"

Hard pressed for words, Noe cried and screamed all the more loudly. Though she blurted out she was going to live separately, Tsuji took no notice of her remark.

"Let's have another go at it. Chiyoko, appearances to the contrary, is a practical woman. She's managing her own home satisfactorily. I'll never again do such an irresponsible thing. Makoto is with us, and we'll be having another child soon, won't we?"

From about February Noe had again become pregnant. She really felt dreadful when she looked back now to her own mind on a night she had once rejected Tsuji by using her pregnancy as an excuse.

"Try to calm down. Though you're excited at having been betrayed in your trust and love for me, I guess your shock at the present moment comes merely from the wounding of your pride and from your jealousy."

"Supposing it is. Are you in a position to be pointing that out to me?"

"Well, do as you wish then."

"I'll have to ask others to help me."

"Ah yes, go and appeal to Mr. Osugi."

Again Noe groaned like an animal and sprang at Tsuji. And while shouting, "Let me die! Let me die!" she did not know what she was actually saying. With Noe crying herself to sleep, all they could do was let the matter drop.

Noe published her reactions to this event as "Random Thoughts" in the June issue of *Seito*. The humiliation of being betrayed by her husband was so painful she could not keep it to herself, and it was due to her unappeased anger that she announced her shame to the world. Nevertheless, she could not help writing as if she recognized through this event her own passionate love for Tsuji. To have as a husband a man whom she could cast off without regret and divorce for some frivolous betrayal would have been an even greater wound to her pride. As Noe's notoriety advanced with another article also entitled "Random Thoughts" in the same June issue, she desperately defended Tsuji against society's criticism that he was a laggard and nincompoop, and she could not help emphasizing his superiority. Unless she made the world recognize him as a man of worth, her pride could not, after all, be appeased. The more she tasted her own disillusionment with Tsuji and awakened to her love for him, the more desperately she defended him to the world.

While Osugi was closely observing Noe under these conditions, he felt that the day of her separation from Tsuji was quietly drawing near. It could only seem to Osugi that all her words and actions were nothing but the last desperate struggle of her pride and vanity.

But this difficulty took the form of Noe's reviving her attachment to Tsuji, whom she had begun to ignore. When she was to return to her birthplace at Imajuku at the beginning of July to have a child born for the first time at the home she had run away from, she decided to take Tsuji with her. Ever since that episode of betrayal she had not been able to have any peace of mind unless she could see him before her very eyes.

Already it was summer. It had become Osugi's intention to revive *Modern Thought* as a replacement for *Heimin Shinbun*, but in the preparatory period he decided to put his energy into meetings. He rented the former office of the Watercolor Study Center on Suidobashi and initiated his Society for the Study of French. With Georges Sorel's *Réflexions sur la Violence* and Romain Rolland's *Théâtre du Peuple* as texts, Osugi's real intention was to study French syndicalism. Though Noe told him she would attend the meetings, she had not gone once, on the pretext that she was returning to Kyushu. Instead, it was Ichiko Kamichika who was the most earnest member from the start, always present, never missing a meeting. She even invited Kikue Aoyama, who had been ahead of her in school.

At that time Ichiko Kamichika had already become a gallant career woman as a female reporter for the Tokyo *Nichi Nichi* newspaper. Since she was good at English, she was asked to meet foreigners and get copy from them, and since it was an era in which female reporters were quite rare, advantage was taken of that rare existence by even giving her the task of interviewing ministers of state. Though a woman, she did not have a position in the women's column, and taking her place with dignity among the male reporters, she was acknowledged a talented interviewer in the local-news and political-affairs sections of the paper. Her first interview had only one item which had to be corrected by Ken'ichiro Ono, who had assisted her in procuring the position, and having grasped at once the essentials of a newspaper article, she was afterwards so very active that even competent male reporters were put to shame.

The attractiveness of her clear-cut features and her proud intellectual face, rare for a Japanese, her clear, crisp, and frank way of telling a story, and her large relaxed body were quite enough to attract the eyes of any male, and under the influence of her fresh charm connected to her new profession as a female reporter, which had become the object of public attention, many men approached her with interest and longing. However, from the first moment she had met Osugi at the Syndicalism Research Association, which had been the predecessor of the Society for the Study of French, Ichiko herself was strongly attracted by his human appeal. Ichiko, who from childhood on had grown up obsessed with an inferiority complex that she had been born plain, had never dreamed she had any charm as a woman. Her longing for the intellectual and the beautiful was so strong she had thought she wanted to choose literature as her path in life. Although it had been her belief that love as idea could be fully understood through literary works, she had no experience in love that even remotely resembled the subject. At the time she graduated from a girls' school, she became engaged after her parents had arranged the preliminary interview with a prospective bridegroom, but forcing a quarrel with her fiancé, she broke off with him and went up to Tokyo. It was similar to Noe's first marriage yet only in appearance, for Ichiko, after freeing herself by force from her fiancé, had not run under the protective roof of another man but into the palace of learning. It was for this reason that even though Ichiko was seven years Noe's senior and already twenty-eight by the Japanese way of counting, she was quite intellectual but almost totally ignorant and immature in the realm of sexual experience.

At that time Ichiko's power of comprehension as she participated so enthusiastically in the meetings and her serious attitude toward study were closely noticed by Osugi. In his attitude toward Noe, his calculation that he had to win her over to his side as an able comrade even more than as a sweetheart had been grappling with his natural affection for her. At the same time he could not help comparing her to Ichiko and her much greater learning and understanding of principle and theory, so he had to admit more than anything else the possibility of Ichiko as his future comrade due to her reliability, which if called upon she could quickly respond with.

He had for some time received no news from Noe, who had returned to Imajuku, and Osugi himself had no inclination to send a letter to her there, which might be dangerous if Tsuji happened to notice it. Distance and time had naturally cooled Osugi's passion. While he steadily advanced his preparations for the reissuing of *Modern Thought*, he was gradually incorporating Ichiko's talents into his staff. And through her own choice Ichiko was not at all reluctant to cooperate.

In October *Modern Thought* was finally reissued. Ichiko helped wholeheartedly on the editing and proofreading for the first number of this second *Modern Thought*, which was like a cross between *Heimin Shinbun* and the previous *Modern Thought*. Though the issue barely got through safely, its second, third, and fourth numbers and all its sequels suffered banning.

In December Osugi moved to Zushi because he had to locate his business office in an area connected to the guarantee money for the magazine. A few times a week he came up to Tokyo for the editing of *Modern Thought* and his meetings of the Society for the Study of French. During these periods the relationship between Ichiko and Osugi grew rapidly in intimacy.

When Ichiko realized she was gradually being drawn toward Osugi by her own feelings of love, she wanted to achieve this love. Now that she had decided to live fully, she desired to live even to the very bottom of the abyss, without regret, no matter how painful her existence might be. Before she realized it, such had become the earnest wish that had taken root inside her. To love a man with a wife could not from the start be expected to run smoothly. However, now that she was attracted to this man only, she believed the one way to live was to carry through this love. That Osugi himself was not indifferent to her Ichiko detected with the intuition of a person in love.

One day in late fall the two were walking along Kudanzaka. Suddenly Ichiko came to a halt, and her eyes, overflowing with passion and sharp as a bird's when she was tense, caught Osugi's gaze. All he had to do was see her expression to know what she was about to say at that moment.

"I can no longer stand this kind of condition. I can no longer put up with this deception of being conscious of the fuzzy emotion toward each other and then going on living with our eyes purposely averted. To love one another or to separate—I want one or the other!"

"I know."

"What should I do?"

"I really am fond of you. A bright woman like you, a woman who can get along with men on equal terms, has been my ideal for a long time. I have never seen a woman like you."

"What should I do?"

"Yasuko is living with me. Unlike you she has no learning and is merely ignorant and submissive. But she has the wisdom of the world in her. And as the wife of a revolutionary she has a firm, unfailing spirit. I have given her terrible hardships. What's more, I do love her. I don't want to betray her as some coward would. I want to win her absolute consent."

"I'll wait."

Ichiko was happy.

Then until they parted, while she listened to Osugi's theory on free love, she also listened, without thinking it odd, to the main point of the argument he alluded to, namely, that it was possible for a man to satisfy his wife and his sweetheart, to share each of them.

"For example, I have many male friends. And I have a different estimation of friend A and friend B. Moreover, my respect and my affection for each are also different. But in that they are my friends they are equal. And each one must be satisfied with the degree of respect and affection given him. I will not say such a foolish thing that because I am not respected by someone as much as another man is, I do not want to become his friend. This is not only my theory on friendship, it is also my theory on love."

Ichiko was already well acquainted with Yasuko from having gone many times to see Osugi at his home. Though Yasuko was certainly gentle and steadfast, she had looked to Ichiko like a toy doll. It had hardly occurred to her to regard Yasuko as an object of jealousy. Even while Osugi broached the subject to Yasuko, Ichiko did not feel the least bit pained. And since she listened silently, smiling even, Osugi was sufficiently flattered to say, "I also like

Noe Ito even though I haven't gotten intimate enough to hold her hand. Only until recently was I much fonder of her than I am of you."

Even though he had told this to Ichiko, she still remained as she had been, her face pleasant and radiant. She had heard rumors about Osugi's feelings toward Noe and had read his *Shinchō* article on chastity, but she did not on this occasion feel particularly concerned. For the present at least, she believed she was the closest to Osugi's affection, much closer than Noe and Yasuko were.

Later, after Ichiko had gone on a business trip for half a month and returned, Osugi went up to Tokyo as usual from Zushi and for the first time stayed at her boardinghouse. Ichiko felt she had received his reply. She was not inclined to ask him how he had managed to persuade Yasuko.

Ichiko shuddered in delight at having acquired him. She was receiving the caresses of the man she loved. Until then how incomplete the life she had been leading as a woman!

"No matter what my destiny, no matter what difficulties await me, I'll never regret this move. I want to penetrate to the very bottom of the abyss of man's life!"

These were her thoughts as she wept in happiness while she was being embraced by Osugi.

Since then each time he went up to Tokyo, he stayed at Ichiko's. He no longer tried to conceal from anyone his relationship with her. This did not mean he had managed to persuade Yasuko to accept his new connection. When she was suddenly told by him that he was in love with Ichiko, Yasuko was totally distracted.

"Though I've come to love Ichiko Kamichika, it doesn't mean in the least that I dislike you. I still love you as I have until now, and I respect you as well. So calm your feelings for my sake and close your eyes for a while without saying anything."

Yasuko could only hear Osugi's excuse as that of a selfish man. Though she knew all along he had been brandishing his dreamlike theory of free love, she had thought it strictly an abstraction in his mind, doubtful as she was that such a strange phenomenon could ever occur in the actual world. And despite the fact that she knew about his relations with women before he had married her, he had never had affairs since their marriage. His sexual appetites were stronger than the average man's and he was by nature greatly attracted to women, but he had not put these tendencies into practice. She had warned herself that his affection toward Noe was at least sly and subtle, yet she had felt she could manage to prevent something before it happened. Although she had been forced to suffer extreme hardship since her marriage to him, her husband in one prison after another, she had never once regretted marrying him.

As her husband, he was gentle and considerate. He took care of her in her infirmity, during her illness laying out the beds and putting them away and even doing the laundry. Whenever he went on an outing, he was eager to take her with him. He had never once made his wife three years his senior feel inferior about her age. An onlooker might have thought that for these eight years they had been leading a precarious and poverty-stricken married life, but day in and day out for Yasuko, hers had actually been a happy existence.

Since she had been fully on guard against Noe, she could not help persuading herself this unexpected new situation was merely a dream. She could not exhibit her usual submissiveness, and as she cried to him, she said she would not consent.

"Such a relationship is totally impossible. If Miss Kamichika is so appealing, definitely divorce me now."

"You *are* foolish, aren't you? How many times do I have to tell you that you are still loved the same as I've loved you up to now! My wife will be you to the very end. I don't see any reason to divorce you!"

It was to Kanson Arahata, who was so much Osugi's best friend as to be like her husband's alter ego, that Yasuko cried and complained about Osugi's new love. Just then Kanson was thoroughly depressed by the successive bannings of their publications. He could only entertain feelings all the more unpleasant toward Osugi, who under such depressing conditions was beginning to abandon himself to illicit love affairs.

Betrayed during his imprisonment by having his wife Sugako Sugano stolen from him by his elder comrade Shusui Kotoku, Kanson could not approve of Osugi's attitude, no matter what his reasons, for exposing to such behavior his wife who had been enduring poverty with her husband during their married life. Kanson began to separate himself at least emotionally from his close friend Osugi, with whom he had cooperated so devotedly in their movement.

That the censure and dissatisfaction of other colleagues should ensue after Kanson's was natural. Since Yasuko was the younger sister of the wife of the famous socialist Kosen Sakai, the reactions of Osugi's comrades were even more complicated.

Ichiko was so thoroughly absorbed in her love for Osugi she was not at all intimidated by the cold glances of the people around him. She willingly volunteered to raise necessary funds, more for Osugi's sake than for the sake of *Modern Thought*. She had gained remuneration enough from her newspaper to live as an independent woman. She felt no regret in liberally pouring all her savings and wages into this joint enterprise with Osugi.

When at the close of the year Noe and Tsuji returned to Tokyo from Imajuku after a long absence, bringing with them the new baby Ryuji, the love between Osugi and Ichiko had just reached its climax.

Chapter 6

IT WAS A day late in January after the dawning of the fifth year of Taisho.

After a lapse of six months Osugi was visiting Noe at her home. Having once sent a postcard to him at Zushi, Noe greeted him with a fresh expression on her face as if she had pulled off her old skin after the birth of her child.

"Tsuji's away. What a pity!"

The moment Noe told him this at the entrance, Osugi's passion of six months earlier revived.

Osugi invited her out. On the pretext that she had to proofread for *Seito*, she joyously left with him. They had the memory of having once met by chance outdoors and walking a short distance side by side. It was almost as if this day's stroll was their first experience together. When she stood beside Osugi, who was taller than Tsuji, her diminutiveness was all the more conspicuous. There was no shortage of talk. While they took turns speaking to one another as if they were obsessed by the necessity to, about their not answering letters, about Tsuji's infidelity, the situation of *Modern Thought*, and an account of Imajuku, their affection reverberated in each other's heart though they had not mentioned the subject. They followed a path in Hibiya Park shaded by trees. On their way along a line of trees whose leaves had fallen, the evergreens cast dark shadows. Before they realized it, the short winter day had faded and not a soul was around. The two of them were so physically and mentally aglow they did not feel the cold. Almost simultaneously they came to a halt. When Osugi took her hand, Noe found herself drawing close to his bosom as though she were falling unsteadily. Tightly embracing the small Noe as if scooping her up, Osugi bent forward to put his lips to hers.

"Are you cold?"

Though her cheeks were aglow, her lips were chilled, her body trembling. Instead of answering, she stood on tiptoe and put her arms around Osugi's back. When she was securely in his embrace, her swollen breasts brimming with milk moistened her kimono.

"I probably smell from milk."

Noe was so tightly embraced by a strong force she felt as if she were suffocating. She heard her teeth sound as she received the impact of Osugi's lips with their foul-smelling breath.

Later that night on seeing Osugi's face when he dropped into her lodging on Kasumicho in Azabu, Ichiko said with a smile, "Have you just had a pleasant experience? Your face is all lit up. Did you meet Noe-san?"

Ichiko had known that Noe had returned to Tokyo and that Osugi was concerned about her.

"Did you detect that? The fact is I just now left her. I kissed her for the first time."

"Congratulations!"

After this immediate response Osugi interpreted Ichiko's expression on her still smiling face as coming from her liberality and generosity. He had not noticed that her smile was frozen fast to help her bear her momentary shock.

Overflowing with the joy of his own egotism, he felt her magnanimity quite natural, and he continued to give vent to his words, which to Ichiko were quite cruel.

"That husband and wife are already hopeless. Noe will separate from Tsuji. It's only a question of time. The day is finally coming in which she will join our group."

"Our group?"

"Yes. I've been thinking so from long ago. As Yasuko has admitted you, you will admit my new connection to Noe. The experiment on my pet theory of a many-sided free love is finally coming to perfection with this new relationship."

Ichiko remained silent. Her indignation and humiliation after this shock made her feel nauseated to the very depths of her being. Occurring to her for the first time was Yasuko's position, which Ichiko had given no thought to. She vividly called to mind the way the gentle Yasuko had been so hurt by her husband's falling in love she had become half-insane and had never consented to his relationship with her. To make matters worse, how could Yasuko possibly approve of a new love affair between her husband and Noe?

For the first time Ichiko could not help feeling Osugi's conceited theory of love was only the brutal egotism of a man so callous he believed he could keep as many mistresses as he wished in addition to his wife. As usual, Osugi wanted Ichiko physically as if that were his natural right, rather openly revealing a passion aroused by this fresh development of his love for Noe.

By no means could Ichiko submit to him that night, either in her own sensitive nerve fibers or her own sexual desires. Though it had been more than two months since she had entered into a physical relationship with him, from the very first she had not awakened at all to the pleasures of sexual love. Because her spirit had overflowed with love for him, her pleasure had been strictly spiritual in that the enjoyment of giving the man she loved what he himself wanted had welled within her. Still remaining in Ichiko, who had been raised a Christian, was the girlish sensation which viewed physical love as unclean, and she could only regard sexual activity as a kind of obligatory custom. Her knowing that Yasuko was in delicate health and that for a long time had been unable to satisfy Osugi's intense sexual desires was probably one of the reasons no jealousy toward Yasuko had stirred inside her. While Osugi was embracing Ichiko as she listened to him impudently telling about the sweetness of his first kiss with Noe and the sensitivity of Noe's physical response, Ichiko for the first time tasted through sexual desire a violent jealousy toward a woman. In the same way a woman who has not awakened to sexual desire feels some intense sublimation of carnal desire from a kiss, so Ichiko had also tasted more happiness in a quiet embrace and kiss from Osugi than from the sexual act itself. All the more could she not endure Osugi's expanding on Noe's animal passions and even her body, not to mention his first kisses with her, thus exciting his sexual desire further—and all the while even as he was holding Ichiko in his arms!

That entire night Ichiko so pondered the problem she hardly slept. She perceived that the relationship between Osugi and Noe could no longer be held back. Moreover, since she could not be the least bit content to be loved as one of Osugi's mistresses, she drove herself to the conclusion that she ought to definitely sever their relationship now. Although she had not liked Yasuko, she felt sympathetic to her for the position she was in, and could Ichiko overcome her own interest in the affair, she thought Yasuko a woman she could associate with. However, from the very first time she had met Noe as a member of the *Seito* group, Noe fell within the category of those women Ichiko had no feelings for. Due to Ichiko's unconscious elitism in breeding and in graduating from Tsuda College, she could sense almost nothing intellectual in Noe with her small body that gave off a foul odor of wildness and of woman, her distasteful manner of dressing, and the offensive smell of poverty drifting out from her entire person accompanied by something unclean. Ichiko could not help but watch in disgust a Noe who almost unconsciously changed her facial expression and even her voice depending on whether it was a man or a woman she was talking to. In short, if there was a person born under a star whose character did not totally conform to that of another, she could not help but feel from the very beginning that Noe was this one member of the human race whose personality was not agreeable to her. Apart from the question of Yasuko, Ichiko's self-respect would not in the least allow her to compete for a man with this Noe seven years her junior. Ichiko even had her doubts about Noe's talent and potential, which Osugi had acknowledged so extravagantly. In Noe's dispute with Kikue Aoyama on the women's movement in *Seito* for the past few months, Noe had suffered a crushing defeat in exposing her ignorance of social problems and mass movements. Her hysterical way of speaking in *Seito* recently as if it were all right to snap at anybody merely called forth Ichiko's intellectual contempt. Ichiko could never allow herself to compete with a Noe of this sort on equal grounds, no, not that of equality, rather, as the underdog who has been deprived of her lover.

As if in pursuit of Osugi, who had returned to Yasuko, Ichiko hurled after him on the following day her letter of separation.

Surprised, Osugi hastened back to her. In two nights she was so haggard her face had become completely transformed. Her plan of separation, which had seemed quite clear to her, returned to its former state of indecision the moment she saw Osugi, and she had to realize she was still a slave to this love she could not give up.

On the other hand, Noe had been trying to obliterate from inside herself the embrace which she, beguiled by the Hibiya twilight, had exchanged with Osugi. She wanted to convince herself that they had probably been at the mercy of some playful mood. While strongly attracted to Osugi, Noe had so exposed her own violent anger over Tsuji's infidelity and had so severely denounced him she could not sanction the ease of her own inconstancy. She cherished a friendly feeling toward Osugi, but she was not in love with him. That was how she kept trying to explain to herself her feelings toward him.

But she came to be obsessed with the idea that her life with Tsuji could no longer continue. Why had she not returned alone to Imajuku, and why after giving birth to Ryuji had she not taken the measure of separating from Tsuji? While she herself had invited him, she regretted it at this juncture. The life in Tokyo after her return was no different from what it had been six months earlier. The only difference was that the baby had increased her family by one and her freedom was all the more restricted. The editing of *Seito* was also a matter of some difficulty. In her dispute with Kikue Aoyama, Noe had admitted to herself she had been made a fool of. Her plan of "my own *Seito*," which she had imagined when she had taken charge of the magazine from Raicho, was really no more than an illusion. Actually, she was forced to recognize her own incompetence, her immaturity of youth, her deficiency in the fundamentals of learning. She ought to separate from Tsuji after all, and by standing on ground not restricted by anything, she should make an experiment of her youth and potential. This resolution was weakened instantaneously by the thought of Tsuji's disgrace after he was abandoned and by the contemplation of her children's unhappiness. Since she had the hidden hope of leaving home by relying on Osugi and by using his love as a springboard, she wanted to parade in turn before herself, before Tsuji, and before the world that her relationship with Osugi was as pure as blank paper. To do that it was essential to verify Osugi's own feelings and to have him agree with her assertion. From her own practical point of view, to improve her situation even a little by abandoning her home, Noe visited Osugi's lodging one day without notice. A short while before, Osugi had left Zushi and after moving to Minami-Igacho in Yotsuya had made his office at the Fukushimakan, a boardinghouse located at Sanbancho, Kojimachi.

Ichiko happened to be at Osugi's. On seeing Noe, Ichiko suggested they clarify at this juncture the relationship among the three. From Ichiko's tone of voice Noe realized she had already been completely drawn in as one of the women connected to Osugi. Now that Ichiko knew about the Hibiya episode, Noe's excuse was not listened to. Repeating the argument of his usual theory on free love and citing three conditions, (1) to be mutually independent economically; (2) to lead separate lives without living together; (3) to respect mutual freedom (even sexual freedom), Osugi put emphasis on the fact that this complicated quadrilateral relationship would be realized only if the four of them observed these stipulations.

Ichiko tentatively agreed. Since Noe sensed Ichiko's irrepressible tension, jealousy, and hatred toward her, her competitive spirit and will to win welled up unexpectedly in her. Noe, in the same way Ichiko had, took no notice of Yasuko at this juncture. However, she could not tolerate Ichiko for having stolen Osugi's heart while she had been away and for posing as her senior in love. Because she was confident Osugi's love was directed toward her, Noe was obsessed by the conceited feeling that she could immediately annihilate Ichiko and Yasuko.

"Is it really possible for you to accept our own sexual freedom too?"

With this retort to Osugi, Noe was trying to stress her latitude in not being cornered by her love for him. She enjoyed her superiority over Ichiko, even feeling pity for her, who desperately trying to subdue her displeasure toward Noe was gazing in extreme tension at the image of this strange alliance of love.

"Let me think it over. Let me defer the matter a little longer."

With this sharp parting remark behind her, Noe left the two of them at the boardinghouse.

When she was alone, Noe found herself agitated by feelings quite opposite those she had shown when the two others were present. Noe's practical idea of thinking over this problem with Osugi after she resolved to separate from Tsuji had been completely overturned. Since Osugi and even Ichiko had included her in their circle, it was an inescapable fact that her separation and her affair with Osugi would serve as bait for the rumors of society, which in fact would be looking expectantly for something to happen. The self-respect and vanity of Noe, who had been unsparingly talked about as one of the New Women, would not allow her to be seen as unchaste and inconstant, a woman without maternal love, a woman only of lust and passion featured as "the female whispered about" in the human-interest columns of newspapers.

She would not be able to confront the censure she anticipated from the world unless her actions took the form of happening to meet Osugi by chance after liquidating her life with Tsuji, who had begun to obstruct her growth and development, and by all means not the form of discarding Tsuji and her children for the sake of her love for Osugi. However, while she continued to be perplexed about lessening the criticism against her as much as possible in taking this new path, she came to be unable to deny her desire to secure Osugi for herself. The only way left to force the world to consent to her separation was to put a stop to her love for him and even after separating from Tsuji to have no further connection to Osugi. She would abandon her love for him! When this bitter realization was confirmed, stinging her to the quick, Noe discovered for the first time her means of escape. Her egocentric self-satisfaction in compelling this much of a sacrifice of herself would relieve her of moral censure in abandoning her husband and children. She would deceive even Tsuji and even his family and even the world, and she would be free, herself still a chaste woman.

After making this firm resolution, Noe went to visit Osugi to leave him once and for all. He laughed away her words. Clearly perceiving her secret feelings, he unsparingly pointed out her tricks. The more severely she was attacked by him, the more she felt her guilt being washed away. At last she offered a weak challenge.

320 · BEAUTY IN DISARRAY

"As long as you have Yasuko-san and Miss Kamichika with you, I'm unwilling."

Osugi turned a deaf ear to her.

"Then this is my last time with you!"

Osugi did not run after Noe, who turned her back as she hurled this last remark at him.

Osugi found Noe weakly inclining forward, her back clearly revealing a lingering and tenacious attachment to him, the very opposite of her words. He could perceive as if holding Noe's true intentions in his hand that she wanted to turn around and return to him. Just as his self-confidence and conviction had told him, Noe sat in front of Tsuji in his study as soon as she got home that night and brought forward her intention of leaving.

"Please separate from me. I've been continually thinking about it."

The moment she made this remark, she felt the shameful perplexity she had maintained up to that time cleared away at once. Her honesty, her sincerity to herself and others, and her unpretentiousness, which were her essential qualities, suddenly came swarming within her.

"The truth is I've come to love Mr. Osugi. That's why I can't live with you any longer as your wife. That would be too miserable for you."

"Will you be all right with his wife and Miss Kamichika there too?"

Having been asked this question, she wanted to tell Tsuji that if she were in earnest, she had to oust these two women. Able to read this remark in the facial expression of the silent Noe, Tsuji did not ask her anything further. They decided the elder child would be under Tsuji's care, Ryuji to be taken along with Noe.

"I'm sorry for so many things. And I'm so grateful to you."

"Be happy."

With a quiet expression on his face throughout their talk, he did not speak in a loud voice. As for Noe, she was so disturbed she violently broke down into tears as if she were a wife who had been sentenced to leave her husband. The following day she abandoned Tsuji's home, taking Ryuji with her, but the only place she could go to was Osugi's lodging.

The moment Noe resolved to expose herself to all sorts of direct censure from the world and confessed to Tsuji her betrayal of him, which was more shameful and painful than anything else, she was for the first time liberated from her entire past and acquired the freedom she so craved. From the moment she was held in Osugi's arms after placing Ryuji beside her, she found she was also set free from her snobbish feelings toward the other two women. She persuaded herself that no matter how many mistresses Osugi had, she would freely give her love only to him, and Osugi could have whatever he wanted from her.

Seito, which had barely maintained its slender thread of existence, was brought out as a last issue with the second number of volume six in February, the fifth year of Taisho, a little more than twelve months since it had been handed over to Noe by Raicho.

The experimental management of free love under Osugi's plan of three women to one man could not in point of fact advance easily in accordance with his theories and ideals. The person most convinced of his theory was Noe, who had come to live at Osugi's expense at his boardinghouse and who not only could not help living with him but had also affirmed to herself that he loved her the most. Ichiko could hardly be expected to assent to the existing situation in which Osugi's three basic principles had been violated.

Noe herself was unavoidably living with him, and for her very existence Osugi was providing her with meals. In addition to Yasuko's being compelled to silently bear Osugi's relationship with Ichiko was added, a little more than two months after this first shock, his further connection to Noe, so it was hardly possible for Yasuko to remain acquiescent. Gentle and understanding as she was, she could not be expected to be merely the compliant wife this time.

Occasionally Osugi had to visit Yasuko and Ichiko at their homes to soothe and humor them. He found himself in the inevitable dilemma of regarding each of these three women as not only an object of his passion but a necessary and excellent comrade as well. Among the three only Ichiko was economically independent. Although she had been willing to offer Osugi money without hesitation whenever it was necessary, she came to feel disinclined to after Noe appeared on the scene.

This complicated relationship was immediately divulged to the world, the newspapers snatching at it like bait and continuing to play it up as a real scandal.

At this time too Noe was so impatient she thought she had to become economically independent as soon as possible. Of course, when she left Tsuji's house, she had brought hardly more than a few parcels and no extra money whatsoever. The day following her departure she had already found herself being fed with Osugi's money. In anticipation of her financial independence she planned to write a novel based on her present affair and to serialize it in the Osaka *Mainichi* newspaper, which had once printed a story of hers. In order to lose no time in completing her work, she took Ryuji with her and went to the Uenoya Inn at Onjuku in Chiba prefecture. This was the very inn Raicho and Hiroshi had hid at in escaping from the inquisitive world. It was April 29 when, on reserving a room at the inn she knew only from Raicho's correspondence, Noe departed with Osugi, who escorted her as far as Ryogoku.

The Onjuku train station was desolate, and in a downpour that threatened to turn into a storm, Noe made her way at last to the inn along the sea, quite distant from the station. When she settled into her four-and-a-half-mat room on the entresol and listened to the violence of the wind and rain outside, a loneliness and the depression of being alone seized her, separated from Osugi for the first time since she had abandoned Tsuji's home.

For those ten days and more, by completely indulging herself in her love for Osugi, Noe had forgotten the tragic resolution and independence of mind with which she had gone away from Tsuji's home:

> While I am writing in this way, I really feel we are quite separated from each other. When you left me yesterday, all you did was go away without even looking back. You are cruel! I'm completely alone, completely depressed. Can you not come as soon as possible? If not, what shall I do? Is it possible to be this far separated for so long a time? Because I won't disturb you while you are working, please come quickly! As I am writing this down, I again feel my mind becoming distracted, and so I'll stop now. If you can bear the four hours on the train, you can

come, and so please do! The person who makes me
continue to have these feelings for several days must
really be cruel! You see, I'm completely alone! When I
realize that even this letter won't reach you today, my
feelings become unbearable . . .

These words flowing from her pen were due to her open
coquettishness and her incessant attachment to Osugi. At
this juncture the rigorous mental attitude to do her work
and to reflect intently was swept away. Though she had
spread out her manuscript paper, she could not write even
a line. She suddenly found herself remembering and
retracing only the violent pleasures with Osugi up to the
previous day. Again she read Osugi's *Struggle for Life*,
which was the one book she had put among her belong-
ings. Just as during her first reading of this work, Osugi's
sentences clearly entered her mind. And even while she
was reading, her affection for him came gushing up, and
she lifted her pen to begin writing him once more. Now
that she was alone and had come this far, she became aware
she was so captivated by Osugi that she could not live a day
without him. She was unable to seriously reflect and search
her heart for her own essential qualities, which to be used
to their best advantage had to have the bolstering rope of
a man's power each time she broke loose from whatever
hindered her growth. Her life with Tsuji came to be
thought of as already many years previous. These more
than ten days were a period in which she passionately and
intently abandoned herself to her love for Osugi.

The night he had sent her off, Osugi had returned to
Yasuko's home at Yotsuya to take her a portion of the
advance royalties for his forthcoming book. Until that
hour he had been with Jun Tanaka and others and had been

rattling on about his current love affairs, so it was already midnight. When he got into bed and immediately started to tell her Noe had gone to Onjuku, Yasuko said, "That fox!" and was about to use further abusive language, but Osugi silenced his wife by covering her mouth with his outstretched hand. She had grown quite thin over her agonies of the past half month. Moreover, when she heard Osugi had handed Noe the money for her trip to Onjuku, she was hurt even more. Not only had Ichiko never cast any financial burden on Osugi, but in addition she had not hesitated to occasionally appropriate money for his magazine and even sometimes to supplement his household budget. Each of the several times Yasuko had been helped out of some crisis with Ichiko's money, the degree of humiliation, rather than any feeling of gratitude, had deepened, but confronted by Ichiko's economic power, Yasuko could not defeat Osugi's pet theory through any argument of her own. On the other hand, not only was Noe a trespasser on their love, but she even took their money with her. If so, was not Noe quite definitely a mistress? If Yasuko felt humiliation in being helped financially, the insult was worse in sustaining a loss economically. And yet Osugi as usual paraded his egotistical theory with the remark "Not only have I not developed a dislike for you, but my love for Kamichika has not been weakened either. The fact is I can get from Kamichika something I can't get from you, and I can gain something from Noe I can't get from Kamichika. The fact also remains I can give to Kamichika something I can't give to Noe, and I can give to you something I can't give to Kamichika."

"Then you're saying it's still possible for a second Miss Kamichika and a second Noe-san and even more to turn up, aren't you?"

"Well, something like that."

Yasuko was plunged into despair and, unlike the Yasuko she had been up to this time, cried hysterically and moped and denounced these women. If only Osugi threatened to break with her completely, she could resign herself all the more easily, but he wept right next to Yasuko, who collapsed in tears, as he said to her, "You poor dear. Get hold of yourself and put a stop to these miserable feelings," telling her that her sorrow and anguish were those very emotions any woman who found herself in this position was bound to suffer. For all that, he could not abandon his love for these two other women. He insisted it was for the sake of principle and doctrine. Yasuko was completely exhausted, a nervous and physical wreck.

On the other hand, Ichiko herself came to visit Osugi at his Kojimachi boardinghouse, which Noe had vacated. And it was the same with Ichiko as with Yasuko as she informed him she had not taken any meals for several days, the cheekbones of her chiseled features even more remarkable than they used to be, the flesh on her cheeks much thinner. Something hollow had formed about her eyes, the skin around them split finely.

"It's bad for you, isn't it, to have gotten so thin? Try not to let things get you down."

Osugi could not help but speak to her with these gentle words.

"I've decided to resign from my company."

She said she could no longer accept employment by her newspaper due to the clamor raised over her present situation, though her company had valued her ability and had tried to detain her. But even if she resigned, she felt confident she could earn as much as she had up to now by translating. In the same bed with Osugi, Ichiko, her eyes closed at his side as he was rereading the letter that had just come from Noe, did not only not want to see Noe's words but had no desire to even hear how she was getting along.

The logic that had told her she wanted to escape from this pitiful relationship as quickly as possible was lost the moment Ichiko met Osugi, bewitched as she was by his gentleness and his unique theory of love in which he had so much confidence. Ultimately her lingering attachment incomprehensible to her reason made even her firm resolve pass away. Watching the silent Ichiko, Osugi interpreted this silence as evidence of her splendid conquest through reason in her mental struggle as well as evidence of her growth in understanding his principles and ideas.

While he was placating Yasuko and Ichiko, he sent to Noe at Onjuku his sweet words as if they were those in a love letter of youth:

I want to meet you. I want to come. I want to cover you with this burning passion of mine! And once more I want to dissolve into your own passion. I have already been completely taken possession of by you.

Impatient while waiting for him, Noe would gather the maids at the inn for a wild spree, go mountain climbing, drink whiskey desperately, and even in the middle of the night start strumming a samisen. The people at the inn were apparently under the impression she was a patient trying to recuperate from hysteria. By the sixth day after Noe's arrival at Onjuku, Osugi had already been there for a visit. After spending three days indulging in love, he returned to Tokyo. His way of writing was to appeal to her as if he were lost in ecstasy:

Last night and this morning provided one more thing I felt sorry about. I'm worried about having so abused your weak body by such activities, and I'm anxious it may affect your health. However, I was truly happy. I woke up when the train was at Hon-Chiba, and on coming to my senses, I took out your letter and read it, and then in the midst of various recollections of those three pleasant days, I reached Ryogoku as if I had been dreaming. Even now those pleasant, dreamlike feelings are continuing.

In the meantime, the scandal involving the two of them was given full play in the newspapers. Whenever Noe happened to read these articles, she was enraged at herself for not yet having established her economic independence. Osugi wrote that to be on her own financially was, of course, one of the three important rules, but he consoled her by adding,

I cannot insult you or Kamichika with what is referred to as maintenance . . . but in a situation of unavoidable necessity, why is it bad to help one another?

Nevertheless, while they were abandoning themselves to the ecstasies of this love, they found themselves in an economic deadlock in no time at all.

Though Noe had struggled hard to finish her story for the Osaka *Mainichi*, their promise to her was broken, and it was not published. Only the magazine *Women's World* agreed to the plan that the three of them, Osugi, Ichiko, and Noe, would comment on this many-sided love affair, each from his own point of view, the result of which was their merely receiving some money for their contributions. But the sale of *Women's World* was banned, and the public not only failed to appreciate the writing of this trio but also felt a violent antipathy toward them, Osugi and Noe losing the many friends that had remained faithful. Even Yaeko Nogami, who had been the most sympathetic to Noe, sent her a letter of bitter warning.

Noe could not pay the inn at the end of May, and she remained in the predicament of being unable to return to Tokyo even if she wanted to.

Should Osugi send remittances out of his own living funds to Noe, he would be in the miserable situation of having to burden Ichiko with Yasuko's expenses and his own boardinghouse payments. Moreover, Ichiko had finally resigned from her company that month. Had it not been for her pension on leaving, their economic condition would have been beyond control.

Under these circumstances Ichiko found herself becoming even more critical of Osugi. Not only had the three fundamental rules been unilaterally violated by Noe, but the prospect of extricating herself from the situation was far from being certain. She came to feel contemptuous of Noe, of course, but even of Osugi, who had made allowances for such a woman. Ichiko had gone so far as to have doubts about Osugi's ideas on revolution since his theory and practice, as far as love was concerned, contradicted each other this much. Furthermore, on hearing that Noe's plan to earn money by putting her present affair up for sale had backfired, Ichiko was speechless with astonishment over Noe's superficial optimism. Even while Ichiko's rational faculty was at work telling her she ought to break loose from this relationship, what made her prolong it was Osugi's constant remark, "This problem has really matured Noe. Though I told her nothing about you, she has a surprisingly good understanding of your situation and Yasuko's, and her frame of mind is improving. She really understands my situation and these love affairs too. Compared to Noe, you definitely have not tried to understand them at all." Ichiko had not even noticed that Osugi's being accommodated by money from her had made it a psychological burden for him.

"Isn't it strange for you to say you'll die or you'll kill Noe merely because you, who stole me away from Yasuko, have had me stolen by Noe?"

Ichiko felt this censure and derision in Osugi's argument an unjustified insult. Nevertheless, what was it that definitely would not let her extricate herself from this quagmire-like quadrilateral relationship? Ichiko could not help but hang her head in dejection before the inevitable carnality of the human being, which was too much for both intelligence and breeding.

Having been driven to the wall economically, Noe placed Ryuji in the custody of a wet nurse at Onjuku and relieved of this responsibility went to Osaka to live at Junsuke Dai's expense. She wanted above all to repay her debts to Ichiko, and if chance favored her, it was also her aim that instead of Ichiko, who was no longer willing to actively cooperate, she herself would obtain money through the influence of her uncle for the guarantee bond of a new magazine. To once more live penniless at Osugi's expense at his lodging was to Noe, as might be expected, a circumstance she could not allow because of her stubbornness and her obligation to Ichiko:

> My uncle says I should immediately go to America. And he also says I should drop socialism and become a scholar . . . It's annoying to remain silent listening to my

aunt who talks incessantly despite the fact that she knows nothing at all. In short, even though they intimate I should cut my connection to you, they don't say it outright.

It's unbearable to be separated from you in this way, and I long for you. To be separated from the object of my love, from you, means that I can't think of anything at all. And yet I can remain quiet. In spite of the fact that any kind of image may be formed in my mind which speculates on what you are doing at the moment, my heart is calm. I am truly quiet, composed. I wonder why this feeling cannot be maintained when I am with you. Remember when I once talked to you and said I wanted to sever our relationship whenever it became troublesome? Well, I also said something to the effect that whether I severed our connection or not, my feelings would be the same. Now that I am here in this calm way, I really think it possible to break up. However, no matter how serene and calm I am, I can't believe our relationship is mere friendship. I feel it's a mistake to think everything can be solved quite simply if only we dissolve our sexual union. I don't know how to thank you when, receiving some hint from you, I can discover one by one the unexpected fallacies which have been lulling me sweetly to sleep. I can only strain my eyes in amazement at your deep and strong powers in so many areas. I really feel I understand now how bad it is to be separated from you, no matter what the reason for the separation.

How is Miss Kamichika getting along? I honestly feel sorry for her. Every day, whenever I got a telephone call, I could not help feeling pained thinking it might be from her. When I considered how much I had marred her freedom, I was truly disgusted with myself. And I was also pained about the many kind things you have done for me. I couldn't help feeling strangely sad. After I return next time, I think I want to immediately find a house and live in it quietly.

I'm worrying whether your work is progressing. I have certainly disturbed you. Please forgive me.

On June 15 in the fifth year of Taisho, the day after she had arrived at the Dai home in Osaka, Noe, who had written this letter to Osugi in the morning, sent him another on the evening of the same day:

Because I want to take advantage of your kindness, I'm writing again. Your Noe is already completely disheartened. From the moment I got here, I have been bullied. Am I not in misery? Your Noe already wants to return to you. Is it all right to? Both my uncle and aunt think I have been led into temptation by you, and if only they keep me separated from you, they believe I will return to my former self. There has never been such a ridiculous statement! It is, after all, best for me to be beside you. Your Noe has completely deviated from her plan, and even though I'm disgusted with myself, it can't be helped.

Because Junsuke Dai loved his precocious and daring niece who was like a man and because there were aspects of her he felt proud of, he was seriously devising a scheme to send her to America to study. Due to some unexpected business matter he had set out on the very day of Noe's arrival, his journey supposed to last about twenty days, so Noe was compelled to stay put at her uncle's home in

Osaka. Her being apart from Osugi in order to make herself all the more calm had been Noe's frequent theme song from the time she had lived separately at Onjuku. Even afterwards she never abandoned her dream of an ideal relationship of a man and woman who could form an appropriate mutual union on the basis of work and affection, to be realized after gaining her economic independence, living completely on her own, and separating herself from Osugi and not merely for the sake of appearance.

Having sent Noe off, Osugi again quarreled with Ichiko, who came later to visit him. Although she had come with the promise of a short stay, the resentment she had felt ever since Onjuku permeated her gloomy displeased expression, and no matter what words she used, they immediately jarred against Osugi's nerves. Ichiko found it quite difficult to forgive him for wanting again to continue living with Noe in Tokyo in spite of the fact that not only had the two of them dallied in Onjuku with no travel expenses for their return, but they had asked Ichiko herself to send them money. Furthermore, even though Osugi had said Noe had set out for her native town to raise some funds, her travel expenses for this trip were handed to her by Osugi by way of Ichiko's purse. Though she had the feeling Noe would by no means be able to raise any considerable sum, Ichiko merely wanted to make some cutting remark to Osugi when she saw his undisguised expression of loneliness after sending Noe off.

"If you must abuse her, you can go back home."

"Your attitude's never impartial, is it? You always wish to side only with Noe-san. And what about my point of view?"

When Ichiko thought about the problem when she was away from Osugi, she sensed it was already the right moment to withdraw from this completely confusing whirlpool of love, and she came to believe that the respectful and comrade-like affection she had cherished for him was no more than a complete illusion. No matter how she analyzed the situation, she could not help feeling disgusted with her own position in playing the role of a mere bystander and being fleeced out of her money. She wanted as soon as possible to free herself from her self-ridicule, her self-aversion, and the quagmire she was in. And yet whenever she saw Osugi, she found overflowing inside her not only some lingering attachment to him, but also a self-respect that insisted she could never silently withdraw. Her feelings could not be satisfied unless from Osugi's own mouth he at least apologized to her in a manly way by admitting he had made miscalculations in his pet theory on free love, had dragged her into this entanglement, and had caused her spiritual and material damage. No matter from which angle she viewed the problem, the thought took hold of her that she was the one who had sustained the heaviest losses in this quadrilateral relationship. Ichiko could not endure the fact that Osugi, so understanding and so capable of perceiving feelings in others, had only in this particular situation pretended to be completely insensitive and had become day after day coldly indifferent to the wounds of her heart.

When Osugi saw Ichiko becoming so pained, weakened, and enervated that she could easily be comforted by a pleasant remark or a brief caress, he was extremely disgusted with her for showing such frailty. The moment she became peevish, he openly revealed a look of displeasure, and he would not even listen to half the things she said. In what seemed a thrust against her, he opened before her eyes Noe's letters and extolled Noe for the merit of her understanding. As the morning dawned, Ichiko, who had not slept sufficiently, felt all the more dissatisfied.

"You *have* changed."

"I haven't changed at all. Only your way of viewing things has changed."

"Aren't your theory and practice replete with contradictions? Though your *theory* on love is quite splendid as usual, our present situation is no more than one of those innumerable stupid scandals of amour found anywhere in the world."

"If your self-respect has fallen so low that you hold yourself in contempt, there's nothing more to talk to each other about."

"I'll never withdraw under these miserable conditions. I must take the responsibility for what I've done to myself. I know how to settle everything."

"By killing me? That's what Miyajima said. He said you were screaming that."

"Even now I still have in me the right and the ability to kill myself."

"You may do what you like. You people who talk of dying or killing yourselves don't usually put it into practice."

As she stared at Osugi's back, her eyes dry now that tears no longer came from them, Ichiko turned aside and went out. As her figure disappeared, Osugi's heart could not help but succumb, after all, to his grief for her. When he saw her face to face, the guilt in him over her decency and bravery oppressed him, and he became despondent, but when she was away from him, the virtues of her largeheartedness, innocence, and candidness strongly moved him, and he could only feel an unbiased compassion for the unfair position and difficulties she had been placed

336 · BEAUTY IN DISARRAY

in. To Osugi, both Yasuko and Ichiko were women who had always been kind to him, and the warm memories of their service in love bordering on self-sacrifice and devotion could never fade, even while he admitted to himself he had begun to love Noe so much it was impossible to compare these two women with her!

After Ichiko had indignantly left, Osugi had to visit Yasuko at Yotsuya to inquire about her health. At the time of Noe's departure he had learned in a phone call from a friend that Yasuko had been ill in bed for several days with a temperature of 104. Yasuko's face looked feverish as she greeted him.

"This isn't any good, is it? Not to tell me anything until you've become like this."

Remaining silent, Yasuko smiled slightly. His dear old wife, who had been married to him for nine years, felt that at this moment he was seriously concerned about the condition of her illness.

"I'm already beginning to recover," she whispered.

With Osugi's large palm on her forehead, she had, while closing her eyes, murmured these words under the shadow of that palm. That night Osugi slipped into bed next to the feverish Yasuko and slept there. Though he told her that he had quarreled on parting with Ichiko in the morning and that Noe had left, Yasuko merely listened in silence. No longer did she wish to speak out against Noe as she had once done. Suddenly Osugi wondered if Yasuko were not about to die. At the same time he also felt this woman was, after all, the one more than any other who could give him relief. With his arm around her feverish body he fell into a deep sleep for the first time in a long while, continuing in his dream, however, to behold Noe's image.

Without a word the following morning, Yasuko took a

one-yen note from under her pillow and handed it to Osugi, who was about to return to his lodging to see if Noe's letter had come. The previous night Yasuko had noticed in the purse Osugi had thrown down on his pillow that he did not have enough in it even for streetcar fare.

Even while basking from both directions in the violent, tenacious, and strong radiation of the love of Yasuko and Ichiko, Osugi, with a passion that could not be denied, had no other choice but to incline toward Noe alone, who was separated from him now:

You seem quite dejected. It's good you've been abused a great deal. It's good medicine for you. Since you've done this much wrong, you deserve it. Have a real good quarrel now that you are under such circumstances and then come back to me right away. As your reward I'll make love to you in any way you wish. So let's cooperate and do as many crimes as possible in every direction. Or should you postpone these evil deeds and go to America as your uncle says? Only as for the latter, it is in my opinion too cruel. It's too unsatisfying. We have had too few flirtations together! Too few hugs! But this is probably not the time to be saying such things. Be that as it may, this is Noe's victory . . . As I have so often said before, this time for the first time have I really appreciated this kind of love. These last several months I have indulged myself only in craving for love, and I have not experienced the least bit of satiation. Instead of putting it that way, I want, rather, to indulge myself more and more deeply only in craving for that love. And this indulgence is so great I have almost no self-control over any of it. I am trying to separate for a while even from the Noe I love. Moreover, I am even trying not to have us correspond for a while. It is hardly necessary to tell you, who think the same as I do, how I feel spending each night since you left . . . That you will settle in your own home quickly and really find your own livelihood is my one and only hope for you at present . . . However, if things go wrong, Noe, it's better first of all to return home rather than writhe and struggle. As for your own affairs, we can somehow manage if the two of us work a little.

It was natural for Noe, who had so liberally been given such affection, to feel satisfied as the victor in love over Yasuko and Ichiko, and it was also a natural development for Noe to have ample compassion for these two rivals.

In spite of her efforts, Noe's plan to raise money ended in failure as Ichiko had expected. Although Noe ran about from Osaka to Kyushu approaching her prominent acquaintances, her efforts were so hopeless she could not even raise enough money for travel expenses to Tokyo, to say nothing of the hundred yen she had set as her goal. Through the influence of Junsuke Dai, however, Noe requested an interview with Mitsuru Toyama, and with an introduction from the latter, she went to see Shigemaru Sugiyama. He made her leave after saying he wanted to meet Osugi personally. She had no other course except to return to Tokyo at the end of September and live off Osugi at his boardinghouse. Because he had been driven from the Fukushimakan for not paying his lodging fees, Osugi, with an introduction from Shichibu Oishi, had moved to the Kikufuji Hotel, a high-class boardinghouse on Kikusaka in Hongo. The Kikufuji Hotel offered room and board, and although its charges were high, about twice those of an ordinary place, it was convenient to be able to eat free of charge due to the fact that the hotel's request for payment was leisurely in the extreme.

During this time Osugi was busy trying to raise the guarantee bond for the publication of a new magazine. He could not live unless he had an outlet for his own thoughts, and he believed there was no other way to bring order to this intricate and complicated love affair. It so happened the money dropped into his lap from an unexpected source.

Suddenly remembering that he had met Shigemaru Sugiyama through Noe's endeavor, Osugi received the money by directly negotiating with Home Minister Shimpei Goto. When Shimpei Goto himself met Osugi, who visited him without warning and who told him he had come for money, Goto simply and directly gave Osugi three hundred yen, the requested sum. At the time Shimpei attached the condition that he wished the matter kept confidential even from Osugi's comrades. Other than Noe, Osugi did not tell anyone about its origin. He had no intention of informing Yasuko or Ichiko. Of these funds he brought fifty yen to Yasuko, to whom he had not offered anything in a long time, and with thirty yen he took out of pawn Noe's striped crepe kimono and her haori. For a long while the only clothing she had had was the Japanese nightgown she slept in. The guarantee bond was possible if Osugi earned a little more to put with the balance of about two hundred yen. He was in high spirits, thinking it possible to finally make arrangements for Noe to live in her own home. Even while continuing out of necessity to live together in a room at the Kikufuji Hotel, the two of them had never felt the condition a normal one. With a part of the money Osugi wanted to go to his favorite inn at Hayama, the Hikage-no-chaya (the Shady Inn), with the intention of finishing his unfulfilled contracts for articles. Visiting Ichiko after quite a lapse of time, he told her about some money he had received and about his trip to Hayama.

"I'm now finally able to take a step toward living separately from Noe."

Even while Ichiko was inclined to have doubts about his suddenly receiving so large a sum, she was unable to hide her joy over his unexpected pronouncement. Through the assistance of Reiichiro Yuki, a sizable amount of translation work had been sent to her, so if only she worked, Ichiko would not be troubled economically since leaving her company in the wake of her affair with Osugi. However, she had been depressed to the core of her being by the gloom of desperately supporting through her own labor four people. What with her jealousy toward Noe and her mistrust and suspicion of Osugi all the more violent these days, her mind even when she was at her desk was filled, before she realized it, with confusion over the follies of her love, which she could not forget for even a moment, and she could not do any work. Just at the moment of a terrible state of depression, she had been told by Osugi of his plan for remedying his situation, and she was drawn toward a hope which in her confusion she had been about to abandon.

"Alone to Hayama?"

"Of course, alone."

"Oh, that's fine. Well, go ahead and do some good work. But let me know when you're leaving. Is it all right if I come with you for about a day?"

"Yes, let's go together. I'm leaving in a few days."

Looking at Osugi, whom she felt herself drawing closer to after the long interval of not seeing him, she found, after all, her self-confidence that she could endure the bitterness of parting from him disappearing.

However, Noe, who was to remain at home during his absence, began importuning him the night before his departure.

"I want to see Miss Hiratsuka tomorrow."

It was, of course, Noe's coquettish way of bringing out her regret in separating from him for a while. Chigasaki, where Raicho was staying, and Hayama were as close to each other as an eye to a nose. Although Osugi at the outset had no intention of breaking his promise to Ichiko, he could not refuse Noe's proposal.

It was the sixth of November. Raicho, who was having the convalescent Hiroshi bask in the sun on the veranda of their home at Chigasaki, received Noe and Osugi's unexpected visit. Hiroshi had been consumptive, and after entering Nankoin Hospital, associated with earlier memories, and recuperating there, he continued to remain at the seashore in Chigasaki. Raicho was totally absorbed in a calm uneventful life which could not have been imagined in her *Seito* period, the center of her existence the child Akemi, born at the end of the previous year.

"Well, you certainly are welcome!"

While greeting her two guests, Raicho was unable to hide her surprise. Although she had heard a great many of the rumors about their love affair, these continuing even after Noe's divorce, Raicho was confused at seeing with her own eyes the two persons in question. Was this the same unpretentious Noe, the Noe who had shown a naiveté and an undisguised rusticity? She was wearing a striped crepe kimono, more stylish than gorgeous, its collar pulled back offensively low, her hair braided in the ginko-leaf style, her *haori* over her kimono hanging ostentatiously from her shoulders. Her white face powder was too thick, her rouge too red. Thinking Noe looked like a maid in a brothel, Raicho wanted to turn her eyes away. Even Osugi in a kimono without the *hakama* skirt gave the appearance of being her slovenly and licentious keeper. Raicho also felt displeased by the fact that the two of them snuggling against one another insinuated an overfamiliarity toward her. It pained Raicho to think that within a short year they had changed this much. When she recalled the thin back of Jun Tsuji, whose development she had watched so affectionately as if he were the darling of her eye, Raicho came to feel oppressed by what he was going through now that things had come to this state. Raicho continued to be favorably disposed toward Jun Tsuji.

"How is Ryuji-chan?"

While watching Osugi holding Akemi in his arms, Raicho had asked Noe this question in a low voice. Her face showing an unwillingness to talk about it, Noe told her briefly that the child had been sent out to be nursed at Onjuku. To Raicho's most searching question about what Noe intended to do with *Seito*, Noe replied in a voice full of her unyielding spirit, "Once these complications get settled, I'll start it over again with a new plan."

Even when Raicho began to talk about Yaeko Nogami, with whom Noe had been so friendly, Noe intentionally evaded the subject. Raicho felt that in this woman who had gone through such an extraordinary transformation, not even a glimpse of the simple and naive Noe of old could be detected. As for Noe, she merely ate lunch, and after an hour or so they left Raicho's place, Noe clinging to Osugi's arm as they found themselves in a grove of pine trees.

"Oh, I feel relieved now! At any rate, she won't even try to understand us. Oh, that cold and critical attitude of

Raicho's! It's all right now! I was overly optimistic in thinking if I met her and talked with her, she at least would understand us. It's all right now. It's all right because I do have you!"

Osugi wanted to console Noe in her loneliness, all her friends lost, the circle of her acquaintances narrowed. The following day too he detained her to take her boating, and he was completely happy. After bathing with her in the evening, he was about to have supper. Just as he looked back on hearing the announcement of a maid, "A guest has come for you," he saw Ichiko standing there.

Kneeling in front of the mirrorstand to put on her makeup, her breasts and shoulders exposed, Noe caught sight of Ichiko's piercing eyes burning with wrath. In a second Noe's face, as if not to be outdone, stiffened to match Ichiko's hard expression. Noe immediately put her kimono over her shoulders and affecting indifference ignored Ichiko while continuing to do her makeup.

"I didn't realize Noe-san was here."

Ichiko's tone might have been taken either as an explanation or a protest. As might have been expected, Osugi could not hide how awkward he felt.

"I thought I'd drop in at your house, but . . . "

His apologetic tone of voice was low. It was evident Ichiko was a boorish uninvited intruder. With the feeling that she wanted to shield her eyes from the awkwardness of her situation, Ichiko sat down before her meal, which was hurriedly added. The expression of contempt and displeasure Noe had so openly revealed in the mirror still adhered to Ichiko's eyes. Ichiko also ignored Noe from the first and talked only to Osugi, and Noe did not even nod in recognition, much less speak. It was quite obvious no one could eat while the three sat at the table.

Suddenly Noe stood up and suggested, "I'll go back."

With the feeling "You may do as you like," Ichiko merely fixed a sharp glance on her. Nor did Osugi stop Noe. When she finally finished her preparations, she went out by herself.

After asking the maid to clear the table, Osugi had her quickly lay out the beds. He thought that by lying on his bed he could manage not to look at Ichiko's face. He was worried about Noe who had returned. His guilty conscience in breaking his promise to Ichiko and acting in a way that had wounded her in the most serious manner possible was willfully ignored. The awkwardness of being caught in the act attacked him in the form of humiliation so that his unreasonable disgust toward Ichiko, who had driven him into this corner, intensified. Even the feeling of discontent that he had been followed by her and had been restricted in his freedom welled within him.

"I didn't come to deliberately spoil the fun you two were having. Yesterday and the day before I got tired of waiting for your message. I got worried."

"I understand. That's enough already, isn't it? I'm worn-out from a cold and I have a fever. Let me get some sleep," Osugi said as if giving in to his anger over her words. Suggested in his voice was a sullen harshness he could not control.

With a heavy sigh Ichiko also got into the bed next to his. When she realized this was the very bed Noe had slept in the previous night, her jealousy seemed to be burning within her.

Osugi, his closed eyes directed toward the ceiling, sensed a line of vision as if Ichiko were staring at him and penetrating his very face. As he could understand Ichiko's chagrin and indignation on this day, he also realized he could not speak thoughtlessly. When he asked her before dinner if she wanted to take a bath, Ichiko said she had a cold and looked away. At that time she had told him her actual reason for not taking a bath, but the glance she gave him he could easily interpret. Due to Ichiko's gesture Osugi felt secretly relieved not to have to hold her in his arms that night. In his closed eyes only the image of Noe returning alone along some dark path at night stretched on endlessly. Until then each time Ichiko had blurted out she would leave him, which was quite often, Osugi had pacified her. He still believed he loved her as a mistress and comrade, and he also thought her a woman worth loving. He also knew his uncontrollable and seething disgust toward her of late was, in brief, a reflection of his own egotism as a man who had been too much indulged by Noe. And since he was well aware of that, each time Ichiko's violent anger came under control and was weakened and she requested a reconciliation, he had come to grant it as quite natural. But he decided he had almost reached the limit.

As Osugi recalled the serious expressions of each of the three of them that night, he came to feel desperate. He sensed Ichiko was crying, but he stubbornly pretended to be asleep. It was almost ten o'clock when a telephone call came from Noe. She was at the train station in Zushi. Noe said that she had turned back at Yokohama because she suddenly realized she had forgotten the key to their room.

"She's totally helpless."

While offering Ichiko this excuse as a pretext, Osugi hurriedly threw on his padded dressing gown and after having the inn call a jinrikisha went out to the station.

The tears Ichiko had been able to control began to spill over at that moment. She could not help feeling everything was due to Noe's cunning histrionics. Any hotel would have duplicate keys. From the very beginning Noe must have taken that into account. It was all a cheap trick. At one bound Ichiko thought over the entire misery of her situation since she had entered the room. She was tormented by a pain as if her entire body were spouting flames.

She remembered the cold touch of the blade of the dagger she kept next to her in her handbag these days. Before her floated the scene of gloomy twilight along the street on the day she had requested this dagger at the cutlery shop on Nihombashi. That was the day after Osugi had told her he had kissed Noe for the first time. How much better it would have been if she had decided to separate from him that very day. As each day extended into the next, she was unable to say anything to Osugi, and her shame ended by covering her body and soul with something thick and black.

She did not know how many hours had passed. When she became more fully conscious, she heard Osugi's voice along the corridor, and Noe, as if hiding behind his back, came into the room. It was almost midnight. Another bed was laid out next to Ichiko's, and with Ichiko in the middle, Osugi and Noe lay down. Both of them looked exhausted, and after entering the room they hardly spoke. With her thoughts beginning to clear, Ichiko revived in her mind's eye all her past with Osugi, as if she were trying to drag each scene out.

In the morning which dawned after an oppressive night, Noe hardly touched any of her breakfast and hurriedly left. Again with her cold eyes following Noe going away, Ichiko did not even try to speak to her. Osugi sat at his desk, his manuscript paper spread out. He had promised to write a criticism of the administration advocated by the Terauchi cabinet. From behind Osugi, who was trying to write, Ichiko in her characteristic way of distinctly pronouncing the ends of her words started a quarrel to annoy him.

"Noe-san . . . though she's gone back, isn't she hiding out at some inn and waiting for my *own* return?"

"You *are* an idiot!"

With his words indicating he would take no further notice of her, Osugi bent deeper against his desk. Ichiko left the room without saying anything more. As she walked alone on the beach, something feverish was once again burning and seething inside her. The image occurred to her that right then Osugi and Noe were conspiring about something over the telephone. Ichiko could not allow herself to suffer from the misery of being continuously afflicted night and day with nothing but such wild fantasies. Was Osugi's beautiful theory on free love actually no more than this shameful mass of jealousy and suspicion and mistrust? In the midst of the bright and calm of the beach at midday where no other person appeared, Ichiko was seized by a dizzy sensation of solitude and desperation. As she crouched in a posture as if gathering shells, she let her tears overflow uninterruptedly into the sand.

Even when night came, Osugi's manuscript paper was still blank. As Ichiko put herself in Osugi's place and considered the direction of his thought the entire day, she felt a cold laughter welling up inside her. Even sitting face to face at dinner was awkward, and their talk was not the least animated.

That Osugi was disgusted with her existence itself and was merely tolerating her was sensed in her very flesh. Why was she to blame? While fixing her eyes on her own anger and enmity which gradually diminished as the night deepened, Ichiko heaved a heavy sigh.

Even now she could not help but feel tender toward the passion with which she could not keep herself from loving Osugi. Why had this attachment, which she had not been able to experience toward any of the several men who had courted her, come into existence for Osugi alone? She had not felt the slightest resistance in rendering him any service. In front of him she was always seized by a feeling of inferiority as if she were petty and incompetent. And yet with what a pleasant and sweet sensation it enveloped her! Ichiko recalled that she had admired and almost worshipped Osugi, who had recognized and loved her as she was, she who had continually underestimated herself by noting her weak points: her aggressiveness, her lack of charm as a woman, her immaturity as a human being. She could only view herself as one of those minor stars unable to emit any light by itself unless she basked in the sunlight named Osugi. Osugi was the source of light for her existence which her youth, in its pace later and longer than that of ordinary persons, had groped for and finally discovered. Through her love for Osugi, Ichiko felt as if she had suddenly been transformed from some lusterless material like charcoal into a dazzling precious stone which scatters its own light. The back of Osugi's head, larger than that of most men, the nape of his neck full of masculine power, the hollow of that nape in which some boyishness remarkably remained—while she was staring at these, she suddenly felt a pain. It was as if her body were being squeezed out of her and were being filled with affection toward his skin, his odor, his bodily heat, toward everything in Osugi that immediately appealed to her carnal desires when her eyes fell on these things with which she was now very familiar.

Osugi, who turned his face to her for some sign, gazed

at her coldly with his large eyes and asked her what was wrong. With her eyes strained, she could not utter a word. She felt that if she spoke, all of her anguish, which was about to reach its limit without any outlet, without any expectation of relief, could end only in a short cry of "I'll die!" or "I'll kill!" Even after they got into bed, she continued to be oppressed by the premonition that again, that any moment even, he would receive a phone call from Noe as he had the previous night.

"I guess you're worried. And about Noe."

Unable to endure the heaviness of the silence, Ichiko had called out to Osugi, whose back was turned away from her. She grabbed Osugi's arm and pulled it, saying almost unconsciously, "Please get up!" the meanness of her words wounding her.

"Don't go too far!"

"Dear, we . . . I think it's better to talk to one another."

As she spoke, the violent emotions she had been controlling overflowed, and she felt a dizziness as if she were being carried away. She desired some power to remove all the shame and humiliation she had been exposed to.

"It's already more than the limit of my endurance! I'm sure that at this juncture you have something to tell me. For example, that you've been wrong."

"If it's the limit, you are free to do as you wish, aren't you? I have nothing to tell you, so you can do what you want."

"Are you saying you feel no responsibility for our situation that has been completely corrupted this way? And what *is* Noe-san? Although you constantly talk about the fact that she understands you and is developing, what about the fact that she's always clinging to you and tempting you when you're trying to work? Where are her understanding and development then? She doesn't even work and only sits around shamelessly sponging off you and Yasuko-san's economic livelihood. Where can her self-awakening be seen when she merely wears some good yet showy kimono and keeps her hair set?"

"Stop it! All that slander about Noe!"

"I will speak out! Why do you defend her? Why do you always defend only Noe-san? Your theory of revolution is equally unconvincing. It only means that I was foolish, that I was deceived by you. Even Mr. Takabatake and his followers say so. He says that if a revolution can be made in Japan on the basis of your petty theory, he'll become a Buddhist priest, and I'm sure he's absolutely right!"

Osugi suddenly turned in bed and sprang up. In his anger and excitement his pale face twitched, his large protruding eyes bloodshot.

"I'll not forgive you any longer! This time's the very last! I know your true colors now. Because of the money you lent me, you make reckless remarks by lording it over me. I'm paying back that money. Here, take it and leave! From now on I'm a stranger to you! Tomorrow go back at once!"

Seeing Osugi removing a handful of bills from his bag, Ichiko felt the blood being drawn out of her entire body. When she realized all her connections to Osugi were being severed with this scant bundle of money, she felt as if she had exhausted her power to think. Was the value of the love for which she had wagered herself at the cost of everything—relatives, friends, society, job—worth no more than those several sheets of paper currency?

Only the sensation that she had become a stone remained. No longer were Noe and Yasuko in her mind. A cold wind was violently raging inside this self of hers that had turned into a cavern. And only that sound gradually filled all her being and overflowed inside her.

Lying in front of her eyes was Osugi's large head. Like a huge gray plaster of Paris neck, that head was cold and had no blood circulating in it. It was a stone neck which did not answer whether called out to or spoken . . . and an insensate neck unresponsive to a blade whether it stabbed or cut . . .

Ichiko was not aware of the hand reaching into the bag which had fallen on her knees. When she came to, the unsheathed dagger on her lap was attracting light from a lamp. It was a posture Ichiko had accustomed herself to at those times of loneliness that had taken hold of her when she could not endure her agony.

The stone neck did not move an inch. Ichiko realized that gigantic cold neck had no identity at all, except for it to be stabbed. If *now*, it could be stabbed.

Her right hand holding the dagger was heavy like iron. Leaning over, Ichiko drew up her heavy arm and stretched forth the dagger. Her body, which had become a cave, was exceedingly light. Like the falling of a leaf, Ichiko fell slowly with her entire body, the dagger blade directly above the stone neck.